SKTUCKER
1984

CORPORATE INFORMATION SYSTEMS MANAGEMENT □ The Issues Facing Senior Executives

CORPORATE INFORMATION SYSTEMS MANAGEMENT

The Issues Facing Senior Executives

F. Warren McFarlan
James L. McKenney

Both of the
Graduate School of Business Administration
Harvard University

1983

RICHARD D. IRWIN, INC.
Homewood, Illinois 60430

To Karen and Mary

This book is also published as the text portion of
*Corporate Information Systems Management: Text and
Cases* by Cash, McFarlan, & McKenney.

Library of Congress Catalog Card No. 82–82122

Printed in the United States of America

3 4 5 6 7 9 0 MP 0 9 8 7 6 5 4 3

Preface

    This book is aimed at senior business managers and managers of information services (IS) activities, and is intended to communicate the relevant issues in effectively managing the information services activity. No assumptions are made in the book concerning the prior background of the readers with regard to the details of IS technology. It is, however, assumed that the reader has a broad background of administrative experience. Our purpose is to provide perspective and advice to senior executives coping with the information explosion. This expansion is characterized best by the doubling of the Library of Congress from 1933 to 1966 and again from 1967 to 1979, and it is expected a third time before 1987. The acceleration in the growth of knowledge in science is stimulating a dramatic increase in the number of new products based on the new technology. This growth, coupled with the increasing international nature of most business, puts an enormous burden on the individual to keep abreast of events. Although it is a sound scientific conjecture that a human can retain 25 billion characters of information[1] it has proven impossible to retrieve and use everything one knows, let alone keep our knowledge up to date. As Keen and Scott-Morton[2] have suggested, man-machine systems can function to assist the individual in coping with this information overload. We feel the broader issue is to help organizations adapt the new technology in order to better compete. This book is devoted to helping senior managers guide their organizations to better deal with information management.

    The book is organized around the authors' concept relating to a management audit of the information services activity. Chapter 1 begins with an overview of the key questions to resolve in assessing the health of an IS

---

    [1] Carl Sagan, *The Dragons in Eden* (New York: Random House, 1977).

    Michael Scott-Morton and Peter Keen, *Decision Support Systems* (Reading, Mass.: Addison-Wesley Publishing, 1978).

activity. Chapter 2 then presents a series of frameworks which the authors have found useful in analyzing and structuring the problems in this field. The subsequent chapters very specifically deal with issues relating to how the activity can be best organized, planned, and controlled.

The material in this book is the outgrowth of a series of research projects conducted by the authors at the Harvard Business School over the past several years. We are indebted to both former Dean Lawrence E. Fouraker and Dean John H. McArthur for making the time available for this work.

We are particularly indebted to the many firms and government organizations which provided us with so much time and insight during the course of our research. This book is based heavily on observations of real practice and without this support would have been impossible to prepare.

We are especially grateful for the many valued suggestions and insights provided us by our colleagues, James Cash, Kenneth Merchant, Gregory Parsons, Leslie Porter, and Shoshanah Zuboff. In addition we acknowledge the valuable work done by Philip Pyburn and Kathleen Curley during their time as doctoral students. Lynn Salerno, in her editorial capacity at the *Harvard Business Review*, provided valuable assistance. We would also like to express our appreciation to our office staff, Lillian Braudis and Alys Reid, who typed and edited numerous versions of the work.

The authors take full responsibility for all the material in this book.

F. Warren McFarlan
James L. McKenney

Contents

Chapter 1 □ Introduction

Over the past 30 years, the rapid evolution and spread of information systems (IS) technology (in this book, IS will include the technologies of computers, telecommunications, and office automation) has created a major new set of managerial changes. Attempting to resolve these challenges has resulted in creation of new departments, massive recruiting of staff, major investments in computer hardware and software, and installation of systems which have profoundly impacted both how the firm operates and how it chooses to compete. The impact of this technology has not been confined to the large corporations but, in its current form, is impacting the very small (i.e., $1 million sales) firms as well. Further, in the large corporations, its impact is now very pervasive, reaching into both the smallest departments of the company and into managerial decision-making processes in a way which could not have been visualized even 10 years ago.

Facing these challenges is complex because many members of senior management received both their education and early work experience in a time prior to the wide-scale introduction of computer technology. Consequently, many feel somewhat uneasy about the subject and lack confidence that they have the appropriate handles to provide managerial oversight. Many IS managers face similar problems, since their firsthand technical experience was with technologies so different from those of the 1980s as to pose unrecognizable problems. Understanding the programming challenges of the rotational delay of the drum of an IBM 650 (a popular machine in the late 1950s) provides no value in dealing with the challenges posed by today's sophisticated computer operating systems. Further, understanding of what makes acceptable management practice in this field has changed dramatically since 1971. Virtually all major, currently accepted conceptual frameworks for thinking about how to manage in this field have been de-

1

veloped since 1971. Consequently, a special burden has been placed on IS management, not just to meet day-to-day operating problems and new technologies, but to assimilate and implement quite different ways of managing the activity. If they are not committed to a process of self-renewal, very quickly they become obsolete.

This book is aimed at two quite different audiences in a firm. The first is the general management which is responsible collectively for providing general guidance for the IS activity. For these readers, this book identifies a set of frameworks for looking at the IS activity in their firm, crystallizes the policies they are responsible for executing, and provides insights on how they can be executed. Also for this group, the attempt is to move from a world view down to an overall perspective of the IS forest and its management challenge.

The second audience is senior IS management. For these readers, we have attempted to develop an integrated view of the totality of IS management for the 1980s. We have tried to identify the key patterns which organize and make sense out of a bewildering cluster of operational detail. The attempt for these senior managers is to move from analysis of bark composition on individual trees to an overall perspective of the IS forest and its management challenge. The book thus tries to integrate the needs of two quite different audiences (who are very operationally interdependent) and provide them with a common set of perspectives and a language system for communicating with each other.

It would be a serious mistake, of course, to consider the problems of IS management as being totally unique and separate from those of general management. While the authors freely admit to having spent most of their professional lives dealing with IS technical and managerial issues, much of their thinking has been shaped by literature dealing with general business. The issue of IS organization, for example, are best thought of as special applications of the work on integration and differentiation first started by the behaviorists Paul Lawrence and Jay Lorsch. Issues of IS planning and strategy are influenced, on the one hand, by the work of Michael Porter and Alfred Chandler in business policy and, on the other hand, by Kirby Warren and Richard Vancil in the area of planning. Notions of budgeting, zero-based budgeting, transfer pricing, profit centers, and so forth, from the general field of management control, are relevant here. The work of Wickham Skinner and Richard Rosenbloom, in the area of factory management and transfer of technology, has shed light on how the computer operations function can be better managed. Many individual aspects of the IS management problems thus are not unique. What is unique is the peculiar confluence of these notions in running an efficient and evolving IS function. In thinking about this, some authors have found it useful to regard IS as a business within a business. Integrating the IS business into the rest of a firm may be conceived of as having special organizational, strategy-formulating challenges.

This book is organized around four concepts of how this kind of business can be better managed.

Strategic Relevance—The strategic relevance to the firm of an efficiently and effectively managed IS activity is not a constant but varies both between firms and over time for an individual firm. It is also of more significance to some operating units and functions of a company than to others. This notion of different strategic relevance is critical in understanding the wide diversity of potential organizational, planning, control, and other practices for managing and integrating this function.

Corporate Culture—"Within a business" is a very important phrase in understanding how the IS business itself should be managed. The values of senior management, approaches to corporate planning, corporate philosophy of control, speed of technological change in the company as a whole are one set of determinants. The other is the dynamics of its external marketplaces. Both have a major influence on what is appropriate management practice in both managing IS internally and integrating it with the rest of the firm. What works in one corporate environment may fail abysmally in another one.

Contingency—IS management in the 1980s is much more influenced by contingent notions than it was in the 1970s. In the 1970s, as IS management systems were being implemented where chaos existed before, simplistic and mechanistic approaches to management control, planning, and so forth were a great improvement over what was there before. As these systems were assimilated into the firm, the initial surge of value from their introduction, has given way to frustration in many cases because of their apparent rigidity. They answered some challenges well and others not at all. Dealing with this problem has required introduction of more complexity and flexibility in the approaches used to adapt them to the changing environment.

Technology Transfer—The diffusion of IS technology can and must be managed. If poorly managed, it will not evolve into a well-functioning support system but more likely a collection of disjointed islands of technology. We draw upon the general work in technology transfer in our thinking but have expanded that experience because of unique aspects of a technology which must deal with information. What makes the introduction and evolution of IS technology so challenging is that in many of its applications, success comes only when people have changed their thinking processes. Hence, we will refer to it as an "intellectual technology." In the field, too frequently, we have a technical success but an administrative failure.

COMPLEXITY OF THE IS MANAGEMENT TASK

There are a number of factors which have made the assimilation of IS technology a particularly challenging task. An understanding of these factors is essential if a sensible IS management strategy is to be developed. The more important of these factors are enumerated below.

1. IS technology, at least in its modern form (with high-speed computers), has had a very short life. Its earliest commercial application occurred in 1952. Thirty years is a very short time for the distilled outline of a new management profession to develop. Fields like marketing, accounting, finance, and production had a thriving body of literature and know-how in place in 1920. An incredible amount of knowledge and changes in thinking have occurred in these fields in this century, but it has been able to be assimilated within an organized field of thought. Evolution, not revolution, has been the challenge in these fields. The challenge in IS has been to develop from a zero base during a period of time where applications grew from being very narrow and specialized to being quite broad and integrated, with budgets and staffs exploding in size. In this environment, not surprisingly, the half-life of administrative knowledge has been quite short. Not a framework or avenue of thinking in this book predates 1973 in a published form, with much of the thinking taking place in the late 1970s and early 1980s. The authors of this book are under no illusion that this will be the last word on the subject but indeed hope to contribute through their further research to better insights.

2. Another source of administrative challenge lies in the fact that the field has undergone sustained and dramatic evolution in its technologies. Over a 10^6 improvement in processing and storage capacity has occurred since 1953, and the rate of change is expected to continue at the same pace at least through the 1980s and early 1990s. As in all technologies, a point of maturity will come, but we are not yet at this point. This technical explosion has continuously cast up new families of profitable applications as well as permitting old ones to be done in different ways. One painful aspect of this has been that yesterday's strategic coup often becomes today's high-overhead, inefficient liability. There is a natural tendency to harvest a particular approach too long. This tendency has been exacerbated by the prevailing accounting practice of writing off software expense as incurred rather than capitalizing it and then amortizing it over a period of years. These practices conceal both the fact that the organization has an asset and that it is becoming an aging asset.

3. The complexities of developing IS systems has forced the creation of specialized departments resulting in a series of strained relationships with the users of their service. This has been an enduring headache from the start of IS, and there is probably not a better example of C. P. Snow's two-culture problem in existence in the 1980s than the relationship between IS and general management. IS has specialized in order to harness the various necessary technical skills to get the job done. The specialists have appropriately developed their own language systems. They speak of *bits, bytes, DOS, CICS,* and so on to communicate among each other. General management,

however, has a quite different language, featuring words such as *sales growth, return on investment,* and *productivity.* While it is clear that some of the newer technologies, such as user-oriented programming languages and microcomputers, will help users, no substantial relief is in sight. A long-term need will exist for continually developing new integrating devices, such as steering committees and user department analysts, to help handle the problem. This problem is not remarkably different from that faced by the accounting profession with its special language. Despite 6,000 years of accounting history, substantial friction and misunderstanding still exist between accounting departments and users of accounting information. It is surprising to the authors that significant numbers of people who enter general management have only a sketchy ability to handle accounting information.

For numerous reasons, education will continue to only partially address these problems. The experience that students have in colleges and high schools in writing one-time, problem-solving programs—while useful and confidence-expanding—develops a very different set of skills than the skills which will be required to generate programs for processing business transactions reliably on a day-in, day-out basis. Unfortunately, this education often does not address the existence of these differences, and it produces graduates who are ill-trained for these tasks but don't know that they are ill-trained, and thus have excessive self-confidence. Another educational issue is that, cognitively, some individuals are better equipped to assimilate IS technology than others. One of our colleagues has colorfully described this as the world being divided into "poets" and "engineers" (roughly equally prevalent in general management).

4. The increased specialization of contemporary technology and the explosion of skills needed to staff it have posed a fourth, major, managerial challenge. As IS technology has evolved, it has created a proliferation of languages, data base management needs, operating systems support staff needs, and so on, all of which have increased significantly the complexity of the IS management job from an internal perspective.

5. A fifth challenge has been a significant shift in the types of applications being automated. Early applications were heavily focused on highly structured problems, such as hard transaction processing, where one could usually be quite precise about the potential stream of benefits. These applications involved automation of a number of clerical functions and operational control functions, such as inventory management, airline seat reservation, and credit extension. In the case of airline seat reservations, it was able to bring a level of structure and decision rules to the activity not previously present.

Increasingly, today's applications are providing new types of decision support information for both management control and strategic planning decisions. Evaluation of the payout of these expenditures on an objective basis either before, during, or after they are expended is almost impossible.

Individuals may have opinions about these values, but quantification turns out to be very elusive. On top of this, the best way to develop these decision support applications is quite different from the conventional wisdom for the transaction-driven systems.[1] The detailed systems study, with its documentation and controls prior to programming, is turning out to be too rigid. For these systems, prototyping or doing it rough-and-dirty is proving to be the best approach. In short, the new types of application are forcing a shift both in the ways to evaluate projects and in the best ways to manage them. This is not an argument for a more permissive approach to system design and evaluation but rather a cry to be tough-minded in a positive way.

In combination, these factors create a very complex and challenging managerial environment. They will form the backdrop in the discussions of specific managerial approaches in the succeeding chapters.

SENIOR MANAGEMENT QUESTIONS

In viewing the health of an organization's IS activity, our research indicated that a series of six critical questions repeatedly emerge in senior management's mind. We will not argue at this stage that these are the questions which *should* be raised, but rather note that they are the questions which *are* raised. Four of these questions are essentially diagnostic in nature, while the remaining two are clearly action oriented.

1. Is my firm being affected *competitively* either by omissions in work being done or by poor execution of this work? Am I missing bets that, if properly executed, would give me a competitive edge? Conversely, maybe I am not doing so well in IS, but I don't have to do well in IS in my industry to be a success. Failure to do well in a competitively important area is a significant problem. Failure to perform well in a nonstrategic area is something that should be dealt with more calmly.

2. Is my development portfolio *effective*? Am I spending the right amount of money, and is it focused at the appropriate applications? This question is one that is often inappropriately raised. An industry survey calculating IS expenditures as a percent of something or other for 15 industry competitors is circulated among the firm's senior managememt. On one dimension or another, it is observed that their firm is distinctly different from the others, which causes great excitement (normally, when their firm's figures are on the high side). After great investigation, two findings often emerge: (a) Our company has a different accounting system for IS than our competitors, and therefore the results are not meaningful. (b) Our company has a different strategy, geographical location, mix of management strengths and weaknesses than our competitors, and therefore on this dimension also, the results are not meaningful.

---

[1] Michael Scott-Morton and Peter Keen, *Decision Support Systems*, (Reading, Mass.: Addison-Wesley Publishing, 1980).

In short, raising the question of effectiveness is appropriate in our judgment, but, attempting to identify it simplistically through industry surveys of competitors is not.

3. Is my firm spending *efficiently?* Maybe I have the right expenditure level, but am I getting the productivity out of my hardware and staff resources that I should get? This is a particularly relevant question in the 1980s, a decade which will be dominated both by extreme levels of professional staff shortages and by intensified international competition.

4. Is my firm's IS activity insulated well enough against the *risks* of a major *operational disaster?* There is no general-purpose answer as to what an appropriate level of protection is. Rather, it varies by organization, depending on the current dependence on smoothly operating existing systems.

5. Is the *leadership* of the IS activity appropriate for the role it now plays in our organization, and the special challenges now in front of it? Historically, senior management has used the mechanism of changing IS management as one of its main tools in dealing with frustrating IS performance shortfalls. It seems clear that this high turnover is continuing in the 1980s. One key reason for this is that it represents the quickest and apparently easiest step for senior management to take when they are uneasy about departmental performance. Also, as noted in Chapter 2, the nature of the job and its requisite skills tend to evolve over time, and a set of leadership skills and perspectives for one environment may not be appropriate for another one. Further, in many situations the problem is compounded by lack of suitable metrics and data to assess performance objectively. As will be discussed in subsequent chapters, we believe the development and installation of these metrics is absolutely vital. In their absence a 50 percent improvement in ability to meet service schedules, for example, may be totally overlooked, with the emotional temperature concerning remaining problems simply being raised.

6. Are the IS resources *appropriately placed* in the firm? Organizational issues, such as where the IS resource should report, how development and hardware resources should be distributed within the company, and existence and potential role of an executive steering committee, are examples of topics of intense interest to senior management. They are not only actionable but are similar in breadth to decisions made by general management in other aspects of the firm's operations.

These questions are intuitive from the general management viewpoint and flow naturally from their perspective and experience in dealing with other areas of the firm. We have not found all of them as stated to be easily researchable or answerable in specific situations and have, consequently, neither selected them as the basic framework of the book nor attempted to describe specifically how each can be answered. Rather, we selected a complementary set of questions which not only form the outline of the book, but whose answers will give insight into the earlier questions. The following paragraphs lay out these questions in summary form, and Chapters 3 through

9 deal with them in far greater depth. Together, they form the outline of a "management audit" of the IS activity which can produce a blue book of action items.

Organization (Chapters 3 and 4).   The text of Chapters 3 and 4 is most closely aligned to the previous set of questions, covering questions 5 and 6 in more depth. The following main themes are important in this area. First and foremost, What is an appropriate pattern for distributing hardware and software development resources within the corporation? The issues of patterns of distributed resources (including stand-alone mini- and microcomputers) have been well studied, and ways of appropriately thinking about them have been developed. These ways are heavily contingent, being influenced by such items as corporate organization, corporate culture, leadership style of the chief executive officer (CEO), importance of IS to achievement of corporate goals, and current sophistication of IS management. Within any pattern of distributed resources, there is need for appropriate policies administered centrally to ensure that suitable overall direction is being given.

A second complicating issue is to ensure that IS is broadly enough defined and that the coverging and increasingly integrated technologies of computing, telecommunications, and word processing are in fact being adequately integrated. These issues are further complicated when breaking out of the domestic arena and dealing with international coordination. (Chapter 9 is devoted to the issues posed by different national infrastructure—such as staff availability, level of telecommunications sophistication, and specific vendor support, great geographic distance, different spoken languages, transborder data flows, national culture and sensitivity, and so forth.) Finally, issues of organization reporting chains, level of reporting, IS leadership style, and steering committees represent additional topics. In the early 1980s, we believe there are better ways to think about these issues. While common questions and methods of analysis exist, however, in different organization settings very different answers will emerge.

Planning (Chapter 5).   The question, "Is my firm competitive and effectively focused on the right questions," we believe is best answered by looking carefully at the IS planning process. The design and evolution of this process had turned out to be much more complicated than anticipated in the early 1970s when some fairly prescriptive ways of dealing with it were identified. Elements creating this complexity can be classified as falling into three general categories. The first is an increased recognition that at any point in time IS plays very different strategic roles in different companies.

This strategic role significantly influences both the structure of the planning process (who should be involved, the level of time and financial resources to be devoted to it, etc.) and its interconnection to the corporate planning process. Firms where new developments are critical to the organization's introduction of new products, and to achievement of major operating efficiencies or speeded up competitive response times, must devote significantly more senior management time to planning than in settings where this is not the case.

The second category of issues relates to both IS and user familiarity with the nuances of the specific technologies being planned. Applications of IS technologies which both IS and user staff have considerable experience with can be planned in more considerable detail with great confidence. The newer technologies to IS and/or the users pose very different planning problems, both as to why planning is being done and how it can best be done. In any individual year a company will be dealing with a mix of older and newer technologies which complicates the planning task tremendously.

The third category of issues relates to the matter of the specific corporate culture. The nature of the corporate planning process, formality versus informality of organizational decision making and planning, geographic and organizational distance of IS management from senior management—all influence how IS planning can best be done. These issues suggest that as important as IS planning is, it must be evolutionary and highly individualistic to fit the specific corporation.

Management Control (Chapter 6).   The questions of efficiency and, to a lesser degree, those of effectiveness are best addressed by ensuring that an appropriate IS management control architecture and process are in place. Planning's role is to ensure that long-term direction is hammered out and that steps to acquire the necessary hardware/staff resources to implement it are taken. The role of management control is to ensure that the appropriate short-term resource allocation decisions are made and that acquired resources are being utilized efficiently. The key issues in this field include the following:

1.   Establishing an appropriate (for the organization) balance between user and IS responsibility for costs. Establishment of IS as a managed cost center, profit center, investment center, etc. is a critical strategic decision for an organization, as is the election of an appropriate IS transfer pricing policy to go along with it. Again, not only does this policy appropriately change over time, but it varies by type of organization as well.

2.   Identification of an appropriate budgeting policy for IS represents a second key cluster of issues. While many components of the IS budget are either fixed or transaction driven, there are others which are discretionary. These discretionary components need to be examined to ensure both that they are still being allocated to essential missions and that an appropriate balance is struck between the needs of many legitimate end users. This balance is necessary in a world where there are not unlimited financial resources for projects and where project benefits in many cases are not

easily quantifiable. Zero-based budgeting has proven to be a useful tool in some IS settings (albeit with some operational difficulties as will be discussed in Chapter 6).

3.   Finally, there is need for a regular weekly and monthly performance reporting cycle, not just against goals but against standards where possible. The move of IS operations from a primarily batch to an online activity not only reduces the territory for objective standard setting but has obsolesced many of the older approaches.

Project Management (Chapter 7).   The questions of efficiency and effectiveness are also addressed through analysis of the project management process. The past decade has given rise to a proliferation of so-called project management processes and methodologies which have helped to rationalize a formerly very diverse area. The installation of these methodologies, an obvious improvement in the 1980s, has created a new set of opportunities.

The first opportunity ties in the area of implementation risk. The advocates of these methodologies have implied that by utilizing their approach implementation risk will be eliminated. A careful examination of the long list of partial and major project fiascoes in the past four to five years suggests clearly that this is not the case. As will be described in the chapter on project management, our contention is that project risk not only exists, but it can be measured, and a decision can be made regarding its acceptability long before the majority of funds have to be committed to a project development effort. In the same vein, it is possible and appropriate to talk about the aggregate risk profile of the development and maintenance portfolio of projects. Not only does risk information provide a better language between general management, user management, and IS management during the project planning phase (where many options can be considered), but it provides a firmer and more valid context for after-the-fact performance assessment.

The second opportunity is the recognition that different types of projects can best be attacked by quite different kinds of project management methodologies. A single methodology is better than the anarchy and chaos which often precede its introduction. Several years of its use, however, can create a straitjacket environment. The approach will normally fit one kind of project very well and others considerably less well. Different organization structures within a project team, different types of user interfaces, and different planning and control approaches are suitable for different types of projects. In the early 1980s it is clear that the most appropriate project management approach for any project should flow out of the project's innate characteristics.

Operations Management (Chapter 8).   Appropriate controls over the IS daily operations ensure both cost efficiency and operational reliability in an important part of the IS activity. The IS operations activity represents a very specialized form of manufacturing environment with some unique problems.

First, operations is in a significant transition from a batch job-shop style to a continuous-process manufacturing or utility style. Not only has this changed the way it can best be organized, but it has dramatically altered the type of controls which are appropriate.

Second, for a number of firms, the IS activity has embedded itself so deeply in the heart of the firm's operations that unevenness in its performance causes immediate operating problems. These firms need significantly greater controls and backup arrangements than firms which have less dependence.

The performance of operations can be measured on a number of dimensions. Cost control, ability to meet batch report deadlines, peak-load response time of no greater than X seconds, and speed of response to complaints or unexpected requests are examples of these dimensions. It is impossible to optimize all of these simultaneously. Each firm needs a clear identification and prioritization of these items before it can come up with a coherent operations strategy. Different firms will have quite different priorities, and hence a search for a universal operations strategy and set of management tools represents a fruitless quest.

Multinational Issues (Chapter 9). International operations pose special problems in dealing with the IS activity. Geographic separation, different cultures, and availability of IS staff skills vary widely from one country to another. When combined with differing cost and availability of telecommunications gear, different vendor support from one country to another, and issues related to transborder data flows, it becomes clear that execution of an international IS strategy is much more complex than when one is operating primarily within the borders of one country.

The IS Business (Chapter 10). The concluding chapter attempts to integrate this discussion by considering the challenge of managing IS technology development and diffusion from the perspective of a business within a business. In that chapter, we emphasize the present marketing posture of the IS business. We characterize the 1950-64 era as one captured by the words R&D—"Could it work, and could we learn to make it work?" The 1964-72 era we characterize by start-up production—"Could large projects be managed in a way which would create useful, reliable services in a high period of growth when technology was new and changing?"

The 1972-81 era was one of striving for control and learning to manage a service organization with a newly established technology as applications continued to proliferate. The era of the 1980s will be one characterized by marketing. The challenge is to blend new-product opportunities posed by new technologies with their new customers in a thoughtful manner.

SUMMARY

This chapter has identified, from a managerial viewpoint, the key forces which are shaping the IS environment, senior management's most frequent questions in assessing the activity, and the questions which we think are most useful in diagnosing the situation and taking corrective action. In this final section we would like to leave you with a set of questions which we believe both IS management and general management should ask on a periodic basis (once every six months or so). They are a distillation of the previous analysis and, we believe, a useful managerial shorthand.

1. Do the perspective and skills of my IS management team fit the firm's changing applications, operations, and user environment? There are no absolute, for-all-time answers to these questions but rather only transitional ones.
2. Is the firm organized to identify, evaluate, and assimilate new IS technologies? In this fast-moving field, an insensitive low-quality staff can generate severe problems. Unprofitable, unwitting obsolescence (which is hard to recover from) is terribly easy here. There is no need for a firm to adopt leading-edge technology (indeed, many are ill-equipped to do so), but it is inexcusable not to be aware of what the possibilities are.
3. Are the three main management systems for integrating the IS environment to the firm as a whole in place and architected? These are the planning system, the management control system, and the project management system.
4. Are the security, priority setting, manufacturing procedure, and change control systems in the IS operations function appropriate for the role it now plays in your firm?
5. Are appropriate organization structures and linking mechanisms in place to ensure both appropriate senior management guidance of the IS activity and appropriate user dialogue?

To answer these questions, we have developed a framework based upon our four organizing concepts of strategic relevance, corporate culture, contingent action planning, and technology transfer. In each of the areas of organization, planning, management control, project management, and operations, we will be examining their implications for action. Realistically, today we are moving in a complicated space of people, differing organization strategies, different cultures, and changing technologies. We have taken as our task the identification of a sequence of frameworks which allow better analysis of the problems and issues facing organizations in relation to IS. We rely upon the reader to apply this discussion to his own business situation to formulate a realistic action plan.

Chapter 2 □ IS Manageable Trends

INTRODUCTION

In the first chapter, we identified some of the key issues which make the assimilation of IS technology so challenging. We then suggested what the implications of these issues were for management practice. The major headings in this book—Organization, Planning, Management Control, Project Management, and Operations Management—collectively are selected to provide a comprehensive treatment of these issues. Analysis of these areas in a firm's situation, complete with appropriate recommendations, is normally called an IS management audit. Underlying our treatment of each of these headings is a cluster of six themes which reflect both changing insight into management practice and guidance for administrative action.

A discussion of the nature and implications surrounding each theme is presented here, as well as our identification of its future. These themes represent, in our opinion, the most useful ways to think about the forces driving transition in the IS unit in the early 1980s. Candidly, our expectation, as mentioned in Chapter 1, is that, inevitably, additional experience, research, and evolving technology will produce new formulation of these and other themes in subsequent years. These themes form the basis of organizing our discussion within each chapter on an aspect of management.

In outline form these six themes include:

1. IS technology impacts firms in different ways strategically. The thrust of this impact strongly influences the appropriate selection of IS management tools and approaches.
2. The merging of office automation, telecommunications, and data processing technologies. Formerly disparate areas of technologies now requires coordination at least at a policy level and later at a line control level.

3. Organizational learning about IS technology is a dominant fact of life. The type of management approaches appropriate for assimilating a technology change sharply as the organization gains familiarity with it.
4. Environmental forces are shifting the balance of IS services on make-or-buy decisions in the direction of buy, which profoundly impacts the kind and quality of IS support an organization can receive.
5. While the functions of the system life cycle remain, the best approaches to executing them, and the problems of implementation, have changed significantly, with a wide diversity of approaches being appropriate for different systems.
6. Effective IS policy and responsibility involves a continuous reshifting and rebalancing of power between general management, IS management, and user management. Each group has a legitimate and important role to play in ensuring an appropriate level of IS support to the firm.

The following paragraphs define the nature of these themes.

THEME 1—STRATEGIC IMPACT

It has become increasingly clear that good management of IS technology is not of equal significance for all organizations. For some organizations, IS activities represent an area of great strategic importance while for other organizations they play, and apprepriately will continue to play, a cost-effective and useful role but one which is distinctly supportive in nature. Organizations of this latter type should expect that a lesser amount of senior management strategic thinking would be devoted to their IS organization. This issue is complicated by the fact that while today the IS function may not have strategic importance to the firm in meeting its goals, the thrust of its applications portfolio may be such as to have great significance for the future.

The opposite, of course, could also be true where IS plays a strategic operational role in the company's day-to-day operations but their future development applications do not seem to offer the same payoff or significance. However, in any case, it is important to understand what role IS is and should be playing.

Exhibit 2–1 summarizes these points by identifying four quite different IS environments.

Strategic. These are companies for whom smooth functioning of the IS activity is critical to their operation on a daily basis and whose applications under development are critical for their future competitive success. Banks and insurance companies are examples of firms which frequently fall into this category. Appropriately managed, not only do these firms require considerable planning, but the organizational distance between IS and senior

EXHIBIT 2–1 □ **Categories of Strategic Relevance**

Strategic impact of existing operating systems		Factory	Strategic
	High	Factory	Strategic
	Low	Support	Turnaround

	Low	High

Strategic impact applications
development portfolio

management is very short. In fact, in some firms the head of the IS function, broadly defined, sits on the board of directors.

Turnaround. These are firms that may receive considerable amounts of IS operational support, but where the company is not absolutely dependent on the uninterrupted cost-effective functioning of this support to achieve either short-term or long-term objectives. The impact of the applications under development, however, is absolutely vital for the firm to reach its strategic objectives. A good example of this was a rapidly growing manufacturing firm. The IS technology embedded in its factories and accounting processes, while important, was not absolutely vital to their effectiveness. The rapid growth of the firm's domestic and international installations in the form of items such as number of products, number of sites, and number of staff, however, had severely strained its management control systems and had made its improvement of critical strategic interest to the company. Enhanced IS leadership, new organizational placement of IS, and an increased commitment to planning were all steps taken to resolve the situation. Another firm had systematically stunted the IS development function for a period of years—until existing systems were dangerously obsolete. Retrieving this situation had become a matter of high corporate priority.

Factory. These firms are heavily dependent on cost effective, totally reliable IS operational support for smooth operations. Their applications portfolios, however, are dominated by maintenance work and applications which, while profitable and important in their own right, are not fundamental to the firm's ability to compete. Some manufacturing, airline, and retailing firms fall into this category very nicely. In these organizations, even a one-hour disruption in service from existing systems has severe operational consequences on the performance of the business unit.

Support. These firms, some of which may have very large IS budgets, are neither fundamentally operationally dependent on the smooth functioning of the IS activity nor are their applications portfolios aimed at the critical strategic needs of the company. A recently studied large manufacturing company fit this category perfectly. It spent nearly $30 million per year on IS activities, with more than 500 employees involved. There was no doubt that this sum was being well spent, and the firm was getting a good return on its investment. It was also clear that the firm could operate, albeit unevenly, in the event of major operational difficulties and that the strategic impact of the application portfolio under development was limited. IS was at a significantly lower organizational level than in other settings, and the commitment to planning, particularly at the senior management level, was quite low. Our research has uncovered a surprisingly large number of companies in this category.

In attempting to diagnose where a firm or business unit should be on the dimension of the strategic impact of the applications development portfolio, examination of the business strategy of the corporation as a whole provides useful context. Chapter 5 describes two of the currently widely used frameworks of competitive analysis and suggests how the bridge can be built between their frameworks and the identification of the strategic impact of the IS development portfolio.

THEME 2—MERGING OF TECHNOLOGIES

It is our contention that management of DP or computing can no longer be considered as a useful concept around which to organize a program of management focus. Rather, the technologies of computing, telecommunications, and office automation must be thought of as providing in aggregate a common cluster of policies and management focus. When we refer to the information systems (IS) departments or policies, we will be including all three of these technologies under this umbrella. At present there is a clear trend toward coordination of these technologies in most firms.

There are at least two major reasons why they must be viewed and managed, at least at a policy level, as a totality. The first is the enormous level of physical interconnections which increasingly must take place between the three technologies. Online inquiry systems, electronic mail, and end-user programming terminals are a few examples of the type of applications which require the physical integration of two or more of the technologies. The second major reason is that, today, execution of projects utilizing any one of these technologies poses very similar management problems. Each tends to involve large projects in terms of expenditures, rapidly changing technology, substantial disruptions in many people's work styles, and often the development of complex computer programs. As will be discussed in Chapter 3, the integration of these technologies has been complicated by the fact that 10 years ago not only were they not integrated but they had come from vastly different managerial traditions. These traditions made them independent, and unless actively managed to move together, they will remain apart. In dealing with the three technologies as a totality, we see the need for integration of them, at a minimum at a policy setting level, and, in many settings, a common line management for all three.

THEME 3—ORGANIZATIONAL LEARNING

Throughout the development of IS there has been an ongoing effort to understand the managerial issues associated with implementing and evolving automated systems in an organization. Starting from Whisler and Leavitt's article[1] on the demise of middle management and going on to Dick Nolan's and Cyrus Gibson's stages[2] and Chris Argyris' espoused theory versus theories in actions,[3] there have been a range of concepts on how to deal with the problem of getting individuals to use automated systems appropriately. After field studies over a seven-year period on 28 organizations, we have concluded that the managerial situation can be best framed as one of managing technological diffusion. Successful implementation of a technology requires individuals to learn new ways of performing intellectual tasks. As this learning takes place changes in the information flows as well as in individual roles occur. Often this results in organization changes substantiating the Leavitt and Whisler conjecture and reinforcing Nolan's and Gibson's original four stages.

We consider this process to be closely akin to the problems of organizational change identified by Lewin[4] and described in action form by Ed Schien[5] as an unfreezing, moving, and then refreezing again. They can best be summarized by rephrasing Nolan's and Gibson's original *four stages* (calling them *phases* here) and considering the process ongoing with a new start for each new technology, be it data base, office automation, or CAD/CAM. This approach usefully emphasizes the enduring tension that exists between efficiency and effectiveness in the use of IS. At one time it is necessary to relax and let the organization search for effectiveness while at another it is necessary to test for efficiency to maintain control.

---

[1] Thomas L. Whisler and Harold J. Leavitt, "Management in the 1980s," *Harvard Business Review* (November–December 1958).

[2] Cyrus F. Gibson and Richard L. Nolan, "Managing the Four Stages of EDP Growth," *Harvard Business Review* (January–February 1974).

[3] C. Argyris, "Double Loop Learning in Organizations," *Harvard Business Review,* (September–October 1977), p. 115.

[4] K. Lewin, "Group Decision and Social Change," in *Readings in Social Psychology,* ed. G. E. Swanson, T. M. Newcomb, and E. L. Hartley (New York: Holt, Rinehart & Winston, 1952).

[5] E. Schien, "Management Development as a Process of Influence," *Industrial Management Review* 2 (1961), pp. 59–77.

Phase 1—Technology Identification and Investment. This phase involves identifying a technology of potential interest to the company and funding a pilot project. In this phase, the pilot project may be considered akin to R&D. The key outputs of the project should be seen as expertise on technical problems involved in how to use the technology, plus a first cut at the types of applications where it might be most useful. It is generally inappropriate to demand any hard profit and loss payoff identification either before or after the implementation of this pilot project.

Phase 2—Technological Learning and Adaptation. The objective during this phase is to take the newly identified technology of interest to an organization where a first level of technical expertise has been developed and to encourage user-oriented experimentation with it through a series of pilot projects. The primary purpose of these pilot projects is to develop user-oriented insights as to where the potential profitable applications of this technology might be, and to stimulate user awareness of the existence of the technology. Repeatedly, what the IS department thought were going to be implications of a technology turned out to be quite different in reality. As is true of phase 1, there is a strong effectiveness thrust to phase 2.

Phase 3—Rationalization/Management Control. Phase 3 technologies are those which are reasonably understood by both IS personnel and key user personnel as to their end applications. The basic challenge in this phase is the development of appropriate tools and controls to ensure that it is being utilized efficiently. In the earlier phases, the basic concerns revolve around stimulating awareness and experimentation. In this phase, the primary attention turns to development of controls and appropriate IS hygiene to ensure that the applications are done for a minimum amount of money and can be maintained over a long period of time. Formal standards, cost-benefit studies and user chargeout mechanisms are all appropriate for technologies in this phase as their use is rationalized.

Phase 4—Maturity/Widespread Technology Transfer. Technologies in this phase have essentially passed through the gauntlet of organizational learning, with technological skills, user awareness, and management controls in place. Often the initiating organization will move on to new technologies and spend no energy on transferring the expertise. If not managed, organizational rigidity may slow the process of adaption to the new technology.

The key point in this discussion is that technologies in all four phases exist simultaneously in an organization at any point in time. The art of management in the 1980s is to bring the appropriate perspectives to bear on each technology simultaneously (that is, supporting IS phase 1 research, IS phase

2 aggressive selling to the end user, and intensive IS phase 3 generation of controls). This calls for a subtlety and flexibility from IS management and general management that too often they do not possess or see the need for. A monolithic IS management approach, however, will not do the job. This will be discussed further in Chapters 3 and 5.

THEME 4—MAKE-OR-BUY

A source of great tension and repositioning of IS in the 1980s is the acceleration of the pressures which are pushing firms towards greater reliance on external sourcing of software and computing support as opposed to the internal delivery of these services. Escalating costs of development of large systems, limited staff, availability of proprietary industry data bases, and dramatic increase in the number of potential applications are some of the factors driving this trend.

Make. Key pressures pushing in the direction of the make decision include the following:

The firm has the potential to develop a customized product totally responsive to its very specific needs. This is true not only for initial development but for necessary system enhancements and maintenance throughout its life. Further, one has the psychological comfort gained by having key elements of one's firm under one's supervision (corollary of "not invented here").

The ability to maintain confidentiality about data and type of business practices being implemented. This point is particularly important in situations where IS-type services are at the core of how the firm chooses to compete.

Ability to avoid vulnerability to the fluctuating business fortunes of outside software or data services suppliers.

Increased ease in developing one's systems due to the growth of user-oriented programming language, online debugging aids, and other user-oriented pieces of software.

Ease of adapting made software to rapidly changing business needs without having to coordinate your requirements with other firms.

Buy. Key pressures moving in the direction of the buy decision include the following:

Ability to gain access to specialized skills that either cannot be retained or where there is insufficient need to have them continuously available.

These include skills in end-use application, skills in programming, etc. to construct a system, skills to operate a system, and skills to maintain a system. Both demographic trends (in reduced work force entrants) and increased end-use specialization needs are making this a more important rather than less important item.

Cost: The ability to leverage a portion of the development cost over a number of firms can drive the costs down for everyone and make the in-house development alternative unattractive. This is particularly significant for standard accounting applications and data base systems.

Staff utilization: Scarce in-house resources can be saved for applications that are so company-specific or so confidential that they cannot safely be subcontracted. Saving these resources may involve buying into a set of systems specifications for the common applications which are less than optimal.

Ability to get the job done faster either through bypassing the corporate priority queue or buying access to a piece of totally or partially developed software.

Ability to make a short-term commitment for IS processing support instead of having to make a major facilities investment.

Immediate access to high standards of internal control and security offered by the large, well-run, service organization.

A proliferation in the types of information services that can be bought, and the active marketing of those services. The key categories involved include the following:
- Programmer availability (contract programmers, etc.).
- Proprietary data bases.
- Access to service bureau computer processing.

The change in balance of these pressures in favor of the *buy* alternative has significantly impacted IS management practice, as internally supplied services lose market share. Care must be taken to ensure that adequate management procedures are in place. For example, the management control system must be checked to ensure it is not tilting the balance too much in favor of buy through excess charges. Another example is that as project management for software is being delegated more to the outside, procedures to ensure that these suppliers have suitable project management systems must be developed. Implementation risk on a fixed-price contract becomes strongly related to vendor viability. (A good price is no good if the supplier goes under before completion.) Managing this shift to buy is a dominant concern in planning the necessary IS human resource. A critical factor in implementing new programs to complement existing activities (which must be maintained), this shift is discussed further in Chapter 8 on operations.

THEME 5—SYSTEMS LIFE CYCLE

The activities necessary to be undertaken to provide a specific information service can be characterized classically as the following series of steps:

DESIGN/CONSTRUCT/IMPLEMENT/OPERATE/MAINTAIN

The test of the appropriateness of an IS organization and set of policies is how successful they are in encouraging and controlling each of these steps for multiple systems. While changing technology and improved managerial insights have significantly altered the way each of these steps can be implemented, the functions of each have remained relatively unchanged for a considerable period. However, with an increasing shift to buy (versus make) occurring, some significant changes in many of these steps have to be made, with IS management in many cases becoming more like a broker.

Design.   The objectives of the design step are: a definition of the information service desired and the important criteria for selection of the service, identification of the users and the initial tasks to be implemented, and, if relevant, the long-run form of service and support. The first step has traditionally been either a joint IS-user proposal based on the IS plan or a user request. More and more it is being initiated by a user request, often stimulated by the marketing effort of an IS hardware/software/service supplier. The design step is a critical activity which demands careful attention to short- and long-term information service requirements as well as to ensuring the delivery of reliable service. This step was traditionally dominated by the IS technical staff but more and more is being assumed by the user. The shift should be managed carefully.

The substance of the design work normally begins with an analysis to determine the feasibility and potential costs and benefits of the proposed system, which, if favorable, leads to an explicit decision to proceed. This is followed by substantive joint work by the potential user and a systems professional to develop a working approach to a systems design. Depending on the systems scope, these design efforts may cover the range from formal systematic analysis to informal discussions and a flowchart. The end product of this work is both a definition of the desired service and an identification of a means of providing it (including in-house or purchased).

Construction.   A highly specialized activity, the structuring of automatic procedures to perform a timely, errorless, information service is a combination of art and logic. Professional judgment is needed in area of:

1.   Selection of form and brand equipment and/or service bureau.
2.   Selection of programming language, data base system, etc.

3. Documentation of operating procedures and content of software.
4. Identification and implementation of appropriate testing procedures.
5. Review of adequacy or long-term viability of purchased software service.

Very technical in content, this work depends on both good professional and IS management skills. In the past it was very dependent upon good organization linkage to the users. As more services are purchased this phase may be eliminated in entirety, although often a portion exists to adopt the standard system to the specific details of the situation.

Implementation. This activity still involves extensive user-IS coordination as the transition is made from the predominantly technical IS-driven tasks of the construction step to its completed installation and operation in the user environment. Whether the system is bought or made, the implementation is still a joint effort. Establishment and testing of necessary communication links, bringing new skills and an assortment of intrusions into the normal habits of the organization, are critical. A key general management concern is to ensure adequate technical support to a user of a purchased system during implementation.

Operations. In most settings the operation of systems has received the least amount of attention and creates an enormous residue of frustration and ill will. Further, as more users are becoming operators the subtleties of operations are becoming common to all managers. A significant amount of the difficulty, as will be discussed in the chapter on operations management, stems from inadequate attention being paid to clear definition of the critical performance specifications to be met by the new system and from failure to recognize that there are often inherent conflicts between specific service goals. At the front end of operations is the need for specific procedures to test and document services, including a formal acceptance procedure by operations. This clearly separates responsibility for construction of a service from responsibility for its operation. This separation of roles is particularly important when the same department (or even individuals) is responsible for both construction and operation of the system. In addition, operations approval procedures are needed for systems enhancements and maintenance. At the back end of operations is the actual delivery of service and measurements to assess its quality.

Maintenance. Ongoing design, construction, and implementation activities on existing services are labeled maintenance. When action is desired on a steadily growing need, normally caused by an outside change or user desire, it requires some technical support. (The word *maintenance* is a complete misnomer because it implies an element of deferrability which does not exist. It could better be labeled modernization. Much of maintenance stems from real-world changes in tax laws, organization shifts, such as new offices or unit mergers, business changes, such as new-product line creation or elimination, new technology, etc. It can be as simple as changing a number in a data base of depreciation rates or as complex as rewriting the tax portion of the payroll. Effective execution of maintenance faces three serious problems:

1. It is considered by most professionals to be dull and noncreative as it involves working on systems created by someone else.
2. In actuality, for older systems, it is very complex, requiring competent professionals to safely perform necessary changes.
3. Accounting procedures do not recognize that software is an asset or that over time it tends to age, making eventual conversion vastly more complex and in extreme cases putting the entire organization at risk as it struggles to free itself from both obsolete hardware and software.

Newer systems are permitting users to develop their own adaptations by including report writers or editors. Because these complex systems require maintenance, however, a cost comes with the benefit. Managing maintenance continues to be a troublesome problem, but organization, planning, and management control all provide critical context to ensure that these issues are resolved appropriately.

Summary.   The description of the systems life cycle helps capture much of the complexity of IS management. At any point in time an organization has hundreds of systems, all in different positions along this life-cycle line. Of necessity, the IS management system in the overwhelming majority of cases must be organized by IS function rather than by specific application system. This inevitably creates significant friction because IS organization forces the handing off from one unit to another of responsibility for an application system as it passes through these steps. The user is often the only link (although changes often take place here) as the system's responsibility is passed from one group of technical specialists to another.

Further complicating the situation is that the execution of this process (and the dividing line between the steps) varies widely from one type of application system to another. For example, a structured transaction-oriented system requires an intensive up-front design effort to get firm specifications which can then be programmed. A decision support system, however, involves more a process of user learning. An appropriate methodology here is often a crude design followed by a simple program. Use of the programs by the user leads to successively different and more comprehensive design as its performance is analyzed and then to a series of new programs. Interactively, one cycles through this sequence a number of times. Such a design process (pragmatically useful) flies in the face of many generally held nostrums about good development practices.

In Chapter 8 we deal with the issues of operations management and the impact of *buy* on the systems life cycle.

THEME 6—POWER BALANCE AMONG THREE CONSTITUENCIES

Much of the richness of IS management problems stems from managing the conflicting pressures of three different and vitally concerned constituencies. There are IS management, user management, and the general management of the organization. The relationship between these groups quite appropriately varies over time as the organization's familiarity with different technologies evolves, as the strategic impact of IS shifts, and as the company's overall IS management skills grow. The next five chapters are largely devoted to identifying the various aspects of managing this relationship.

IS Management. A number of forces drive the creation of an IS department and ensure its existence. It provides a pool of technical skills which can be developed and deployed to meet complex problems facing the firm. Appropriately staffed, an important part of its mission is to scan leading-edge technologies and make sure that the organization is aware of their existence. It represents a critical mass, responsible for conveying knowledge of the existence of this technology, and of how to use it, to appropriate clusters of potential users. By virtue of its central location it can conceive where potential interconnection between the needs of different user groups exists, and it can help to facilitate their connection. In a world of changing and merging technologies, this unit is under continued pressure to modernize if it is to remain relevant. Basically, the raison d'être of the unit is that its specialization permits implementation of otherwise undoable tasks. As the technology has evolved the problem has become more complex because IS staff members themselves have become *users* of the system (through development of operating systems, etc.). Further complicating the situation is the growing availability of user-friendly systems and experienced users who do not feel the need to call on IS for help.

User Management. The specialization of the IS function has taken place at the cost of eroding some of the tasks of the user department while not relieving users of responsibility for ensuring that ultimately the tasks are well done. In the past, requirements of the technology served to disenfranchise users in the designing of services. This was coupled with a complicated chargeout system which further estranged the user from IS. Also complicating matters is the aggressively marketed availability of outside services which go directly to the user.

As the ultimate customer of IS service, the user best understands and has internalized the key operating problems. If the existing service is poor, the user feels the full impact in terms of inability to execute the corporate mission and wants to buy without IS help.

In the early stages of a technology, particularly, the user is a specialist in living with the problem and not a specialist in the technologies which can be brought to solve the problem. Another complication is that the term *user* often implies more precision than actually exists in a real situation. Often the user involves many individuals at different levels scattered across multiple departments. Further, as the user is becoming more sophisticated through experience with the older IS technologies, and as the technologies are becoming more user-friendly, some (not all) of the reasons for having a specialized IS organization have disappeared. Finally, user management, through increased experience with personal computing, is gaining more confidence (unwarranted) in its ability to manage all stages of the project life cycle (the same is true of general management; see below). Thus the balancing point of services between the specialist department and the consumer is appropriately being reappraised continuously.

General Management. The task of general management in this environment is to ensure the appropriate structure and management processes are in place to referee the balance between user and IS to fulfill the overall needs of the organization. Their ability and enthusiasm for playing this role varies widely, both as a function of their comfort with IS and their perception as to its strategic importance to the firm as a whole. Since many have reached their positions with little exposure to IS issues early in their careers or to radically different types of IS issues, this discomfort is often extremely acute. Much of this book is aimed at helping this group to feel more comfortable about their grasp of this activity. As the years pass, however, this group, through their experience with personal computing and encounters earlier in their careers with different (now obsolete) IS technologies, have gained confidence (often misplaced) in their ability to handle the policy issues implicit in IS technology.

In brief, each group's perspective and confidence is evolving. This change, however, while solving some problems is creating new ones.

SUMMARY

In this chapter we have identified six manageable trends that are intimate to all aspects of managing information services in the 1980s. Exhibit 2–2 is our map of the remaining chapters and identifies the emphasis in each chapter in relation to these organizing themes. Chapter 3 considers, in depth, the management issues of merging of the three technologies of OA, DP, and TP. It treats this issue as an organizational learning problem requir-

EXHIBIT 2-2 ☐ Map of Chapters and Themes

Chapter / Manageable Trend	Strategic Impact	DP/TP/OA	Organization Learning	Make/Buy	Life Cycle	GM/ User/ IS
IS Technology Organization Issues **Chapter 3**		●	●			●
Organizational Issues in IS Development **Chapter 4**	●		●	●		●
Information Systems Planning **Chapter 5**	●		●			●
IS Management Control **Chapter 6**	●		●	●		●
A Portfolio Approach to Information Systems Development **Chapter 7**	●				●	●
Operations Management **Chapter 8**	●			●	●	●
Multinational IS Issues **Chapter 9**		●				●
The IS Business **Chapter 10**	●		●	●		●

ing a series of contingent actions in order to effectively manage the diffusion of technology. In Chapter 4, we deal with the organization issues of shifting power and role among GM-User-IS in order to balance innovation and effectively control new IS technologies in environments where IS has different strategic impact. The planning discussion in Chapter 5 focuses upon the strategic relevance of IS and its potential impact on the organization. This includes both corporate culture and the type of contingent actions needed to assimilate the technology. In management control (Chapter 6) the emphasis is on how corporate cultures influence the managerial roles and the nature of how to integrate the services. Chapter 7 on project management focuses on developing a set of contingent actions for IS, users, and general management for different types of projects. Managing the life cycle and the make-or-buy decisions are the prime subjects of both Chapters 8 and 9. In Chapter 8 the discussion is on ensuring an efficient operation. In Chapter 9 we extend the culture concept to include the range of complexities present in international situations. Chapter 10 uses the marketing mix model to synthesize the overall issues to interface the IS activity to the company as a whole.

Chapter \ Manageable Trend	Strategic Impact	DP/TP/OA	Organization Learning	Make/Buy	Life Cycle	GM/ User/ IS
IS Technology Organization Issues **Chapter 3**		●	●			●
Organizational Issues in IS Development **Chapter 4**	●		●	●		●
Information Systems Planning **Chapter 5**	●		●			●
IS Management Control **Chapter 6**	●		●	●		●
A Portfolio Approach to Information Systems Development **Chapter 7**	●				●	●
Operations Management **Chapter 8**	●			●	●	●
Multinational IS Issues **Chapter 9**		●				●
The IS Business **Chapter 10**	●		●	●		●

The vice president of services of a large durables manufacturing firm recently faced a dilemma. She had just discovered that her request had been denied for a stand-alone word processor to solve operating problems in her fastest growing sales office. It seemed a trivial request, yet its review created a mess, and she felt the decision set a dangerous precedent. The reason given for the denial was incompatibility with the division's information services network. When she had asked why it was incompatible, an incomprehensible series of technical arguments ensued which appeared to have no relationship to her very real productivity problem. Should she fall in line, fight the decision, or resubmit the request as an operating expense instead of a capital expenditure?

A major manufacturing company over the past four years has reduced the hardware processing capacity and staffing of its corporate data processing center by 60 percent. Dramatic growth, however, has taken place in divisional data centers to such an extent that overall corporate data processing expenditures have risen more than 50 percent during the period.

After careful analysis, senior staff of a major decentralized company recommends an orderly dissolution of the company's $25 million data center and the creation of eight smaller diversified data centers over a 30-month period.

INTRODUCTION

These incidents are not unusual. Repeatedly in the past decade technological change has obsolesced previously valid organization structures for information services in many companies and forced (or will force) major reorganization. There are several key reasons for this.

First, for reasons of both efficiency and effectiveness, in the 1980s information services must include office automation, data and voice communications and data processing, managed in a coordinated and, in many situations, an integrated manner. Development of this coordination is not easy in many organizations because each of these activities in the 1960s and 1970s not only had different technical bases but were marketed to the company quite separately and were usually managed independently. Internally, quite different organization structures and practices for handling them developed. Frequently these old organizations include neither staff levels nor the mix of skills necessary to the new technology. The different managerial histories and decision-making habits associated with each of these technologies in the past has made their current integration exceptionally difficult.

Second, it has become increasingly clear that to ensure success information services technologies new to the organization require quite different managerial approaches than those technologies the organization has had more experience with. These different approaches are often facilitated by reorganization. For example, the problems of implementing new office automation technology projects are quite different from those associated with the more mature technologies of data processing.

Third, where the firm's data and computer hardware resources should be located organizationally requires rethinking. The dramatic hardware performance improvements (of all three technologies) in the past decade *permits* this issue to be addressed quite differently today than in the early 1970s.

These dramatic shifts have been facilitated by the technology shift from the vacuum tube to the very large-scale integrated circuits with their vastly improved cost/performance ratios. These productivity changes are continuing as still smaller, more reliable useful circuits are being developed. Exhibit 3-1 shows the cost trends per individual unit and circuit over the past 20

EXHIBIT 3-1 □ Costs and Performance of Electronics[1]

Technology	1958 Vacuum tube	1966 Transistor	1972 IC	1980 LSI*
$/unit	$ 8.00	$ 0.25	$ 0.02	$0.001
$/logic	160.00	12.00	200.00	.05
Operation time	16×10^{-3}	4×10^{-6}	40×10^{-9}	200×10^{-12}

* Large-scale integrated circuit.

years, trends which will continue for the next decade. The cost reduction and capacity increases caused by these changes have reduced computer hardware cost as a fraction of total IS department cost below 30 percent in most large information services environments. Today, computer cost often does not exceed corporate telecommunications expense and for many firms is significantly less than software development and maintenance charges. Equally significant, this technology has permitted development of stand-alone minicomputer systems or office automation systems which can be tailored to provide specific service for any desired location.

This changed technology has permitted a dramatic shift in both the type of information services being delivered to users and the best organizational structure for delivering them. This structure has evolved and will continue to involve not only the coordination of data processing, teleprocessing, and office automation but also redeployment of both the physical location and organizational placement of the firm's technical and staff resources that provide information services. By technical resources we mean items such as computers, word processors, private telephone exchanges, and intelligent terminals. In staff resources we include all the individuals responsible for either operating these technologies, developing new applications, or maintaining them.

Special Nontechnical Information Services
Environmental Factors

Today, several noncomputer technology related issues have propelled the need for reexamination of how information services can be most effectively organized inside the firm. The most important of those issues are the following:

1. An increasing shortage of competent, skilled people in the United States to translate this technology into ongoing systems and processes within organizations. These shortages, severe in 1982, will worsen in the coming decade for the following reasons:

---

[1] W. D. Frazer, "Potential Technology Implications for Computers and Telecommunications in the 1980's," *IBM Systems Journal* 18, no. 2, pp. 333–36.

    a. The number of individuals reaching their 18th birthday in the 20 years between 1978 and 1998 is estimated to plunge by 27 percent.

    b. The 15 percent decline in Scholastic Aptitude Test scores in the past decade and the reworking and simplification of college freshman curricula.

    c. The shrinking availability of professional information systems curriculum as potential faculty choose industry over university careers. In the spring of 1982 over 100 unfilled openings in information systems existed in major universities.

2. The development of highly reliable, cheap, digital telecommunications systems in the United States and expanding growth in Europe. The economics and reliability of worldwide telecommunications, however, are not consistent with the United States and Canada representing unique environments for the immediate future. In Western Europe, tariffs run an order of magnitude greater than that of U.S. tariffs, often coupled with inordinate installation delays once an order is planned. However, as European countries better coordinate their government-owned system they may develop a more cost-effective environment. In Latin America and other parts of the globe, these problems are further compounded by reliability problems. For example, one South American company was forced to shut down a sophisticated online system supporting multiple branches because of unplanned, unacceptable communication breakdowns (sometimes more than 24 hours in duration). In another situation, the company was able to achieve acceptable reliability only by gaining permission to construct and maintain its own network of microwave towers.

3. Legitimate demand for information services support by users continues to vastly exceed available supply. Supplies of cost-justified applications waiting to be implemented and exceeding available staff resources by three or more years tend to be the norm rather than the exception. This has created widespread user frustration. Further, perceived unsatisfactory support and unhappy interpersonal contacts with the central information services organization continue to persist. This has increased users' natural desire to gain control over this aspect of their work. The new technologies increasingly permit users to gain this control. In addition, users' confidence in their ability to run a computer (through personal experience, such as a home APPLE, for example) is not only growing but is likely to continue to grow (admittedly an often unwarranted self-confidence).

4. A fundamental conceptual shift has occurred in computer-based systems design philosophy. The prevailing practice in the 1960s and early 1970s involved writing computer programs which intermixed data processing instructions and data elements within the computer program structure. In the 1980s world, the management of data elements is

clearly separated from the computer program instructions. The implementation of this shift has placed enormous pressure on information services organizations as they balance investing human resources in new systems developments versus redesign of old systems, while ensuring reliable operation of the old systems until the updated ones can be installed.

The combination of these items with changing hardware economics has meant that organization structures correctly designed in the early 1970s may be seriously flawed for the 1980s and that a major reappraisal is in order. The succeeding sections of this chapter will cover the need for, and challenges in, merging the disparate technologies, the different approaches to assimilating as IS technology (depending on the organization's familiarity with it, and the issues involved in deciding on an approximate centralization/decentralization balance of data and hardware.

MERGING THE ISLANDS OF IS TECHNOLOGY

The problems in speedily integrating the three technologies of data processing, telecommunications, and office automation are largely a result of the very different management practices relating to these technologies (as shown in Exhibit 3–2); the following paragraphs analyze these differences in more depth.

In 1920 an operational style of information services in most corporations—elements of which continue to this day—was in place. The manager and his secretary were supported by three forms of information services, each composed of a different set of technology. For word processing, the typewriter was the main engine for generating legible words for distribution. A file cabinet served as the main storage device for output, and the various organization units were linked by secretaries moving paper from one unit to another. Data processing, if automated at all, was dependent upon card-sorting machines to develop sums and balances, using punched cards as input. The cards served as memory for this system. The telecommunications system involved wires and messages that were manipulated by operator control of electromechanical switches to connect parties. The telecommunication system had no storage capacity.

Also in 1920, as shown in Exhibit 3–3, the designer of each of the three islands had significantly different roles. For word processing the office manager directed the design, heavily influenced by the whim of his or her manager. Although office system studies were emerging, word processing was primarily a means of facilitating secretarial work. The prime means of obtaining new equipment was through purchasing agents and involved selecting typewriters, dictaphones, and file cabinets from a wide variety of medium-sized companies. Standardization was not critical. Data processing

EXHIBIT 3-2 □

Functions of the technology	1920 islands of technology			1965 islands of technology			1980 islands of technology		
	Word processing	Data processing	Communication	Word processing	Data processing	Communication	Word processing	Data processing	Communication
Human-to-machine translation	Shorthand/dictaphone	Form/keypunch	Phone	Shorthand/dictaphone	Form/keypunch	Phone	Shorthand/dictaphone/terminal	Terminal	Phone/terminal
Manipulation of data	Typewriter	Card sort	Switch	Typewriter	Computer	Computer	Computer	Computer	Computer
Memory	File cabinet	Cards	(None)	File cabinet	Computer	(None)	Computer	Computer	Computer
Linkage	Secretary	Operator	Operator	Secretary	Computer	Computer	Computer	Computer	Computer

EXHIBIT 3-3 □

Roles of use	1920 islands of technology			1965 islands of technology			1980 islands of technology		
	Word processing	Data processing	Communication	Word processing	Data processing	Communication	Word processing	Data processing	Communication
Designer	Office manager	Card designer	AT&T	Office system analyst	System analyst	AT&T	System analyst	System analyst	System analyst
Operator	Secretary	Machine operator	AT&T	Secretary	Operator	AT&T	Manager/secretary/editor	Manager/secretary/operator	Manager/secretary/AT&T
Maintainer	Many companies	Single supplier	AT&T	Many companies	Single supplier	AT&T	Many companies or single supplier	Multiple suppliers	AT&T/other
User	Manager	Accountant	Manager	Manager	Manager/accountant	Everybody	Everybody	Everybody	Everybody

was the domain of the controller-accountant, and the systems design activity was carried out by either the chief accountant or a card systems manager whose job it was to design the protocols for the flow of information to the processing steps. Both data processing and teleprocessing were sufficiently complex and expensive that they required that managers develop an explicit plan of action.

However, a key difference between data processing and telephones, starting in the 1920s, was that the service of data processing was normally purchased and maintained as a system from one supplier. Thus, from the beginning, a systems relationship existed between buyer and seller. Teleprocessing, however, evolved as a purchased service. As AT&T had made available a network of cheaper inner-city telephones, companies responded by ordering the phones, and the utility developed a monopoly of the phone system. All three islands, therefore, were served in a different manner in 1920; one by many companies, one by a single systems supplier, and one by a public utility.

In 1965 the servicing and management of all three islands was still institutionalized in the 1920s pattern. Word processing had a design content but was still very much influenced by the manager and centered around the secretary. Services, such as typewriters and reproducing systems, were purchased as independent units from a range of competitors offering similar technology. There was little long-term planning, with designs and systems evolving in response to new available technical units. Data processing, however, had emerged as an ever more complex management process. It was dominated by a serious evaluation of major capital investments in computers and software as well as multiyear project management of the design and development of systems support. In addition, extensive training sessions for all employees and users were required to effectively take advantage of the productivity of the new system. At times, even the corporate organization was changed to accommodate the new potential and problems caused by computer technology. For communications, however, in 1965 AT&T completely dominated the provision of communication service and, from a user's perspective, its management was a passive purchase problem. In some organizations managing communications implied placing three-minute hourglasses by phones to reduce length of calls.

Today, however, the management concerns for word processing and teleprocessing have become integrated with those of data processing for three important reasons. First, these areas also now require large capital investments, large projects, large complex implementation, and extensive user training. Further, it has become increasingly possible for significant portions of all three services to be purchased from a single supplier. The managers of these activities, however, have had no significant prior expertise in handling this type of problem. For office automation, a special problem is the move from multiple vendors with small individual dollar purchases to one vendor that will provide integrated support. The size of the purchase decisions and the complexity of the applications are several orders of magnitude larger and more complex than those faced a decade ago. For telecommunications the problem revolves around breaking the psychology of relying on a purchased service decision from a public utility and instead looking at multiple sources for large capital investment decisions. In both cases, this represents a sharp departure from past practices and creates needs for a type of management skill which 15 years ago was added to the data processing function.

The second linkage to data processing is that, increasingly, key sectors of all three components are physically linked together in a network; consequently, the problems of one component cannot be addressed independently of the problems of the other two. For example, in one manufacturing company the same WATS line over a 24-hour period is used to support online data communications, normal voice communication, and, finally, an electronic, mail message switching system.

The situation is complicated by the fact that today, for each of the three islands, a dominant supplier is attempting to market his product position as the natural technological base from which the company can evolve into coordinated automation of the other islands. For example, IBM is attempting to extend its data processing base into products supporting office automation and communications. AT&T is attempting to extend its communications base into products supporting data processing and office automation. Xerox is attempting to expand its office automation effort into communications and data processing.

In our judgment, failure to constructively address these management issues poses great risk to an organization. We believe that over the next few years most organizations will consolidate at least policy control, and perhaps management of the islands, in a single information services unit. The key reasons for this include:

1. Decisions in each area now involve large amounts of money and complex technical/cost evaluations. Similar staff backgrounds are needed to do the appropriate analysis in each case.
2. Great similarity exists in the type of project management skills and staff needed to implement applications of these technologies.
3. Many systems require combining these technologies into integrated networks to handle computing, telecommunications, and office automation in an integrated way.

ORGANIZATIONAL PATTERNS OF MANAGING THE TECHNOLOGIES

Organizationally, there are multiple paths which can be followed in effecting the merger of the three islands of technologies as a firm moves toward a merged information services function. The three most common paths are identified below.

Merging Data Processing and Telecommunications

It is clear why data processing and teleprocessing of data merged under DP leadership some years ago in many organizations. In those organizations early data processing applications had to support multisite situations; thus, the DP staff was forced to become conversant with the technical aspects of data communication. Expertise subsequently was developed to deal with minimizing the changes caused by the Bell telephone company rate structure and to resolve the technical issues of getting terminals to communicate to computers. In the early 1970s the technical issues were formidable because there was a clear dichotomy between voice and data communication. The Bell system was designed for voice, and converting it to data transmission was a challenge requiring significant capital investment to obtain quality digital signals between computer-oriented systems. In the mid-1970s, technical changes in the way information was represented to a telecommunications systems permitted voice and data to be dealt with similarly. On several nontechnical dimensions, however, initially they continued to pose dissimilar management problems: voice (the telephone), a purchased service, was still a carefully regulated utility, while data communications demanded increased sophistication in evaluating capital investments in complex technologies from multiple vendors. However, as the size of data communications has exploded, the economic advantages of merging voice and data communications have become significant. Increasingly, the trend is to merge voice and data communications policy and operations in a single department, typically located within the DP department. For example, a large bank recently installed a system to manage voice and data traffic by controlling switches and line utilization. The system reduced their communication bill 35 percent, with improved service to both the data processing effort and voice communication.

Merging Telecommunications and Office Automation

The new technology of the 1970s facilitated the marriage of word processing and office automation to telecommunications. Designers of word processor equipment could now include in work stations the ability to communicate to other work stations as well as to central storage devices through telecommunications systems. These features permitted word processors in the early 70s to quickly emerge, not as automated typewriters but as the basic building block of an automated office with the potential to link the manager to word storage files, other managers, and to data files. This has been vastly simplified by inclusion in the telecommunications system of storage capacity. Now, two parties do not have to be linked simultaneously. Rather, communication can occur through installation of an office station which retains and assembles messages and responses. For some organizations, acquisition of this capability has been an accidental by-product of acquiring systems to improve word processing. However, this capability has often subsequently equaled or exceeded in importance the productivity gained by introducing word processing. The real impact of these linkages is only beginning to be widely exploited today in relation to their potential. Their development is complicated and slowed when organizational distance exists between telecommunications and office automation.

Merging Data Processing and Office Automation

A less frequent linkage today is that between data processing and word processing. This path has been followed by technologically innovative DP managers through extension of their terminals for data processing into remote sites. These managers learned to move words (as opposed to numeric data) through computers from one site to another. As their experience grew, these innovators found a great demand for systems which could store and forward words to other sites. Often, the remote terminals evolved to become more word than numeric data communicators. As word processing software developed, these DP managers upgraded their terminals to include WP activities. Thus DP assimilated all communications, voice and data, and initiated word processing. This pattern's success has been determined by whether the mature DP organization has been able to develop the sensitivity to nurture the new technologies instead of smothering them with excessive controls.

In summary, at present a wide array of organization patterns are possible as an organization advances toward the totality of information services. We see this heterogeneity as transitional, with the eventual merger of these islands into a central hub occurring in most organizations; certainly for policy making, planning, and control purposes, and in many settings, for line control and execution. The timing of these moves in any organization is situation dependent, involving current corporation structure and leadership style, speed at which the firm has been staying modern in these technologies, individual retirement plans, current development priorities, and so forth.

PHASES OF TECHNOLOGY ASSIMILATION

The merger of these technologies is made more complicated by the fact that quite different approaches are needed to manage a technology as an organization gains experience with it. For example, the current mix of approaches for assimilating a relatively mature DP technology may be quite inappropriate for assimilating brand new office automation or brand new DP technologies. Failure to recognize the need for these different approaches has led to both mismanagement of major projects and missed opportunities in terms of projects which should have been done but weren't (no one knew enough about the technology to see the missed opportunity).

Organizations change much more slowly than technology and must grow to productively assimilate new information services. As Nolan and Gibson demonstrated for data processing, an organization progresses through stages in assimilating technology. Recent work in office automation and data process-ing have discovered this model to be a special case of the broader problem in the learning cycle of adapting a technology to an organization's needs.[2] These studies show the introduction of new information technologies and must be carefully managed or disaster can occur. Distressingly, there has been surprisingly poor transfer of skills learned in managing DP to office automation. A recent study of 37 firms found that 30 had not built on their DP technology experience when moving into word processing and office automation.[3] Of equal importance, over two thirds had not progressed beyond Nolan and Gibson's stage 2 of automation of tasks and experimentation with respect to word processing and were in a state of arrested development.[4] A longitudinal study, tracing an organization's use of information services technologies in all three components, found four phases of evolution which relate to Nolan and Gibson's original stages and are also consistent with organizational change concepts developed by Schien.[5] These phases are characterized in Exhibit 3–4 as Investment/project initiation, Technology learning and adaptation, Rationalization/management control, and Maturity/widespread technology transfer.

The *first phase* is initiated by a decision to invest in a new (to the organization) information processing technology: it involves one or more complementary project development efforts and initial individual training. These projects are characterized by impreciseness in both their costs and ultimate stream of benefits. The resulting systems when looked at retrospectively often seem quite clumsy. Each step of the project life cycle is characterized by much uncertainty, and considerable learning takes place. The second phase seems to follow unless there is a disaster in phase 1, such as vendor failure or poor user involvement which results in Stagnation Block A.

Stagnation Block A typically generates a two-year lag before new invest-

---

[2] James McKenney, "A Field Study on the Use of Computer-Based Technology to Improve Management Control" (Harvard Business School Working Paper 7–46).

[3] Kathleen Curley, "Word Processing: First Step to the Office of the Future? An Examination of Evolving Technology and Its Use in Organizations" (thesis, June 1981).

[4] Cyrus F. Gibson and Richard L. Nolan, "Managing the Four Stages of EDP Growth," *Harvard Business Review* (January–February 1974).

[5] Edgar Schien, "Management Development as a Process of Influence," *Industrial Management Review* 2 (1961) pp. 59–77.

EXHIBIT 3-4 □ Phases of Technological Use

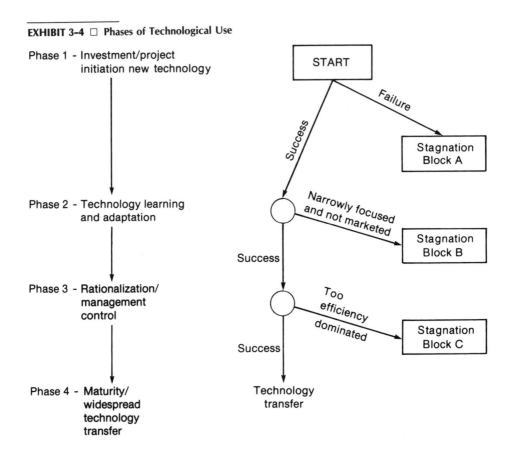

Phase 1 - Investment/project
         initiation new technology

Phase 2 - Technology learning
         and adaptation

Phase 3 - Rationalization/
         management
         control

Phase 4 - Maturity/
         widespread
         technology
         transfer

ments in this technology are tried again—normally along with a complete change of personnel. The decision to disinvest normally is a result of there being increased work and little benefit from the system; sources of these problems may be vendor failure, lack of real management attention, incompetent project management, or merely bad choice. Rarely are the problems leading to Stagnation Block A recognized quickly. The complexity and time requirements of implementing new information technology normally hide understanding of the developing failure for 18 to 36 months. The failure typically is not a clear technological disaster but rather an ambiguous situation which is perceived as adding more work to the organization with little perceived benefit. Hence, rejection of the system follows. All projects studied which aborted had significant cost overruns. Each failure created anxieties and prevented development of coordinated momentum. Typically, organizations frozen in this state end up purchasing more services of a familiar technology and become relatively adept at adapting this technology to their use but become vulnerable to obsolescence.

The *second phase* involves learning how to adapt the technology to particular tasks beyond those identified in the initial proposal. Again, as learning takes place, the actual stream of benefits coming from the projects in this phase are often quite different from those anticipated. Again, retrospectively, the resulting systems look clumsy. The project life cycles in this phase, although not characterized by great technical problems, tend to be hard to plan. In none of 37 office automation sites studied was the first utilization of technology implemented as originally planned.[6] In each case, significant learning took place during implementation. If the second phase is managed in an adaptive manner that permits managers to capture, develop, and refine new understanding of how this technology could be more helpful, the organization moves to phase 3. Failure to learn from the first applications, and to effectively disseminate this learning, leads to Stagnation Block B.

A typical Stagnation Block B situation occurred in a large manufacturing company and involved automation of clerical word processing activities which were under the control of a very cost-conscious accounting function. Highly conservative in its approach to technology in data processing, the firm had developed automated accounting systems centrally controlled in a relatively outmoded computer operating system and had yet to enter into data base systems. Having focused on word processing only to do mass mailing in order to save costs, they forfeited additional benefits. After three years of use, mass mailing is the only activity on their system. They are presently reviewing a proposal for microcomputers as executive aids which could be done by their word processors, but the organization is frozen into their use on only mass mailing.

Phase 3 typically involves a change in the organization, continued evolution of the uses of technology to ones not originally considered, and, most important, development of precise controls guiding the design and implementation of systems which use these technologies (to ensure that later applications can be done more cost efficiently than the earlier one). In this phase, the various aspects of the project life cycle are shaken down with the roles of IS and user becoming clearer and the results more predictable.

If, in phase 3, control for efficiency does not excessively dominate and room for broader objectives of effectiveness is left, then the organization moves into a *phase 4*, which involves broad-based communication and implementation of technology to other groups in the organization. Stagnation Block C is reached when excessive controls are developed, which are so onerous as to inhibit the legitimate profitable expansion of the use of technology. An example of Stagnation Block C with respect to data processing is the case of a manufacturing company which entered into large scale centralization with distributed input systems. To justify the expense of

---

[6] Curley, "Word Processing."

the new operating system, it focused significant attention on gaining all the benefits of a very standardized, highly efficient production shop. In the process of gaining this efficiency, the organization had become so focused on standard procedures and efficiency that it lost its ability and enthusiasm for innovation and change with respect to this technology, and it began to actively discourage users. Further, the rigorous protocols of these standard programs irritated their users and helped set the stage for surreptitious local office automation experimentation (phase 1 in a different technology). Too rigorous an emphasis on control had prevented logical growth. The first incident described at this chapter's beginning was from that company.

Phase 4 can be characterized as a program of technological diffusion. Here, firms take experience gained in one operating division and expand its use throughout the corporation.

Quite naturally, as time passes, new technologies will emerge which offer the opportunity either to move into new applications areas or to restructure old ones (see Exhibit 3–4). Each of the three components of information services is thus confronted over time with a series of waves of new technologies and, at any point in time, must adapt different approaches to managing and assimilating each, as each is in a different phase. For example, in 1981, a manufacturing company studied was in phase 4 in terms of its ability to conceptualize and deal with enhancements to its batch systems over a multiyear period. At the same time, it was in phase 3 in terms of organizing protocols to solidify control over the efficiencies of its online inquiry and data systems whose growth had exploded in the past several years. It had recently made an investment in several word processing systems and was clearly in phase 1 with respect to this technology. Finally, it had just been decided that communications was an important technology to deal with and was at the beginning of phase 1 in terms of considering how to merge data and voice communication.

It requires great subtlety for the IS organization to deal with the quite different control and management problems associated with each phase. One must simultaneously be an innovator, marketer, and controller for different technologies. The phsychological attitudes are so different for these phases that one large consumer products company has found it effective to have two development groups, one for phase 1 and 2 technologies and one for phase 3 and 4 technologies. The controls, aptitudes, and interests of each group are quite different.

As the islands of technology merge, it is critical that the dominant phase 3 approach being used in the technology of one island not be blindly and incorrectly applied to the phase 1 and phase 2 technologies in that island or to the phase 1 and 2 technologies of another island. Depending on the situation, this may be a reason to speed up or slow down a reorganization leading to the merging of the islands.

PATTERNS OF HARDWARE/DATA DISTRIBUTION

As the three islands of technology merge and as structure and procedures emerge to overcome the problem of managing the phases of technology assimilation, a key organizational question that remains is where the data and hardware elements should be located physically. (The issues associated with the location of development staff will be dealt with in the next chapter.) At one extreme is the organization form which has a large centralized hub connected by telecommunications links to remote input/output devices. At the other extreme is a small or nonexistent hub with most or all data and hardware distributed to users. In between these two extremes lies a rich variety of intermediate alternatives.

The early resolution to this organization structure was heavily influenced by technology. The higher cost per computation of hardware in the early 1960s (when the first large investments in computing were instituted) made consolidation of processing power into large data centers very attractive (large machines having a much lower cost per computation than smaller machines). In contrast, the technology of the early 1980s *permits,* but does not demand, cost-effective organizational alternatives. (In the 1980s, technological efficiency of hardware per se is not a prime reason for having a large central data center.)

To retain market share, the vendors of large computers are suggesting (as the comparative difference in efficiency of large computers versus small ones is eroded) that many members of an organization have a critical need to access the same large data files; hence, the ideal structure of an information service is a large central processing unit with massive data files connected by a telecommunications network to a wide array of intelligent devices (often at great distance). While this is certainly true in many situations, unfortunately the problem is more complex as is discussed below. Key factors influencing resolution of the problems include management control, technology, data factors, professional services, and organizational fit. The impact of each of these factors is discussed in the following text, with Exhibit 3–5 presenting a summary.

Pressures toward a Large Central Hub of a Distributed Network

Multiple pressures, both real and perceived, can generate need for a large hub of a distributed network.

Management Control-Related. The ability to attract, develop, maintain, and manage staffs and controls to assure high-quality, cost-effective opera-

---

EXHIBIT 3-5 □ **Summary of Pressures on Balancing the Hub**

Pressures	For increasing the hub	For increasing distribution
Management control	More professional operation Flexible backup Efficient use of personnel	User control User responsiveness Simpler control Local reliability improved
Technology-related	Access large-scale capacity Efficient use of capacity	Small is efficient Telecommunications $ reduced
Data-related	Multiple access to common data Assurance of data standards Security control	Easier access Fit with field needs Data only relevant to one branch
Professional services	Specialized staff Reduced vulnerability to turnover Richer career paths	Stability of work force User career paths
Organizational fit	Corporate style—central Corporate style—functional IS centralized from the beginning	Corporate style—decentralized Business need—multinationals

---

tion of existing systems is a key reason for a strong central unit. The argument is that a more professional, cheaper, and higher quality operation (from the user's perspective) can be put together in a single large unit than through the operation of a series of much smaller units. This administrative skill was what caused the major decentralized company identified at the beginning of the chapter to not eliminate its corporate data center and move to regional centers. In the final analysis, they were unconvinced that eight small data centers could be run as efficiently in aggregate and, even if they could, that it was worth the cost and trauma to make the transition. They felt the corporate data center permitted, through its critical mass, retention of skills for use corporate-wide which could not be attracted or retained if the company had a series of smaller data centers. They decided instead to keep central the operation and maintenance of all three technologies while emphasizing user input to projects in the design and construction phases through development departments in the several divisions.

Further, provision of better backup occurs through the ability to have multiple CPUs in a single site. When hardware failure occurs in one CPU, switching the network from one machine to another can take place by simply pushing a button. Obviously, this does not address the problems of a major environmental disaster which impacts the entire center.

Technology-Related. The ability to provide very large-scale processing capacity for users who need it, but whose need is insufficient to require their own independent processing system, is another strong reason for a large hub. In a day of rapid explosion in the power of cheap computing, it has become easier for users to visualize doing some of their computing on their own personal computer, such as an APPLE or a stand-alone mini. However, at the same time, some users have other problems, such as large linear programming models and petroleum geological reservoir mapping programs that require the largest available computing capacity. The larger the computer capacity available, the more detail they can profitably build into the infrastructure of their computer programs.

Also, in many firms an opportunity is perceived to exist to better manage aggregate computing capacity in the company thus reducing total hardware expenditures. With many machines present in the organization, if each is loaded to 70 percent, the perception is that there are a vast number of wasted CPU cycles that could be eliminated if the processing was consolidated. Although clearly an important issue in the technology economics of the 1960s, the significance of this as a decision element has largely disappeared in the 1980s.

Data-Related. Another pressure for the large central hub is the ability to provide controlled, multiple-user access to common corporate data files on a need-to-know basis. An absolutely essential need from the early days for organizations such as airlines and railroads, with sharp reductions in storage and processing costs, this access has become economically desirable for additional applications in many other settings. Management of data at the hub can also be a very effective way to control access and thus security.

Professional Services. Development of the large staff which accompanies the large IS data center provides an opportunity to attract and keep challenged a specialized technical staff. The ability to work on challenging problems and share expertise with other professionals, not only to attract them to the firms but to keep them focused on key issues, provides a necessary air of excitement. Existence of these skills in the organization permits individual units to undertake complex tasks as needed without incurring undue risks. Furthermore, when the staff has only limited skills, consolidation of such skills in a single unit permits better deployment from a corporate perspective. Further, the large group's resources at a hub permit more comfortable adaptation to inevitable turnover problems. Resignation of one person in a distributed 3-person group is normally more disruptive than 5 persons leaving a group of 100 professionals.

The large unit provides more potential for the technically ambitious individual, who doesn't want to leave the IS field, to find alternative stimuli and avenues of personal development (perceived technical and professional growth has proven to be one of the key elements which can slow down turnover). This is a critical weapon in postponing the so-called burnout problem.

Organizational Fit. In a centralized organization, the above-mentioned set of factors take on particular weight since they lead to congruency between IS structure and overall corporate structure and help eliminate friction. This point is particularly important for organizations where IS hardware was introduced in a centralized fashion and the company as a whole adapted their management practices to its location in this way. Reversal of such a structure can be tumultuous.

Pressures toward a Small Hub and Primary Distributed Environment

Today, important pressures push toward placing significant processing capacity and data in the hands of the users and only limited or nonexistent processing power at the hub of the network.

Management Control-Related. Most important among these pressures is that such a structure better satisfies the user's expectation of control. The ability to handle the majority of transactions locally is consistent with one's desire to maintain a firm grip on their operation. The concept of locally managed data files suggest that the user will be the first person to hear about deviations from planned performance of the unit and hence have an opportunity to analyze and communicate his or her understanding of what has transpired on a planned basis. Further, there now exists a greater number of user managers with long experience in IS activities who have an understanding of systems and their management needs. These individuals are justifiably confident in their ability to manage IS hardware and data.

Also, the user is offered better guarantees of stability in response time by being removed from the hourly fluctuations in demand on the corporate network. The ability to implement a guaranteed response time on certain applications has turned out to be a very important feature from the user's perspective.

This distribution of hardware provides a way to remove or insulate the user from the more volatile elements of the corporate chargeout system. It permits the user to better predict in advance what the costs are likely to be (therefore reducing the danger of having to describe embarrassing negative variances), and not infrequently, it appears to offer the possibility of lower costs.

Distribution of processing power to the user offers a potential for reduction of overall corporate vulnerability to a massive failure in the corporate data center. A network of local minis can keep key aspects for an operation going during a service interruption at the main location. A large forest products company decentralized to local fabricators all raw material and product decisions through installation of a mini system. This reduced the volatility of online demand at the corporate computer center and permitted the service levels to both corporate and distributed users to rise.

A simpler operating environment from the user's perspective is possible in the distributed network both in terms of feeding work into the system and in terms of the construction of the operating system. The red tape of routing work to a data entry department is eliminated, and the procedures can be naturally built right into the ongoing operation of the user department. (Surprisingly, in some cases regaining this control has been viewed with trepidation by the user.) Similarly, with the selection of the right type of software, the problems in interfacing with the basic operating system can be dramatically simplified (to use the jargon of the trade, they are "user friendly").

Technology-Related. The superior efficiency of large central processing units in comparison to that of much smaller units was true in the early days. Today, however, several important changes have occurred in the external environment:

The economics of CPUs and memories in relation to their size have altered, and the common rule that the power of computers rises as the square of the price no longer applies.[7]

The economics of Grosch's law was never claimed to apply to peripheral units and other elements of the network. The CPU and internal memory costs are a much smaller percentage of the total hardware expenditures today then they were in 1970.

The percentage of hardware costs as a part of the total IS budget has dropped dramatically over the past decade as personnel costs, telecommunications costs, and other operating and development costs have become more significant. Efficiency of hardware utilization consequently is not the burning issue it was a decade ago. When these factors are taken in conjunction with the much slower improvement in telecommunications costs (11 percent/year) and the explosion of user needs for online access to data files which can be generated and stored locally, in many cases the economic case for a large hub has totally reversed itself.

As more systems are purchased rather than made, the users are better informed in the procedures of how to select and manage a local system.

Data-Related. Universal access by users to all data files is not a uniformly desired goal. Telecommunications costs and the very occasional

---

[7] Edward G. Cale, Lee L. Gremillion, James L. McKenney, "Price/Performance Patterns of U.S. Computer Systems *ACM* (April 1979). The statement is commonly referred to as Grosch's law.

needs of access to some data files by users, other than at the site where it is generated, means that in many settings it is uneconomical or undesirable to manage all data in a way in which central access is possible. Further, inability to relate data may be in accordance with corporate strategy. A case in point is the large company mentioned at the beginning of the chapter which recently considered abandoning its corporate computing center. The corporate computing center was a service bureau for its eight major divisions (all development staff resided in the divisions). No common application or data file existed between even two of the divisions in the company (not even payroll). If the company's survival depended on it, it could not identify in under 24 hours what its total relationship as a company was with any individual customer. In senior management's judgment, this lack of data relationships between divisions appropriately reinforced the company's highly decentralized structure. No pressure existed anywhere in the organization for change. The corporate computing center, an organizational anomaly, was conceived simply as a cost-efficient way of permitting each division to develop its network of individual systems.

It is exceedingly easy for technicians to suggest interesting approaches for providing information which has no practical use, and the suggestion may even threaten soundly conceived organization structures.

Professional Services.   Moving functions away from the urban environment toward more rural settings offers the opportunity to reduce employee turnover, the bane of metropolitan area IS departments. While the recruiting and training process is very complicated to administer in these settings, once the employees are there, if sensitively managed, the relative lack of headhunters and nearby attractive employers reduces turnover pressures.

When the IS staff is closely linked to the user organization, it becomes easier to plan employee promotions which may take technical personnel out of the IS organization and put them into other user departments. This is critical for a department with low employee turnover, as the former change agents begin to develop middle-age spread and burnout symptoms. Two-way staff transfers between user and IS is a way to deal with this problem and to facilitate closer user IS relations.

Organization Fit.   Also important in many settings, the controls implicit in the distributed approach better fit the realities of the corporation's organization structure and general leadership style. This is particularly true for highly decentralized structures (or organizations which wish to evolve in this fashion) and/or organizations which are highly geographically diverse.

Finally, highly distributed facilities fit the needs of many multinational structures. While airlines reservation data, shipping container operations, and certain kinds of banking transactions must flow through a central location, in many settings the overwhelming amount of work is more effectively managed in the local country, with communication to corporate headquarters being either by telex, mailing tapes, transmitting bursts of data over a telecommunications link, or some other way, depending on the organization's management style, size of unit, etc.

Assessing the appropriateness of a particular hardware/data configuration for an organization is very challenging. On one hand, for all but the most decentralized of organizations, there is a strong need for central control over standards and operating procedures. The changes in technology, however, both permit and make desirable in some settings the distribution of the *execution* of significant amounts of the hardware operations and data handling.

SUMMARY

The combination of the trend to merge technologies and the ability to distribute data and hardware must be carefully managed because they are interdependent. Since firms come from different positions, history, culture, and business strategy, they may reach radically different balances. At present, the business strategy and corporate culture heavily dominate the hardware/data distribution issue, while current technology and business strategy dominate the speed of the merging issue. Further, for firms where IS is strategic, such as banking or insurance, there is a strong trend to accelerate the merging of all services into single-office support systems. Support industries can move more slowly. On the other hand, some banks (where IS is clearly strategic) will continue to have centrally supported systems while others will have distributed stand-alone systems providing similar support. A key reason for the difference will lie in the culture of the bank, its geography, and other factors relating to its business practices.

Reexamination of the deployment of hardware/software resources for the information services function is a priority item in the 1980s. Changing technology economics, merging of formerly disparate technologies with different managerial traditions, and the problems of managing each of the phases of IS technology assimilation in different ways have obsolesced many appropriate 1970 organization structure decisions. To ensure that these issues are being appropriately addressed, we believe five steps must be taken.

1. Establishing, as part of the objectives of a permanent corporate group, the development of a program to manage change. This policy group must assess the current program toward merging the technology islands, guide the process of balancing the desires for a strong hub against the advantage of a strongly distributed approach, and ensure that different technologies are being guided in an appropriate way.

2. The policy group must ensure that uniformity in management practice is not pushed too far and that appropriate diversity is accommodated.

Even within a company, it is entirely appropriate that different parts of the organization will have developed, and will continue, different patterns of distributed support for hardware and data. Different phases of development, with respect to specific technologies, geographical distance from potential central service support, etc., are valid reasons for different approaches.

3. The policy group must show particular sensitivity to the needs of the international activities. Without great care, it is inappropriate to enforce common approaches to these problems internationally, either for companies operating primarily in a single country or for the multinational which operates in many countries. Each country has different cost and quality structure of telecommunications, different levels of IS achievement, different reservoirs of technical skills, different culture, etc. These differences are likely to endure for the foreseeable future. What works in the United States often will not work in Thailand.

4. The policy group must ensure that it addresses its issues in a broad strategic fashion. The arguments and reasoning leading to a set of solutions are more complex than simply the current economics of hardware or which persons should have access to certain data files. Corporate organization structure, corporate strategy and direction, availability of human resources, and current operating administrative processes are all additional critical inputs. Both in practice and in writing, the technicians and information theorists have tended to oversimplify a very complex set of problems and options. A critical function of the group is to ensure adequate R&D investment (in phases 1 and 2). A special effort must be taken to ensure appropriate investment occurs in experimental studies, pilot studies, and development of prototypes. Similarly, the group must ensure that proven expertise is being distributed appropriately within the firm to appropriate places that are often unaware of its existence or potential.

5. The policy group must ensure an appropriate balance is struck between long-term and short-term needs. A distributed structure optimally designed for the technology and economics of 1981 may fit the world of 1989 rather poorly. Often it makes sense to postpone feature development or to design a clumsy approach in today's technology which will be quite efficient in the anticipated technologies of the late 1980s. As a practical matter, the group will work on these issues in a continuous, iterative fashion rather than implementing a revolutionary change.

Chapter 4 □ Organization Issues in IS Development

Chapter / Manageable Trend	Strategic Impact	DP/TP/OA	Organization Learning	Make/Buy	Life Cycle	GM/ User/ IS
IS Technology Organization Issues **Chapter 3**		●	●			●
Organizational Issues in IS Development **Chapter 4**	●		●	●		●
Information Systems Planning **Chapter 5**	●		●			●
IS Management Control **Chapter 6**	●		●	●		●
A Portfolio Approach to Information Systems Development **Chapter 7**	●				●	●
Operations Management **Chapter 8**	●			●	●	●
Multinational IS Issues **Chapter 9**		●				●
The IS Business **Chapter 10**	●		●	●		●

In the preceding chapter, we noted that information services operations in the future will be characterized by a central hub with some data files linked via telecommunications to a variety of remote devices which may or may not have extensive data files and processing power. The balance between work done at the hub and at distributed locations will vary widely from one organization to another. Evolution of this network will require the integration, at least at a policy level, of the formerly separate technologies of computers, telecommunications, and word processors. The rapid evolution in these technologies during their integration means the organization will simultaneously manage a blend of technologies, some which they have familiarity with (such as batch data processing) and others which they have limited experience with (such as electronic mail). The management structures needed for guiding new technologies to the organization are quite different from those for the older technologies. In dealing with these technologies, the corporation must encourage innovation, by both IS and user, in the newer ones while focusing on control and efficiency in the more mature ones.

Policies for guiding the deployment of information services development staff and activity in the 1980s must deal with two sets of tension. The first is the balance between *innovation* and *control*. This follows from our discussion of the phases of technology assimilation in the previous chapter. The emphasis in phase 1 and phase 2 technologies is on discovery of how to operate technologies and their implications for use in the company, while the emphasis in phase 3 and phase 4 technologies is on turning these findings into efficient reality. The relative emphasis a firm should place on aggressive phase 1 and 2 innovation will vary widely, depending on a broad assessment of the potential strategic impact of IS technology on the firm, corporate willingness to take risk, and so on. If there is a perception that this technology could be of great impact in helping the firm reach its strategic objectives, significantly greater emphasis must be given to these investments than if it is seen to be merely helpful.

The second tension is that between *IS dominance* and *user dominance* in the retention of development skills and in the active selection of priorities. The user often has a predilection to drive toward short-term need fulfillment (at the expense of long-term IS hygiene and orderly development). IS on the other hand can become preoccupied with the mastery of technology and an orderly development plan at the risk of slow response to legitimate user needs. Effectively balancing the roles of these two groups is a complex task, which must be dealt with in the context of the potential strategic role of IS technology, in the context of the corporate culture, and in a contingent manner.

Exhibit 4–1 illustrates some consequences of either excessive IS or excessive user domination in environments. It shows clearly that very different application portfolios and operating problems will emerge in each setting. Throughout this chapter a strong focus will be on the need for experimentation because of the repeated inability of organizations to foresee the real implications of their launching into a new technology. The following four incidents are typical of this problem.

1. A Short-Term User-Need Situation—Strategically Important. The present number one priority at a large machine-tool manufacturer engineering department is computer-aided design (CAD). Early success has led to a major expansion of the effort. They are modifying the digital information design output to enable them to control directly computer-driven machine tools. This work has deliberately been done independently of their bill of materials/cost system which is in a data base format and maintained by the IS unit. Short of staff to immediately integrate the new system in their data base structure, it was a user decision to go ahead, despite major future system integration problems. The work was done over the objection of IS management, but user management (engineering) has received full support

---

EXHIBIT 4-1 □ Possible implications of excess dominance

IS dominates control of systems life cycle	User dominates control of systems life cycle
Too much emphasis on data base hygiene.	Too much emphasis on problem focus.
No recent new supplier or new distinct services (too busy with maintenance).	IS says out of control.
New systems always must fit data structure of existing system.	Explosive growth in number of new systems and supporting staff.
All requests for service require system study with benefit identification.	Multiple suppliers delivering services. Frequent change in supplier of specific service.
Standardization dominates—few exceptions.	Lack of standardization and control over data hygiene and system.
IS designs/constructs everything.	Hard evidence of benefits nonexistent.
Benefits of user control over development discussed but never implemented.	Soft evidence of benefits not organized.
Study always shows construction costs less than outside purchase.	Few measurements/objectives for new systems.
Head count of distributed minis and development staff growing surreptitiously.	Technical advice of IS not sought or, if received, considered irrelevant.
IS specializing in technical frontiers, not user-oriented markets.	User buying design/construction/maintenance services and even operations from outside
IS spending 80 percent on maintenance, 20 percent on development.	User building networks to own unique needs (not corporate need).
IS thinks they are in control of all.	While some users are growing rapidly in experience and use other users feel nothing is relevant because they do not understand.
Users express unhappiness.	No coordinated effort for technology transfer or learning from experience between users.
Portfolio of development opportunities firmly under IS control.	Growth in duplication of technical staffs.
No strong user group exists.	Communications costs are rising dramatically through redundancy.
General management not involved but concerned.	

---

from senior management because of the project's potential major impact on shortening the product development life cycle.

The engineers are enthusiastically working on the CAD project to make it work; the IS team is lukewarm. Early results appear to have justified the decision.

2. User Control to Achieve Automation. At a division of a large consumer products manufacturer, a substantial investment in office automation was undertaken with modest, up-front, cost/benefit justification. Managers and administrative support personnel were encouraged by IS to "use" the systems with only modest direction and some introductory training on a Wang word processor which was made available to them. In four months time, three product managers had developed independent networks to support sales force activities; two had automated portions of their word processing, with substantial savings; two others did little but encourage their administrative support staff to "try it out." The users gained confidence and were pursuing new programs with enthusiasm.

The challenge to the IS management now, after only six months, is to develop and evolve an efficient program with these seven different "experienced" users. The IS manager currently estimates it will take roughly two years to achieve this efficient integration. However, both he and divisional management feel, retrospectively, that it would have been impossible to implement office automation (OA) with a standard IS-dominated systems study and that the expense of the after-the-fact rationalization is an acceptable price for these benefits. This word processing program was in sharp contrast to the strong central control IS was exerting over its mature data processing technologies.

3 Step-by-Step Innovation of a New Technology. A third example is the experience of a large grocery chain which acquired a system of point-of-sales terminals. These terminals were initially purchased by the retail division (with the support of the IS manager) to assist store managers in controlling inventory. They were to be used exclusively within individual stores to accumulate daily sales totals of individual items. These totals would permit individual stores to trigger reorders in case lots at a given point in time. Once installed, however, these isolated systems evolved quickly into links to central headquarters. These links were established to supply data to new computer programs which provided a better measurement of advertising effectiveness and the ability to manage warehouse stock levels on a chainwide level.

Implementation of this nonplanned linkage involved significant extra expense because the communication protocols in the selected terminals were incompatible with those in the computer at headquarters. However, the possibility and benefits of the resulting system would have been difficult to define in advance as this eventual use was not considered important when the initial point-of-sale terminals were being installed. Further, in management's opinion, even if the organization had considered it, the ultimate costs of the resulting system would have been seen as prohibitive in relation to benefits (in retrospect, *incorrectly* prohibitive).

4. User Innovation as a Source of Productivity. A final example concerns the separate introductions by a large bank of an electronic mail system and a word processor system strictly to facilitate preparation of bank loan paperwork. However, the two systems soon evolved to link the loan managers (who were initially not planned for as customers of either system) to a series of analytical programs. This evolution developed as a result of conversations between a loan officer and a consultant. They discovered that the word processor loan system included a powerful analytical tool which could be used for analyzing loan performance. Because of the bank's electronic mail system, the analysis could be easily accessed by loan personnel (both at headquarters and in branches). After three months of use, the bank was faced with a series of internal tensions as the costs of both the electronic mail and the word processing systems unexpectedly rose. Further, there was no formal means to review "experiments" or evaluate this unexpected use of the systems by participants not initially involved. Eventually, a senior management review committee supported the project, and it was permitted to continue, with substantial enhancements made to the word processing software.

These examples are typical of emerging new services which support professionals and managers in doing work. They form the underpinning of our conviction that it is impossible to foresee in advance the full range of consequences of introducing IS technology. Excessive control and focus for quick results in the early stages can deflect important learning. Neither IS nor users have had outstanding records in predicting all the consequences of new technology in terms of its impact on the organization. Consequently, a necessary general management role is to help facilitate this assimilation.

This chapter is divided into three main sections. The first focuses on the pressures that are on users to gain control not only over development but, when possible, to have the resulting product run on stand-alone mini or micro systems operating in their departments. The second section identifies the advantages which come from a strong IS development coordination effort and the potential pitfalls of uncontrolled proliferation of user-developed systems. The third section identifies the core policies which must be respectively implemented by IS management, user management, and general management in order to ensure a good result. In our judgment, the general management role is critical in facilitating technological change and organizational adaptation.

PRESSURES TOWARD USER DOMINANCE

The intense pressures which are encouraging stronger control by users over their development resources and the acquisition of independent IS resources can be clustered into four main categories.

Pent-Up User Demand

The backlog of development work in front of an information services department is frequently very large in relation to its staff resources (three- to five-year backlogs tend to be the norm). The sources of these staffing crunches are multiple, and the problems are not easily solved. First, existing systems require sustained maintenance to deal with changing regulatory and other business requirements. As more systems are automated the maintenance needs continue to rise, forcing either increases in development staff or postponing of new work. This problem is intensified by the shift in systems design philosophy (in the early 1970s) from one which incorporated data into programs to one which clearly separates data base management from processing procedures. Effecting this one-time conversion of data systems is expensive in terms of staff resources.

Further, the most challenging high-status jobs tend to be with computer vendors and software houses. This puts great pressure on the in-company IS department because its most talented staff is tempted to move into more challenging (and often more financially remunerative) assignments. Frequently, it is easier for the IS development unit to get the budget allocations than find the staff resources to use them.

There are strong reasons for users to develop their own expertise. Systems people linked to the user organization make it easier to plan employee promotions which move IS personnel to other functional jobs enhancing user/IS coordination. Combining IS experience with user responsibilities creates a knowledgeable IS user. Some care must be taken on local development, however, as user groups often have a tendency to buy or develop systems tailored to their very specific situation, and this may lead to long-term maintenance problems. In an environment characterized by local development, often there is also poor technology transfer between similar users and nonachievement of leverage, issues of low importance to the local unit. A large forest products company, organized geographically, combined a regional-system-minded regional manager with an aggressive growth-oriented IS manager who was promoted to be in charge of all administrative support. In three years, their budget for IS was double that of a comparable region but only one application was exported. Subsequent review of this unit's work indicated that nearly half of their developments had focused on problems of potential general interest to the company.

Finally, the protocols of interfacing into a network and of meeting corporate control standards can be very time-consuming and complex. A stand-alone system purchased by a user which is independent of the network can simplify the job and permit less-skilled staff resources to be utilized. It may require no major changes, particularly, if it is a system familiar to one or more employees from prior experience.

These items, in aggregate, for reasons beyond IS management control, make IS *appear* to be unresponsive to users' demands. These perceived shortcomings of IS management by users (on the dimensions of responsiveness and excessive focus on detail) make user-developed systems and stand-alone minis an attractive nonconfrontational way of getting work done. Using either their own staffs or outside software houses, users significantly speed up the process of obtaining "needed" service.

The IS Market Is Growing in Services and in a Competitive Fashion

Thousands of stand-alone computer systems are available for specific applications ranging from simple accounts payable systems to complete office automation products. Their existence makes them beguilingly easy solutions to short-term problems. Marketed by hardware or software vendors to end-user managers, the emphasis is on functional features, with technical and software problems being soft-pedaled. This is particularly true of most standard word processing systems. Most systems are marketed with no mention of their computer foundation. A stand-alone solution is seen as particularly attractive because faster and more consistent online response times are given than from distributed systems. The stand-alone provides easy access to online systems; it also permits the user to avoid the problems associated with being only one of multiple users of a system who, in aggregate, over the hours of the day and the weeks, provide a highly volatile (in terms of volume) stream of transactions. Additionally, the system appears simple operationally, needing only an operator to run it when developed. Air conditioning, physical maintenance, and power availability are not seen as issues.

Frequently the local solution *appears* to be more cost effective than work done or purchased by the control IS development group. Not only is there no cumbersome project proposal to be proposed and defended in front of IS technicians who have their own special agendas but often a simple up-front price is quoted. Developed under user control, the project is perceived to be both simple and relatively red-tape free.

User Control

The notion of regaining control over a part of their operations, particularly if IS technology is a critical part of their units' operations, is very important to users (often reversing a trend which began 20 years ago in a very different technology). Control in this context has at least three different dimensions.

The first is the ability to exert direct control over systems development priorities. By using either their own staffs or self-selected software houses, users often believe they can get a system up and running in less time than it would take to navigate the priority-selling process in the corporate IS department, let alone get staff assigned to projects. This control ensures that the systems will be closer and more responsive to user needs. Mistakes made by a local group are often more easily accepted than those made by a remote group and rarely discussed; successes are often topics of conversation.

The second dimension of desired control is that users see themselves gaining control over the maintenance priorities. This is done either themselves or by contracting with suppliers that are dependent upon the users for income. Quite often the promotional message is that the maintenance can be performed by a clerk following a manual. A rare occurence!

The third dimension which is of importance for stand-alone computer systems is that users see themselves as gaining control over day-to-day operations. Insulated from the vicissitudes of the corporate computer scheduling, users believe they will be able to exert firmer control over the pace of their departments' operations. This is particularly important to small marginal users of heavily utilized data centers with volatile loads. Today, these points are intensified in many users' minds because of previous experiences with service degradation in large computer systems at month-end, or with jobs not run because of corporate priorities. Additionally, as a result of home computers, managers are becoming more confident in their ability to successfully manage a computer project. Clever computer-vendor marketing has helped to increase their confidence. However, often this experience, is of insufficient depth, and the user has more confidence than is warranted.

FIT TO ORGANIZATION

As the company becomes more decentralized in structure and geographically diverse, a distributed development function becomes a much better fit and avoids heavy marketing and coordination expenses. In conglomerates, for example, only a few have tried to centralize development, with most leaving it with the original units. Another advantage of distributed development is that if you have any intention of spinning off a unit, the less integrated its IS activities are with the rest of the company, the easier it is to implement the divesture.

USER LEARNING

As suggested in the four examples at the beginning of the chapter, it is very hard to predict the full ramifications of the introduction of a new technology. Firsthand, enthusiastic experimentation by the user can unlock creativity and stimulate new approaches to troublesome problems. Systems developed by an IS unit have to overcome more resistance in adoption. This is a special case (in the IS field) of broader work done in the fields of organization development and control where this factor has been identified as one of the principal forces in favor of organizing in multiple profit centers, as opposed to functionally. As noted in Chapter 3, this is increasingly evident in office automation and new professional support such as CAD.

Summary

In aggregate, these items represent a powerful set of arguments in favor of a strong user role in systems development and suggest when that role might be the dominant one. They further suggest that a summary statement capturing the flavor of the pressures driving users toward stand-alone, mini-based systems and local systems development or purchase of software, mini, and locally developed systems is: *short-term user driven.* The stand-alone, mini, and local development offer users solutions today to their problem under their *control* in a perceived enjoyable fashion. While, clearly, benefits associated with phase 1 and 2 learning can be achieved, as noted below often these are gained with not much regard for information hygiene.

PRESSURES TOWARD IS CONTROL OVER DEVELOPMENT

There are heavy internal pressures to consolidate or keep consolidated the development resource in one or more large clusters. The principal pressures are the following:

Staff Professionalism

A large support staff provides an opportunity to attract, and keep challenged, specialized technical individuals. The central unit also provides useful support for a small division or function which does not have its own data processing staff, but needs occasional access to data processing skills.

Further, as the average age of many IS development staffs continues to rise (graying of IS) these opportunities become a critical element in trying to increase productivity. The importance of this is intensified by the fact that salary levels, individual interests, and perceived interpersonal communication problems make lateral movement out of the department for some individuals an unfeasible option.

It is also easier to develop and enforce better standards of IS management practice in a large group. Documentation procedures, project management skills, and disciplined maintenance approaches are examples of critical development-department infrastructure items. In 1971, a large financial service organization faced with a deteriorating relationship between its central development department and key users was forced to split the development department into a number of smaller units and distributed these units around the company, thereby changing both reporting responsibility and office location. The quality of IS professionalism, although initially successful in stimulating new ideas and better relationships with users (many development people came to identify better with users than with technical development issues), had dropped so low by 1977, through neglect, that several major project fiascoes occurred which required assistance from an outside service organization. Today, significant parts of the development function have been recentralized, with much tighter controls installed over management practices in the remaining distributed development groups.

This is particularly important in relating to user-designed or user-selected computer-based systems. Lacking practical systems design experience and purchased software standards, the user often ignores normal data control procedures, documentation standards, and conventional costing practices. Consequently, purchasing from several suppliers, or incrementally from one, results in a clumsy system design which is hard to maintain. For example, one large financial organization discovered that all those involved in the design and purchase of software of three of their stand-alone computer systems used to process data on a daily basis had left the company, no formal documentation or operating instructions had been prepared, and all source programs had been lost. All that remained were disk files with object programs on them. The system ran, but why it ran no one knew, and even if the company's survival depended on it, changes were very difficult and time-consuming to execute.

Feasibility Study Concerns

An important problem is that a user-driven feasibility study may contain some major technical mistakes, resulting in the computer system being inadequate to handle the growing processing requirements. Because of inexperienced staff, such a feasibility study tends to underestimate both the complexity of the software needed to do the job and the growth in the number of transactions to be handled by the system. (The risk rises if there were limited technical inputs to the feasibility study or if the real business needs were not well understood.)

Often users organize a feasibility study to focus on a specific service and fail to recognize that a successful first application leads to the generation of an unexpected second application, then a third, and so forth. Each application appears to require only a modest incremental purchase price and therefore may not receive a comprehensive full-cost review. The result may be that the hardware configuration or software approach selected is unable to handle the necessary work. Unless great care was taken in the initial hardware selection and system design process to allow for growth, expansion can result in both major business disruptions and very expensive software modifications.

User-driven feasibility studies are more susceptible to acquiring an unstable vendor. In this rapidly growing industry sector, it is unlikely that all the current vendors will remain viable over the next five years. The same trends to hit the pocket calculator and the digital watch industry in the late 1970s will hit this industry sector as it reaches a point of maturity. This is critical because many of these systems insinuate themselves into the heart of a department's operations. Because these are software-intensive investments, failure of a vendor will mean both expensive disruption in service provided by the department and intensive crisis-spending efforts to convert the software to another machine. These concerns apply not just to hardware suppliers but also the packages and services provided by software suppliers. A single experience with a product from a failed software vendor provides painful learning.

Corporate Data Base System

Development of corporate data base strategy includes collection of files at a central location for reference by multiple users. The availability of staff in a central unit provides a focal point for both conceptualizing and developing systems which can serve multiple users. If such needs exist, a central department can best develop and distribute such systems to users (or manage the development process in a company where development of these systems is farmed out to local development units). The need for this varies widely with the nature of the corporation's activities. A conglomerate often has less need for this data than does a functionally organized, one-product company.

Inevitably, the first concern raised in discussing stand-alone islands of automation is that the company is losing the opportunity to manage and control its data flows. It is visualized that data of significance to many people beyond those in the originating unit will be locked up in a nonstandardized format, in inaccessible locations. Without denying the potential validity of this (there is substantial truth here), several mitigating factors exist which demand that this objection be carefully examined in any specific situation.

One factor is the issue of timing. In many cases, the argument of the erosion of data as a corporate resource is raised against a stand-alone system. It is alleged that in order to preserve flexibility for future data base design this stand-alone computer should not be acquired. Frequently, however, it turns out that this flexibility is not needed for three or more years in the future. In this context, a well-designed system may be an equally good (if not better) point of departure in evolving toward these long-term systems as would be jumping directly from the present set of manual procedures. This possibility must be pragmatically assessed.

Another mitigating factor, often overlooked, is that on planned frequent intervals data can be abstracted, if necessary, from a locally managed system and sent directly to a central computer. This is further supported by the fact that ordinarily not all information in a stand-alone file is relevant to other users (indeed, often only a small percentage is).

On the other hand, uniquely designed data handling systems can prove expensive to maintain and link. A clear need exists to identify in operational terms the data requirements of the central files and, if relevent, to suggest guidelines for what data can be stored locally. This problem is exemplified by the typical word and data processing systems which generate voluminous records in electronic format. Unless well designed these files may be bulky, lock up key data from potential users, and pose potential security problems. For example, a mail-order house recently discovered that each customer representative was using over 200 disks per day and storing them in boxes by date of order receipt, making aggregate customer information impossible to obtain in a timely manner. A new procedure reduced the number of disks to five.

The organization of and access to electronic files may require central storage to maintain the availability of data and ensure appropriate security. It is often easier to maintain good security when all files are in a single location than when scattered around a number of locations.

Initiative Center for New Ideas

A central unit helps identify new technologies of potential value to the company and communicate their existence to prospective users *(Phase 1 learning)*. It can also function as a research unit and take financial and implementation responsibility for leading-edge projects legitimately too adventuresome for an individual user but which offer significant potential for organizational learning. Several organizations use this group to initiate and to manage corporately mandated productivity improvement programs. In these settings, senior management has viewed the user departments as being relatively weak, needing productivity improvements but incapable of implementing them. They consequently selected a change agent for initiating these changes, running roughshod if necessary over the users.

A problem related to this view, however, is that the central development group may push to "make" decisions, when instead they should "buy." Its high level of professionalism can generate an excessively critical attitude toward any purchase as being too general and incorporating inappropriate features. Recently the IS staff of a large government agency, following a reduction of staff, ended up with very well-trained individuals who had suffered the early stages of all of IBM's new standard systems. A request for a new data retrieval system for the entire agency met with their insistence that it be resolved with an expensive in-house development project. This project soaked up all available systems expertise and forced user management into buying, without help, several outside services to meet immediate operational needs. Subsequently, when the development group started to test the retrieval system, they discovered that unmanaged proliferation of new services made key data files inaccessible, perhaps an unnecessary problem had they used an outside data software package. Procedures are needed to ensure that the true economics of make-or-buy are considered by central groups.

Fit to Corporate Structure and Strategy

Centralized IS's development role is clearest in organizations where there is centrally directed planning and operational control. A large manufacturer of farm equipment which has a tradition of central functional control from corporate headquarters had successfully implemented a program where all software for factories and distribution units worldwide was developed by their corporate systems group. Now as these groups are growing in size the company's structure is becoming more decentralized. Consequently the cost of running effective central systems development is escalating, and they are having to implement a marketing function to educate users and decentralize some functions. It is becoming increasingly common for centralized development groups to have an explicitly defined and staffed internal marketing activity.

Cost Analysis

A significant edge that a centralized IS group has, through their practical experience in other system efforts, is the ability to produce a realistic software development estimate (subject to all the problems discussed in Chapter 7) which takes into account the interests of the company as a whole. Software development estimates turned out to be a real problem in user feasibility studies. There are two contributing factors to this. The first is that in most cases a new system turns out to be more software intensive than hardware intensive. Typically, software costs run from 75 percent to 85 percent of the total costs for a customized system. Since the user often has had little or no experience in estimating software development costs, an order of magnitude mistake in a feasibility study (particularly if it is an individually developed system and not a "turnkey" package) is not unknown.

The second factor is the lack of experience with true costs of service because of complicated chargeout systems. Many corporate chargeout systems present calculations in terms of utilization of computer resource units that are completely unintelligible to the user. The result is that each month or quarter an unintelligible and unpredictable bill arrives. In management control environments where the user is held responsible for variance from budget, this causes intense frustrations. A locally developed system, particularly if it is for a mini, is perceived as a solution to this.

Further, many chargeout systems are designed on a full-cost basis. Consequently, the charges from the corporate center often seem high to the user. Since, particularly in the short run, there are significant fixed cost elements to a corporate information systems center, what appears a cost reduction opportunity to the user may be a cost increase for the company. Policies for ensuring that appropriate cost analyses are prepared must be established.

Summary

A phrase capturing the spirit of these problems would be *long-term information hygiene*. The problems, in many respects, are not immediately evident at the time of system installation but tend to grow in importance with the passage of time. Policies to manage the trade-offs between the obvious short-term benefits and long-term risks are delicate to administer but are necessary. Further, what were long-term problems may be short term as we learn to buy new cheaper software and throw away expensive-to-maintain code.

IS-USER RESPONSIBILITIES

The tension over control can be managed by establishing clear core policies as to what make up the user domain, what make up the IS domain, and what is senior management's role. Senior management must play a significant role in ensuring both that these policies are developed and that they evolve appropriately over time. Both IS and the users must understand the implications of these roles and the possible conflicts.

IS Responsibilities

To manage the long-term information hygiene needs of an organization the following central core of IS responsibilities emerge as the irreducible minimum:

1. Development of procedures to ensure that for potential information services projects of any size a comparison is made of internal development versus purchase. If the projects are implemented outside the firm or by the user this must include establishment of the appropriate professional standards for project control and documentation. These standards need to be flexible, since user-developed systems for micros pose demands quite different from systems to be run on large mainframe computers. Further, a process for forcing adherence to the selected standards must be defined.

2. Maintenance of an inventory of installed or planned-to-be-installed information services.

3. Development and maintenance of a set of standards which establish:
    a. Mandatory telecommunication standards.
    b. Standard languages for classes of acquired equipment.
    c. Documentation procedures for different types of systems.
    d. Corporate data dictionary with clear definitions for when elements must be included. Identification of file maintenance standards and procedure.
    e. Examination procedure for systems developed as independent islands to ensure that they do not conflict with corporate needs and that any necessary interfaces are constructed.

4. Identification and provision of appropriate IS development-staff career paths throughout the organization. These include sideways transfers within and between IS units, upward movements within IS, and appropriate outward movement to other functional units. (More difficult in distributed units, it is still doable.)

5. Establishment of appropriate internal marketing efforts for IS support activities. These should exert pressure to speed up, and coach, the units which are lagging, while slowing down the units which are exceeding technological prudence.

6. Preparation of a detailed checklist of questions to be answered in any hardware/software acquisition to ensure that relevant technical and managerial issues are raised. These questions should concern:

a. How the proposed system meets corporate communication standards (item 3).

b. For word processing systems, questions on upward growth potential and built-in communication and data processing capability.

c. For data processing systems, availability of languages which support systems growth potential, available word processing features, etc.

d. For communication systems, the types of data transfer capabilities, list of available services, storage capacity, etc.

7. Identification of preferred systems suppliers and the conditions for entertaining exceptions to the list of standards to be met by vendors before a business relationship is established. For example, size, number of systems in place, and financial structure should be clearly spelled out.

8. Establishment of education programs for potential users, to communicate both the potential and the pitfalls of new technology and to define the users' roles in ensuring its successful introduction in their departments.

9. An ongoing review of which systems are not feasible to manage and which should be redesigned.

These comments apply with particular force to the design of systems which embed themselves operationally in the company. Decision support systems do not pose nearly the same problems.

These functions, of course, can be significantly expanded with much tighter and more formal controls if the situation warrants it. In this regard, a diagnostic framework presented in 1980 in the *Harvard Business Review*[1] is particularly useful in assessing both the current position of an organization and where it should move.

User Responsibilities

To assist in the orderly implementation of new IS services and grow in an understanding of their use, cost, and impact on the organization, the following responsibilities should be fulfilled by the user of IS service.

1. Maintain a financial control system of all user IS-type activities. Increasingly, in the more experienced organizations a user-understandable IS chargeout system has been installed.

2. Make an appraisal of the user-people investment for each new project, in both the short term and the long term, to ensure a satisfactory service.

3. Develop a comprehensive user support plan for projects that will support vital aspects of the business or that will grow in use. This includes

---

[1] Jack R. Buchanan and Richard G. Linowes, "Understanding Distributed Processing," *Harvard Business Review*, July–August 1980, pp. 143–53.

inputs to networks' architecture, data base policies, filing policies for word processors, and user training programs at both the staff and managerial levels.

4. Manage the IS/user interface consistently with its strategic relevance, as an integral aspect of the business. The mix of central site, prepackaged programs, outside contracts, and all new services expenditure should be approved by the user.

5. Perform periodic audits on the appropriateness of system reliability standards, communications services, and security requirement documentation.

These represent the very minimum sets of policies that the users should develop and manage. Depending on the firm's geography, corporate management style, stage of IS development, and mix of technology phases of development, expanded levels of user involvement may be appropriate, including acquisition of their own staff. As these items evolve over time, the appropriateness of certain policies will also evolve.

General Support and Policy Overview

Distinct from the issues involved in the distribution of IS services are a cluster of broad policy and direction activities which require *senior management perspective*. In the past, these activities were built into the structure of a central IS organization. Now, because of the need to link IS to business planning, they are not infrequently separated. A major oil company recently reorganized to produce a 300-person systems and operations department reporting directly to the head of administrative services. This department does the implementation and operational IS work of the company on a month-to-month, year-to-year basis. At the same time, an 8- to 10-person IS policy group reports directly to the head of corporate planning, which works on overall policy and long-range strategy formulation. A major conglomerate which has all its development hardware distributed to key users has at the same time a three- to four-person group at headquarters level. Key functions of this corporate policy group should include the following:

1. Ensuring that there is an appropriate balance between IS and user inputs across the different technologies and that one side is not dominating the other inappropriately; initiating appropriate personnel and organizational moves if the situation is out of balance. Executive steering committees, for example, are a common response to a user imbalance.

2. Through its broad overview and perspective on the total role of information systems in the company, ensuring that a comprehensive IS corporate strategy is developed. In particular, in an environment where the resources are widely distributed it is critical that a comprehensive overview of technology, corporate use thereof, and linkage to overall corporate goals be put together. The relative amount of resources to be

devoted to this will appropriately vary widely from organization to organization as the perceived contribution to corporate strategy, among other things, changes. (This will be discussed in more depth in Chapter 5.)

3. Auditing the inventory of hardware/software resources to assure that the corporate view is provided in the establishment of purchasing relationships and contracts. In certain settings the corporate group will be the appropriate place to initiate standard vendor policies.

4. Ensuring development and evolution of appropriate sets of standards for both development and operations activities and ensuring that those standards are being applied appropriately. In this regard, the corporate policy group plays a combined role of consultant on the one hand and auditor (particularly if there is a weak or nonexistent IS auditing function) on the other hand. The implementation of this role requires staff that is both technically competent and interpersonally sensitive.

5. Acting as the facilitating authority in managing the transfer of technology from one unit to another. This will occur through recognizing common systems needs between units and the stimulation of joint projects. Actual transfer will require a combination of sustained visits to the different operating units, organizing of periodic corporate MIS conferences, development of a corporate information systems newsletter, and other means.

6. Acting as an initiative center to identify and encourage appropriate forms of technical experimentation. A limited program of research is a very appropriate part of the IS function and an important role of the corporate policy group is to ensure that that does not get swept away in the press of urgent operational issues. Further, the corporate function is in a position to encourage patterns of experimentation that smaller units might feel pose undue risk if they were the sole beneficiary.

7. Assuming responsibility for the development of an appropriate planning and control system to link IS firmly and appropriately to the company's goals. Planning, system appraisal, chargeout, and project management processes should be monitored and, if necessary, encouraged to develop by the policy group. In this context, the group should work closely with the corporate steering committee.

These roles suggest the group needs to be staffed heavily with individuals who in aggregate represent both broad technical backgrounds and extensive practical IS administrative experience. Except in very limited numbers, it is not a very good entry-level department for new staff members.

SUMMARY

The last two chapters have focused on the key issues surrounding organization of the information systems activity for the 1980s. It can be seen that there has been a significant revolution in what is regarded as good managerial practice in this field. Conventional wisdom has changed considerably and seems likely to continue its evolution. Consequently, many IS organization structures effectively put together in the 1970s are inappropriate for the 1980s. A significant contributing component of this change has been the development of new hardware and software technologies. These technologies not only permit quite different types of services to be delivered but also offer the potential for quite different ways of delivering these services.

The subject of determining the appropriate pattern of distribution of IS resources within the organization is both complex and multifaceted. We suggest that the general manager should develop a program to encourage innovation and to maintain overall control to manage the distribution of services. The final resolution of these organization and planning issues is inextricably tied to non-IS-oriented aspects of the corporate environment. Current leadership style at the top of the organization and that person's view of the future provide one important thrust for redirection. A vision of tighter central control sets a different context for these decisions than one which emphasizes the autonomy of operating units. Closely associated and linked to this is the broad corporate organization structure and culture and the trends which are occurring there.

The realities of geographical spread of the business units have a heavy impact on the art of the possible. The large corporate headquarters of an insurance company poses different constraints than the multiple international plants and markets of an automobile manufacturer.

On a less global scale are the realities of quality and location (organizationally and physically) of current IS resources. Equally important is how responsive and competent these resources are seen to be by current users. The unit which is perceived (no matter how unfairly or inaccurately) as unresponsive has different organization challenges than the well-regarded unit. Similarly, the current and perceived appropriate strategic role of IS on dimensions of applications portfolio and operations has important organizational implications. The support unit, for example, must be placed to deal with its perceived lack of relevance to corporate strategy. In dealing with all of these forces one is trying to find an appropriate balance between innovation and control, and the input of the IS specialist versus the user.

Not only do appropriate answers to these questions vary between companies, but different answers and structures are often appropriate for individual units in an organization. In short, there is a right series of questions to ask, and an identifiable but a very complex series of forces which, appropriately analyzed, determine for each organizational unit what the direction of the right answer is (for now).

Chapter 5 □ Information Systems Planning: A Contingent Focus

Chapter \ Manageable Trend	Strategic Impact	DP/TP/OA	Organization Learning	Make/Buy	Life Cycle	GM/User/IS
IS Technology Organization Issues **Chapter 3**		●	●			●
Organizational Issues in IS Development **Chapter 4**	●		●	●		●
Information Systems Planning **Chapter 5**	●		●			●
IS Management Control **Chapter 6**	●		●	●		●
A Portfolio Approach to Information Systems Development **Chapter 7**	●				●	●
Operations Management **Chapter 8**	●			●	●	●
Multinational IS Issues **Chapter 9**		●				●
The IS Business **Chapter 10**	●		●	●		●

A major manufacturing company eliminates its five-person DP planning staff, reassigning three to other jobs in the IS organization, and letting two go. In commenting on this, the vice president-finance stated, "We just didn't seem to be getting a payoff from this. After three years of trying, we thought we could find a better place to spend our money."

The executive vice president-operation of a large financial institution, in speaking of a recently completed business systems planning effort, stated that this effort has been the key to conceptualizing a new and important direction concerning both the amount of IS expenditures and where they should be directed during the next five years. "We would be lost without it," he noted.

The head of IS planning of a major financial services organization, in discussing his recent disillusionment with planning, noted, "When I started IS planning two years ago, I was very enthusiastic about its potential for invigorating the company. It worked for a while, but now the effort seems to have gone flat."

These comments seem typical of a number of organizations where an IS planning effort is launched with great hopes and apparent early results but subsequently runs into difficulty. This chapter explores key managerial issues surrounding this as they have unfolded in the past 10 years and provides guidelines for assuring success.

As information systems applications have grown in both size and complexity over the past two decades, the job of conceptualizing a strategy for assimilating these resources into the firm's operations has grown steadily more important. A key vehicle for developing this strategy has been a sensitively architected planning process. Such a planning process, to be effective, must deal simultaneously with the realities of the firm's organizational culture, corporate planning culture, stage of IS development, and criticalness of IS activities in relation to the company's achieving corporate goals.

Repeated studies have suggested that a clear correlation exists between effectively perceived IS activities in an organization and a focused, articulated, and appropriate planning process.[1] Since good metrics do not exist for measuring the overall effectiveness of an IS activity, however, the evidence absolutely linking effectiveness of the IS activity with planning processes is more diffuse and fragmentary.

This chapter is organized around four broad clusters of topics:

1. Identification of the external and internal pressures on the firm that generate the need for an articulated IS planning process.
2. Identification of the practical restraining pressures which limit the value to be derived from the planning process.
3. IS planning and corporate strategy.
4. Discussion of important corporate environmental factors which influence both the ultimate effectiveness of IS planning and identification of the key levers to be managed in tailoring the planning process.

PRESSURES TO PLAN—GENERAL CONSIDERATION

There are a variety of critical pressures which force one to plan ahead in the information systems field. The more important include:

Rapid Changes in Technology. Hardware/software technical and cost characteristics have and will continue to evolve rapidly, thereby offering substantially different and profitable approaches to applications develop-

---

[1] Philip Pyburn, "Information Systems Planning—a Contingency Perspective," (Harvard Business School thesis, 1981).

ment. On the one hand, this requires continued meetings of the IS staff and management groups to ensure that they have properly identified shifts significant to the company and developed plans to manage them. On the other hand, it is equally important that potential users, such as office managers or analytical staffs (often quite different from the traditional users of data processing systems), be made aware of the implications of these changes (as well as potential problems). In this way they can be stimulated to identify appropriate profitable new applications in their areas of responsibility that would not necessarily occur to the IS staff.

As the technology changes, planning becomes increasingly important to ensure that the organization does not unwittingly fall into a proliferation of incompatible systems. It is also important because the lead times for acquiring and updating equipment is often long. Once acquired, integration of new equipment into a company's existing technical configuration and network of administrative procedures frequently forces extended implementation schedules up to four years.

A recently studied regional bank has a three-year installation program to manage its transition from 140 online terminals to over 1,400 terminals on completion of its online teller network. Preparation of a detailed plan was absolutely critical in developing senior management's confidence in the integrity of the installation program and ensuring that sound operations would continue during the implementation.

Personnel Scarcity. The scarcity of trained, perceptive analysts and programmers, coupled with the long training cycles needed to make them fully effective, is a major factor restraining IS development. As discussed in Chapters 3 and 4, these do not appear to be cyclical problems but rather long-term difficulties which will endure throughout the 1980s. Not only will increasing amounts of software have to be sourced from outside the firm, but tough internal resource allocation decisions must be made. In 1981, not only is the computer services industry booming but an increasing number of U.S. firms are looking overseas for English-speaking technical personnel to meet existing shortages at attractive U.S. salaries.

Scarcity of Other Corporate Resources. Another critical factor inducing planning is the limited availability of financial and managerial resources. IS is only one of many strategic investment opportunities for a company and cash invested in it is often obtained at the expense of other areas. This is intensified by the overwhelming financial accounting practice in U.S. companies to charge IS expenditures directly against current year's earnings. Hence, review of both the effectiveness and efficiency of these expenditures is a matter of great interest and is a critical limiting factor for new projects, particularly in companies under profit or cost pressures.

Scarcity of IS middle management personnel, particularly on the development side, is also a significant constraint. Companies' inability to train sufficient project leaders and supervisors has significantly restrained IS development. This has forced either significant reductions in many applications portfolios or the undertaking of unduly high-risk projects with inadequate human resources.

Trend to Data Base Design and Integrated Systems. An increasing and significant percentage of the applications portfolio involves the design of data bases to support a variety of different applications. A long-term view of the evolution of applications is critical in order to appropriately select both the contents of the data bases and the protocols for updating them to adequately support the family of application systems using them.

Validation of Corporate Plan. In many organizations, new marketing programs, new product design, and introduction and implementation of organizational strategies depend on the development of IS support programs. It is critical that these points of dependency be understood and that, if the corporate strategy is infeasible due to IS limitations, this message be highlighted and resolution of the problem be forced when alternatives are still available. In organizations where the IS products are integral to elements of the corporate strategy, this linkage is more important than for those organizations where IS plays an important but distinctly support function. For example, a large paper company recently had to abandon major new billing discount promotions, a key part of their marketing strategy, because they were unable to translate the very complex ideas into the existing computer programs with their present level of staff skills. Coordination with IS in planning sessions would have both identified the problem and permitted more satisfactory solutions to be identified.

PRESSURES TO PLAN—SITUATIONAL CONSIDERATIONS

It is important to note that, at different points in the evolution of an IS technology, the balance between these pressures shifts and substantially different purposes are being served by planning. Reflecting upon the advent and growth of business data processing, data bases, distributed systems, telecommunications, and other new technologies, one can identify four different phases of technology assimilation, each of which poses a quite different planning challenge.

Phase 1—Technology Identification and Investment Phase. The basic focus of planning in the initial phase of a new technology is both technically oriented and human resource acquisition oriented. Key planning problems include identification of an appropriate technology for study, site preparation, development of staff skills, and managing development of the first pilot applications using this technology.

In this phase, short-term technical problem resolution issues are so critical and experience so limited that long-term strategic thinking about the implications of the technology is limited. This is not bad, since those involved usually do not yet have a strong enough background in the technology and its implications for the company to think long term. As the organization gains experience, selection of appropriate applications for this technology become more equal to technical issues and one evolves to the second phase.

Phase 2—Technological Learning and Adaptation Phase. The basic thrust of planning in this phase is focused on developing potential user consciousness of the new technology's existence and communicating a sense of the type of problems it can help solve, sequencing projects, and providing coordination. Initiation of a series of user-supported pilot projects is key to success. As a secondary output, the planning process focuses on numbers of staff and skills to be hired, equipment to be acquired, and generation of appropriate financial data supporting those projects. The written plan (if any) of consensus direction which comes out of this process is not an accurate indicator for predicting the pace of future events because individuals engaged in a learning process do not yet have the insights to be both concise and accurate concerning what their real desires are in relation to this technology and how practical these desires are. It is important to note that, since technology will evolve for the foreseeable future, there will usually be a phase 2 flavor to part of a company's IS development portfolio. Our observations of successful practice at this phase suggest clearly that:

1. The portion of a planning process focusing on introducing new technology is best developed by getting started with a pilot test to generate both IS and user learning rather than by years of advance introspection and design.
2. The critical success factors here involve attracting the interest of some potential users on their terms and stimulating their understanding on adaptation of the technology. Success here leads to later requests for service.
3. Planning during this phase (and phase 1 as well) involves a program of planned technological innovations, encouraging users to build upon past experience and organization receptivity to change.

Planning for phase 2 technologies has a heavy strategic focus to it. However, as is true in companies which are in a rapid growth phase in new industry sectors, precision of such planning suffers from both user and developer lack of familiarity with the technology and its implications. Hence, it does not have the same predictive value as planning for technology at a later phase. What the technical developer thinks are the implications of the new technology often turns out to be quite different after the users have experimented.

Phase 3—Rationalization/Management Control.   Effective planning for technologies at this phase has a strong efficiency focus on rationalizing the broad range of experimental operations. Where technological learning and adaptation planning has a long-range (if not terribly accurate) flavor to it, planning in phase 3 is dominated by short-term, one- to two-year efficiency and organization considerations. These include getting troubled development applications straightened away and completed, upgrading staff to acceptable knowledge levels, reorganizing to develop and implement further projects, and efficiently utilizing this new technology. During this phase, planning's objective is to draw appropriate limits concerning the types of applications which make sense with this technology and to ensure they are implemented cost efficiently. In terms of the Anthony framework, during this phase, effective planning has much more of a management control and operational control flavor to it and less of a strategic planning thrust to it.[2]

Phase 4—Maturity/Widespread Technology Transfer.   The final phase is one of managed evolution by transferring the technology to a wider spectrum of systems applications within the organization. In this phase, with organizational learning essentially complete and a technology base installed with appropriate controls in place, it is appropriate to look more seriously into the future and plot longer-term trends. Unfortunately, if one is not careful this can become too rigid an extrapolation of trends based on the business and technology as we now understand it. Unexpected quirks in the business and evolution of technology often invalidate what has been done during phase 4 planning.

Given the current dynamic state of IS technology, there is a need for all four phases of planning to be going on in a typical organization. The planning for business batch data processing for most companies in 1982, for example, is phase 4, while word processing and office automation is phase 2. This suggests that uniform orderliness and consistency in the protocols of the planning process are not necessarily appropriate because of organizational variances in familiarity with particular technologies. Not only does the planning process style have to evolve for a particular family of technologies over time, but a consistent, uniform process for the aggregate portfolio of applications for an organizational unit is unlikely to be appropriate. This is so because it is dealing with a cluster of different technologies, each of which is at a different phase of assimilation within the organization. For example, one manufacturing company studied was phase 4 in terms of its

---

[2] Robert Anthony, *Planning, and Control Systems: A Framework for Analysis* (Harvard Business School, Division of Research, 1965).

ability to conceptualize and deal with enhancements to its batch systems over a multiyear period. At the same time, it was phase 3 in terms of organizing protocols and training a broad group of individuals to solidify control over the efficiencies of its online inquiry and data input systems whose growth had exploded in the past several years. Finally, it had made an investment in several word processing systems and was beginning to examine several different methods of office automation, and was clearly in phase 1 with respect to this technology. In summary, planned clutter (as opposed to consistency) in the approach to IS planning for an organizational unit is a desirable rather than an undesirable feature. Similarly, the approach to IS planning for different organizational units within a company should vary, since each often has quite different familiarity with specific technologies.

LIMITATION IN PLANNING BENEFITS

As new products appear, as the competitive environment shifts, as the laws change, as corporate strategies change, and as mergers and spinoffs take place, the priorities a company assigns to its various applications appropriately evolve as well. Some previously considered low-priority or new (not even conceived of) applications may become critically important, while others previously vital will diminish in significance. This volatility places a real premium on building a fexible framework to permit change to be managed in an orderly and consistent fashion to match evolving business requirements.

In a similar vein, every information systems planning process must make some very specific assumptions about the nature and role of technological evolution. If this evolution occurs at a different rate from the one forecasted (as is often the case), then major segments of the plan may have to be reworked in terms of both scope and thrust of work.

For example, if the present speed of access to a 100-million character file were suddenly increased in the coming year by an order of magnitude beyond current expectations, with no change in cost, most organizations' plans would require careful reexamination, not just concerning the priority of applications but, more important, their very structure.

Some individuals have used this as a reason not to plan but rather to be creatively opportunistic on a year-to-year basis. We have found the balance of evidence supporting this viewpoint unconvincing.

PLANNING AS A RESOURCE DRAIN

Every person, or part of a person, assigned to planning diverts resources away from systems and program development. The extent to which financial resources should be devoted to planning is still very much a question. Not only will the style of planning evolve over time, as parts of the organization pass through different phases with different technologies, but the amount of commitment to planning will also appropriately shift. This suggests that there is incompatibility between the notions of stability in an IS planning process and its role of stimulating a creative view of the future. If not carefully managed, IS planning tends to evolve into a mind-numbing process of routinely changing the numbers as opposed to stimulating a sensitive focus on the company's real problems.

FIT TO CORPORATE CULTURE

An important aspect of IS planning is to implement it in a way which ensures congruence with the realities of the corporate culture. Organizations, for example, which have a very formal corporate planning process, whose relevance is actively supported by senior management, have a pre-sold internal user-management climate which supports formal approaches to IS planning. In middle management's eyes, planning is a legitimate activity, and devoting time to it is appropriate. Other organizations, however, have quite different cultures and approaches to corporate planning. These factors significantly alter both the form and the degree of commitment that can be won from users in an IS planning process and consequently shape the most desirable way to approach the planning task. This is discussed further later in the chapter.

STRATEGIC IMPACT OF IS ACTIVITIES

For some organizations, IS activities represent an area of great strategic importance, while for other organizations they play, and appropriately will continue to play, a cost-effective and useful role but one which is distinctly supportive in nature. It is inappropriate for organizations of this latter type to expect that the same amount of senior management strategic thinking be devoted to the IS organization as for organizations of the former type. This issue is complicated by the fact that while today the IS function may not have strategic importance, the thrust of its applications portfolio may be such as to have great significance for the future and, thus, planning is very important. The opposite, of course, could also be true where IS plays a strategic operational role in the company's operations, but their future applications do not seem to offer the same payoff or significance. Here a less intensive focus on strategic planning is in order with clearly different people involved than in the previous case.

The above points (which were discussed first in Chapter 2) are illustrated below by the identification of four quite different IS environments. (Also see Exhibit 5–1.)

EXHIBIT 5-1 □ Information Systems Strategic Grid

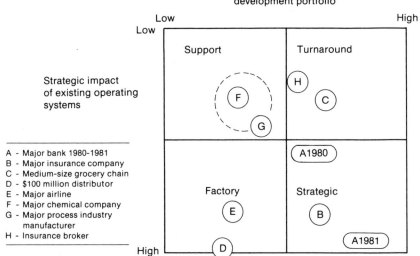

Strategic impact application
development portfolio

Strategic. These are companies which are critically dependent on the smooth functioning of the IS activity. Appropriately managed, these firms not only require considerable IS planning but IS planning needs to be closely integrated with corporate planning in a two-way dialogue. Not only does IS need the guidance of corporate goals but the achievement of these goals can be severely impacted by IS performance and capabilities or lack thereof. The impact of IS on the firm's performance is such that significant general management guidance in IS planning is appropriate.

Recent comments by the CEO of a large financial institution to his senior staff captured this perspective as he noted: "Most of our customer services and much of our office support for those services involve some kind of systematic information processing. Without the computer hardware and software supporting these processing efforts, we would undoubtedly drown in a sea of paper—unless we were first eliminated from the market because our costs were so high and our services so inefficient that we had no customers to generate the paper. Either way, it is abundantly clear that information systems are critical to our survival and our success."

"In our businesses, the critical resources which ultimately determine our marketing and our operating performance are *people* and *systems*."

Turnaround. In a similar way to companies in the strategic box, these firms also need a substantial IS planning effort, which is linked to corporate planning in a two-way dialogue. Corporate long-term performance can be severely impacted by shortfalls in IS performance and capabilities. Again, the impact of IS on the firm's future is such that significant general management guidance in IS planning is appropriate.

These are firms which may receive considerable amounts of IS operational support, but where the company is not absolutely dependent on the uninterrupted cost-effective functioning of this support to achieve either short-term or long-term objectives. The impact of the applications under development, however, is absolutely vital for the firm to reach its strategic objectives. A good example of this was a rapidly growing manufacturing firm. IS technology embedded in its factories and accounting processes, while important, was not absolutely vital to their effectiveness. The rapid growth of the firm's domestic and international installations in number of products, number of sites, number of staff, etc., however, had severely strained its management control systems and had made its improvement of critical strategic interest to the company. Enhanced IS leadership, new organizational placement of IS, and an increased commitment to planning were all steps taken to resolve the situation. Companies in this block not only have an increased need for IS planning but frequently it takes place along with a number of other changes to enhance senior management's overview of IS.

Factory. Strategic goal setting for IS and linkage to long-term corporate strategy is not nearly as critical in this environment. IS planning can take place with appropriate guidance as to where the corporation is going; only limited feedback on IS constraints needs to go in the other direction. Senior management involvement in IS planning appropriately is much less. Detailed year-to-year operational planning and capacity planning is absolutely critical.

Support. Again, strategic goal setting for IS and linkage to long-term corporate strategy is not nearly as critical as for the turnaround and strategic environments. IS constraints are not a critical input to corporate success. Overachievement or underachievement of IS departmental performance will not cause critical problems. Senior management involvement in the IS planning process can be much less here than in the first two situations.

Example of Use of Grid

Not only should the planning approach differ for each of the environments discussed above, but the situation is further complicated when a mismatch exists between where an organization is in the grid and where senior management believes it should be. In general, more planning is needed when a firm is trying to deal with a mismatch.

The following example illustrates the complexity of this problem in terms of a situation recently faced by a large financial institution. The institution's senior management was very comfortable with the company's IS performance although it came up only infrequently on their agenda. Its IS management team, however, was deeply concerned that they lacked the necessary conception of what the firm's goals were and what its products would be four to five years hence. They wanted to ensure that they could provide the necessary support for the achievement of these goals.

The institution is a large international one with a very sophisticated, but closely held, corporate planning activity. Appropriately in a world of potential major shifts in what financial institutions can and should do, there was great concern at the top about the confidentiality of this information, and only a handful of four or five individuals knew the full scope of this direction. Neither the IS manager nor his boss were among this handful. Consequently, they were substantially in the dark about future direction of the organization and could only crudely assess it in terms of trying to guess why some projects were unfunded while others were funded.

The company had a full-time IS planning manager who had three assistants and who reported to the IS manager. For the last two years, the IS planners had worked closely with both middle-management users and the DP technologists to come up with strategies and applications portfolios which were commonly seen by both sides to be relevant to their needs. Because there was little direct linkage of either a formal or informal nature between the IS planning activity and the corporate planning department (repeatedly, corporate planning had communicated "don't call us, we'll call you"), the IS staff had two overriding concerns:

1. The plans and strategies developed for IS might be technically sound and meet the needs of user management, but could be unproductive or indeed counterproductive in terms of its ability to support the institution's corporate thrust.
2. The corporate plans as developed by the four or five at the top in the know but also isolated from IS could unwittingly place onerous or unworkable pressures on IS in terms of future support requests.

At this stage, senior management perceived IS as a factory, believed it was staffed appropriately, was being managed appropriately, and had no concerns about its planning process. IS saw itself as strategic but couldn't sell the concept to anyone. This frustration was recently resolved when an outside review of the institution's overall strategy convinced senior management that they had misunderstood the role of IS and that IS should be treated as strategic. Unfortunately, in the process of evolution, IS management, who were perceived as being satisfactory to run a factory, were quickly perceived as being inadequate for this newly defined challenge and were personally unable to survive the transition.

IS planning on the surface had looked good when one read the written plan. However, in fact, it had failed to come to grips with the realities of the corporate environment and had left an organization for which IS activities are of significant strategic importance in a state of potential unpreparedness and risk. This was fatal where, on multiple dimensions, IS activities were belatedly perceived as being critical to the organization's achievement of its product and productivity goals.

This IS criticality segmentation is useful, not just for talking about corporate IS planning for the company as a whole but for thinking about individual business units and functions as well. IS technology's impact often varies widely by unit and function and the planning process must be adapted to deal with these differences. While making the planning's execution more complex, it also makes it more useful.

Exhibit 5–2 contains a questionnaire used by one firm to analyze the strategic thrust of the development portfolio for each of its organizational units. These questions are designed to uncover whether on balance the development work being done is *critical* to the firm's future competitive posture or whether it is useful *but* not at the core of what has to be done to be competitively successful. Similarly, Exhibit 5–3 contains a questionnaire used by the firm to analyze how critical the existing systems are to an organization unit in achieving its basic operating objectives. Both exhibits are used by the firm as rough diagnostic tools.

EXHIBIT 5–2 □ Information Systems Planning—a Contingent Focus *(portfolio analysis)*

	Percent of development budget	Strategic weight°
1. Projects involved in researching impact of new technologies or anticipated new areas of applications where generation of expertise, insight, and knowledge is the main benefit.	0–5% 5–15% Over 15%	−1 −2 −3
2. Projects involved in cost displacement or cost-avoidance productivity improvement.	Over 70% 40–70% Under 40%	−3 −2 −1
3. Do estimated aggregate improvements of these projects exceed 10 percent of firm's after-tax profits of 1 percent of sales?	Yes No	−2 −0
4. Projects focused at routine maintenance to meet evolving business needs (processing new union-contract payroll data) or meeting new regulatory or legal requirements.	Over 70% 40–70% Under 40%	−1 −2 −3
5. Projects focused on existing system enhancements which do not have identifiable hard benefits.	Under 10% 10–40% Over 40%	−3 −2 −1

		Percent of development budget	Strategic weight*
6.	Projects whose primary benefit is providing new decision support information to top three levels of management. No tangible identifiable benefits.	0–5% 5–15% Over 15%	−0 −2 −4
7.	Projects whose primary benefit is to offer new decision support information to middle management or clerical staff.	0–5% 5–15% Over 15%	−0 −1 −2
8.	Projects which allow the firm to develop and offer new products or services for sale or enable additional significant new features to be added to existing product line.	Over 20% 10–20% 5–10% Under 5%	−4 −3 −2 −1
9.	Projects which enable development of new administrative control and planning processes. No tangible benefit.	Over 20% 10–20% 5–10% 0–5%	−4 −3 −2 −1
10.	Projects which offer significant tangible benefits through improved operational efficiencies (reduce inventory, but direct reduction in operating costs, improved credit collection, etc.).	Over 20% 10–20% 5–10% 0–5%	−4 −3 −2 −1
11.	Do tangible benefits amount to 10 percent of after-tax profit or 1 percent of gross sales?	Yes No	−2 −1
12.	Projects which appear to offer new ways for the company to compete (fast delivery, higher quality, broader array of support services).	Over 20% 10–20% 5–10% Under 5%	−4 −3 −2 −1
13.	Do these projects offer ability to generate benefits in excess of 10 percent of after-tax earnings or 1 percent of gross sales?	Yes No	−2 0
14.	Size of development budget percent of value added.	Over 4% 3–4% 2–3% 2%	−3 −2 −1 −0

*Larger numbers mean more strategic.

Exhibit 5–4 suggests that not only does a firm's placement in this matrix influence how IS planning should be done but has numerous other implications in terms of the role of the executive steering committee, organizational placement of IS, type of IS management control system appropriate, etc. Further, since different organizational units within a company may be at

---

EXHIBIT 5-3 □ **Information Systems Planning—a Contingent Focus (*Operational dependence questionnaire*)** *

1. *Impact of a one-hour shutdown—main center*

    Major operational disruption in customer service, plant shutdown, groups of staff totally idle.

    Inconvenient but core business activities continue unimpaired.

    Essentially negligible.

2. *Impact of total shutdown—main center—two to three weeks*

    Almost fatal—no ready source of backup.

    Major external visibility, major revenue shortfall or additional costs.

    Expensive—core processes can be preserved at some cost, and at reduced quality levels.

    Minimal—fully acceptable tested backup procedures exist, incremental costs manageable, transition costs acceptable.

3. *Costs of IS as percent total corporate costs*

    Over 10%.

    2%–10%.

    Under 2%.

4. *Operating systems*

    Operating system software totally customized and maintained internally.

    Major reliance vendor-supplied software but significant internal enhancements.

    Almost total reliance on standard vendor packages.

5. *Labor*

    Data center work force organized—history of strikes.

    Nonunionized work force, either inexperienced and/or low morale.

    High morale—unorganized work force.

quite different points on the grid, the planning organization and control approach suitable for one unit may be quite inappropriate for another. Finally, an organization and control approach suitable at one point in time may be quite unsuitable at another point in time.

IS MANAGEMENT CLIMATE

In an environment of great management turmoil, turnover, and reassessment, it is unlikely that the same intensity and commitment of effort to planning IS can be productively unleashed as can be in an environment where there is more stability in the structure and where individuals have a stronger emotional attachment to the organization.

In aggregate, while these factors limit the payoff from planning and make its effective execution more complex, they do not eliminate its need. Rather, they both define the multidimensional complexity of the task and place

6. *Quality control—criticalness*

   Processing errors—major external exposure.

   Processing errors—modest external exposure.

   Processing errors—irritating—modest consequence.

7. *Number of operationally critical online systems or batch systems*

   10 or more.

   3–5.

   0–2.

8. *Dispersion of critical systems*

   Critical systems—one location.

   Critical systems—two to three installations.

   Critical systems—run by multiple departments. Geographic dispersion of processing.

9. *Ease of recovery after failure—six hours*

   Three to four days—heavy workload. Critical system.

   12–24 hours critical systems.

   Negligible—almost instantaneous.

10. *Recovery after quality control failure*

    Time-consuming, expensive, many interrelated systems.

    Some disruption and expense.

    Relatively quick—damage well contained.

11. *Feasibility coping manually 80–20 percent basis (i.e., handling 20%*
    of the transactions which have 80% of the value)

    Impossible.

    Somewhat possible.

    Relatively easy.

First answer to each question indicates great operational vulnerability; last answer to each question indicates low operational vulnerability.

bounds on the reasonableness of expectations, which appropriately vary from setting to setting.

IS PLANNING AND CORPORATE STRATEGY

In thinking about the role IS should play in a firm, it is important to understand the nature of the overall competitive position of the firm or business unit and how it competes. This position and the competitive weapons primarily used significantly influence whether IS is strategic to a unit, how investments in IS technology should be thought about, and how IS planning should be executed. For illustrative purposes, two of the most widely used current frameworks for competitive analysis will be discussed here in terms of their implications for IS strategy. These are Michael Porter's

---

EXHIBIT 5-4 ☐ **Examples of Different Managerial Strategies for Companies in Support and Strategic Boxes (assuming they are appropriately located)**

Support	Activity	Strategic
Middle-level management ⟵ membership. Existence of committee less critical.	Steering committee	⟶ Active senior management involvement. Committee key.
Less urgent. Mistakes in ⟵ resource allocation not fatal.	Planning	⟶ Critical. Must link to corporate strategy. Careful attention to resource allocation vital.
Avoid high-risk projects ⟵ because of constrained benefits. A poor place for corporate strategic gambles.	Risk profile—project portfolio	⟶ Some high-risk/high-potential benefit projects appropriate if possibility exists to gain strategic advantage.
Can be managed in a ⟵ looser way. Operational headaches less severe.	IS capacity management	⟶ Critical to manage. Must leave slack.
Can be lower. ⟵	IS management reporting level	⟶ Should be very high.
A conservative posture ⟵ one to two years behind state-of-art appropriate.	Technical innovation	⟶ Critical to stay current and fund R&D. Competitor can gain advantage.
Lower priority—less ⟵ heated debate.	User involvement and control over system	⟶ Very high priority. Often emotional.
Managed cost center IS ⟵ viable. Chargeout less critical and less emotional.	Chargeout system	⟶ Critical they be sensitively designed.
System modernization ⟵ and development expenses postponable in time of crisis.	Expense control	⟶ Effectiveness key. Must keep applications up to date. Other places to save money.
More time to resolve it. ⟵	Uneven performance of IS management	⟶ Serious and immediately actionable.

---

views as communicated in his book, *Competitive Strategy: Techniques for Analyzing Industries and Competitors*[3], and the Boston Consulting Group's widely discussed framework.

---

[3] New York: Free Press, 1980.

Generic Strategies

Porter suggests that there are three generic strategies a firm can adopt. These are noted below together with a brief discussion of their impact on IS as a component of corporate strategy.

Strategy #1. *Be the low-cost producer.* (Appropriate for a standardized product.) Significant profit increases and explosion of market share come from being able to drive operating costs significantly below those of competition. IS offers strategic value in this environment if, for example, it can:

1. Permit major reduction in production and clerical staff. (This will hit labor costs, lowering cost/unit.)
2. Permit better utilization of manufacturing facilities by better scheduling, etc. (There will be less fixed asset expense attached to each unit of production.)
3. Allow significant reduction in inventory, accounts receivable, etc. (That is, reduce interest costs and facilities costs.)
4. Provide better utilization of materials and lower overall costs by reduction of wastage. (Better utilization of lower-grade materials is possible in settings where quality degradation is not an issue.)

If the nature of the firm's manufacturing and distribution technologies do not permit these types of savings, IS is unlikely to be of strategic interest as far as the firm's long-term competitive posture is concerned.

Strategy #2. *Produce a unique differentiated product.* This differentiation can occur along a number of dimensions such as quality, special design features, availability, special services that offer end-consumer value. For example, IS offers strategic value to this corporate environment if:

1. IS is a significant component of the product and its costs, and hence is an important differentiable feature. (Banks, brokerage houses, credit card operations all vie to compete with IS-based service differentiation.)
2. IS can significantly impact the lead time for product development, customization, and delivery. In many industries computer-aided design/computer-aided manufacturing (CAD/CAM) provides this advantage today.
3. IS can permit customization of a product to the customer's specific needs in a way not possible before. (CAD/CAM in specialized textile made-to-order operations such as men's suits.)
4. IS can give a visibly higher and unique level of customer service and need satisfaction which can be built into the end price. (Special-order enquiry status for key items.)

If IS cannot produce perceived differentiable features for firms and business units competing in this way, it is unlikely to be of strategic interest as far as the firm's ability to achieve long-term competitive position is concerned.

Strategy #3. *Ability to identify and fill the needs of specialized markets.* These markets could either be special geographic regions or a cluster of very specialized end-user needs. IS offers strategic value for these firms if:

1. IS permits better identification of special customer need niches and various unevennesses in the market's needs, that is, the ability to analyze company or industry sales data bases to spot unusual trends. (Greeting card companies describe each card in a number of dimensions and can spot, for example, that three-line verses and primarily red cards with contemporary designs, are taking off in the Upper Plain states, and thus take appropriate action.)
2. Their outputs are IS-intensive products, or products whose end features can be modified by IS customization to local needs.

Summary. These paragraphs are to suggest that the generic competitive strategy selected by a firm significantly influences the kinds of things that one looks for from IS if it is to be "strategic" as opposed to "support" for the firm. Different competitive strategies bring very different perspectives to bear on assessing and developing IS strategies. It is critical that these perspectives be taken into account in the IS planning process.

Review-of-Operations Strategy

Another useful cut at assessing the strategic impact of IS is to adopt the Boston Consulting Group's framework of looking at a company's operations over the past decade. Exhibit 5–5 contains their time-honored matrix of dividing firms along the dimensions of market growth and position in the market.

The following paragraphs suggest the differing criteria a unit in each box should bring to assessing its IS strategy.

Stars

1. These firms should accept greater implementation and benefit risk to gain or maintain a meaningful competitive position.
2. Excessive return-on-investment (ROI) focus can get the organization into serious problems. Projects with potentially major intangible benefits in terms of preserving market image, etc. can get deferred through lack of specificity.

EXHIBIT 5-5 □ Position in Market

		Low	High
Market growth	High	?	Stars
	Low	Dogs	Cash cows

Source: Adapted from Barry Hedley, "Strategy and the Business Portfolio," *Long-Range Planning,* February 1977, p. 10.

3. Effectiveness is more important than efficiency in viewing new investment opportunities.
4. Unit should receive #1 priority for applications which support its attainment of market share goals. This includes quality of effort and time to implement.
5. While short-term projects are suitable, this is an appropriate place to make long-term strategic investments.

Cash Cows

1. It is important to invest in intangible products if necessary to *maintain* competitive position. These projects are as critical as those in the star units. Projects which are not aimed at maintaining market share need to be justified on the ROI basis.
2. The risk profile of the applications portfolio should be quite low unless a project is aimed at protecting a vital aspect of competitive exposure.
3. ROI is an important focus as the unit attempts to wring extra profits and efficiency out of its operation.

Dogs

1. Investment in this area must be scanned very carefully. Unless they promise to turn the operation and/or industry around, they should not be made without careful ROI focus.
2. Investments here in an environment of limited resources must take a lower priority than those in other units with a bright future.
3. Care should be taken in designing software which links this department with the rest of the company. In the future this unit is a candidate either to be abandoned or spun off.
4. High-risk projects should be avoided here unless major opportunity exists to turn the competitive structure around.
5. Focus of projects should be short term.

Summary

The notions implicit in these two frameworks are introduced here to suggest the following:

1. The competitive position of a business unit and its generic business strategy profoundly influence how one should think about potential IS investments and the contribution from existing IS systems. Key inputs to the strategic/turnaround/factory/support categorizations flow from analysis of these items.

2. Since different business units in a firm often have quite different competitive positions and quite different generic competitive strategies, a common approach to viewing IS's contribution and role is unlikely to be appropriate in these settings.

3. Since competitive position and generic strategy change over time, a constant approach over time to IS strategy formulation may be quite inappropriate.

CORPORATE ENVIRONMENT FACTORS
INFLUENCING PLANNING

Recently completed research has identified four clusters of corporate environmental factors which influence how IS planning must be structured to improve the likelihood of success.[4]

1. The perceived importance and status of the systems manager. Proper alignment of status of the IS manager to the role IS plays or should play in the overall operation and strategy formulating process of the company is very important. In environments where IS is in a "strategic" or "turnaround" role, a low status IS manager (reporting level and/or in compensation) makes it hard to get the necessary inputs and credibility from general management in the planning process. If the corporate communication culture at the top is heavily informal, this is apt to be fatal, as IS is outside the key communication loop. If the corporate culture is more formal, development and management of appropriate committees and other formal processes can significantly alleviate the situation. For companies where IS is and should be in the "support" role, lower status of the IS director is appropriate and less effort needs to be made to assure alignment of IS and corporate strategy. Further, a lower level of investment (dollars and type of staff) in IS planning is appropriate for these situations. This is illustrated by the recent comments of a director of strategic planning for a large process-manufacturing company. "We relate to IS by giving them insight on what the corporate goals are and

---

[4] Pyburn, "Information Systems Planning."

what the elements and forms are of a good planning system. Because of their role in the company, we do not solicit feedback from them as to what the art of the possible is. The nature of their operation is such that they can provide no useful input to the selection of corporate strategy."

2. *Physical proximity of systems group and general management team.* For organizations where many important decisions are made informally in ad hoc sessions, and where IS is playing a "strategic" or "turnaround" role, it is important to keep key IS management staff physically close to the senior line manager. Regardless of the systems manager's status, it is difficult for him to be an active member of the team in this type of organization if he is geographically distant. In the words of one manager in such a company, when a problem surfaces, those people who are around and easily accessible are those who solve it, and "we don't wait to round up the missing bodies." When the prevailing management culture is more formal, physical proximity becomes less important. In these situations, the formal written communications and the scheduled formal meetings largely substitute for the informal give-and-take. In informal organizations, where IS is "strategic" or "turnaround," even if the systems groups must be located many miles from headquarters for other reasons, it is critical that the IS managers, and preferably a small staff, be at corporate headquarters. For "support" and "factory" organizations in informal organizations, location at corporate headquarters is much less critical.

3. *Corporate culture and management "style."* In organizations where the basic management culture is characterized by the words *low key* and *informal,* and where an informal personal relationship exists between the systems manager and senior management, then formal IS planning procedures do not appear to be a critical determinant of perceived systems effectiveness. Development of this relationship is assisted (as mentioned above) by the geographic proximity and IS manager status. As an organization becomes more formal, IS planning discipline becomes more significant as a countervailing force, even for systems environments which are not highly complex.

4. *Organizational size and complexity.* As organizations increase in both size and complexity, and as applications of information systems technology grows larger and more complex, more formal planning processes are needed to ensure the kind of broad-based dialogue essential to the development of an integrated "vision of IS." Of course, this phenomenon is not unrelated to the previous dimension concerning management culture and style as greater size and complexity often leads to more formal practices in general. In environments where the business unit size is small and relatively simple, formal planning approaches become less critical irrespective of the other factors. Similarly, for business units where the systems environment is not terribly complex, IS planning can safely take place in a more informal

fashion. However, as the portfolio of work increases in size and in integration across user areas, more discipline and formality in the planning process become necessary.

In aggregate, these corporate culture items highlight another dimension as to why selection of a planning approach is so complex and why recommendations on how to do IS planning "in general" almost always turn out to be too inflexible and prescriptive for a specific situation. (Even within a company, these issues may force considerable heterogeneity of practice between organization units.)

CORPORATE ENVIRONMENTAL FACTORS— AN EXAMPLE

The following example shows how these issues have shaped the planning process in a billion-dollar manufacturing organization. Key aspects of the corporate environment include:

1.   The company had both a medium-sized corporate IS facility and stand-alone IS facilities of some significant size in each of its six major U.S. divisions. These divisional IS facilities report straight line to the divisions and dotted line to the corporate IS function. The corporate IS group is part of a cluster of corporate staff activities in an organization where traditionally some considerable power has been located at corporate level.

2.   The vice president of corporate IS also had the corporate planning activity reporting to him. In addition, he had a long personal and professional relationship with both the chairman and chief executive officer which had extended over a period of many years in a company which could be described as having an informal management culture. He was initially given responsibility for IS because the number of operational and development problems had reached crisis proportions. While under normal circumstances, the criticality of IS might be termed "support," these difficulties pushed the firm into the "turnaround" category.

3.   The closeness of relationships between the division general managers and their IS managers varies widely. The size of the application portfolios in relation to the overall size of the division also varied considerably, with IS activities playing a more significant role in some settings than in others.

IS planning begins at the divisional level within the bounds of some rather loose corporate guidelines concerning technological direction. At the divisional level, planning culminates in the preparation of a divisional IS plan. The planning processes and dialogues vary widely from division to division in terms of line manager involvement in developing the plans. In some settings, the line managers are intimately involved in the process of developing the plan, with the division general manager investing considerable time in the final review and modification to the plan. In other divisions, however, the relationship is not so close, and IS plans were developed almost entirely by the IS organization with very limited review by the general management. The relationship of IS activities to the strategic functioning of the various units varies widely.

Critical to the IS planning process is an annual three-day meeting of the corporate IS director and his key staff where the divisional IS managers present their plans. The corporate IS director plays a major role in these sessions in critiquing and modifying plans to better fit corporate objectives. His understanding of the corporate plan, the thinking of the divisional general managers (in his capacity as head of corporate planning), and his firsthand knowledge concerning what is on the chairman's and president's minds enables him to immediately spot shortfalls in IS plans. This is particularly true for those divisions where there are weak IS line management relationships. As a result, plans evolve which fit the real business needs of the organization, and the IS activity is well regarded. A set of planning processes, which in other settings might have led to disaster, has worked out well because of the special qualities of the IS director and development of a communication approach between him and general management which is appropriate for this firm's culture.

SUMMARY

There continues to be evidence that there is a clear link between effective planning and effectively perceived IS activity for many organization settings. Quite apart from the generation of new ideas, and so on, a major role of the IS planning process is stimulation of discussion and exchange of insights between the specialists and the users. Effectively managed, it is an important element in cooling the temperature of potential conflict.

For example, a major financial institution that we studied attempted at least four different approaches to IS planning over a six-year period. Each was started with great fanfare, with different staffs and organizations, and each limped to a halt. However, it was only when the firm abandoned efforts to plan that deep and ultimately irreconcilable differences arose between IS and the user organization. Communication of viewpoints and exchange of problems and potential opportunities (key to developing shared understanding) is as important as the selection of specific projects.

In this context our conclusions are:

1. Organizations where the IS activity is integral to corporate strategy implementation have a special need to build links between IS and the corporate strategy formulation process. As indicated earlier, the process of accomplishing this is complex, requiring resolution along multiple dimensions. Key aspects of this dialogue are:

    a. Testing elements of corporate strategy to ensure that they are doable within IS resource constraints. On some occasions, the resources needed are obtainable, but in other settings, resources are unavailable, and painful readjustments must be made.

  b. Transfer of planning and strategy formulating skills to the IS function.
  c. Ensuring long-term availability of appropriate IS resources.

In other "support" and "factory" settings, this linkage is less critical. Appropriately, over time the need for this linkage may change as the strategic mission of IS evolves.

2. As organizations grow in size, complexity of systems, and formality, IS planning must be directly assigned to someone to avoid resulting lack of focus and the risk of significant pieces dropping between cracks. This job, however, is a subtle and complex one. The task is to ensure that planning occurs in an appropriate form. A strong set of enabling and communication skills is critical if the individual is to relate to the multiple individuals and units impacted by this technology and cope with their differing familiarity with it. Ensuring involvement of IS staff and users for both inputs and conclusions occurrence is key. The great danger is that frequently planners evolve the task with more of a *doing* orientation than an enabling one and begin to interpose, inappropriately, their sets of priorities and understanding. To overcome this problem, many organizations have defined this job more as a transitional one than a career one.

3. Planned clutter in the planning approach is appropriate to deal with the fact that the company is in different phases with respect to different technologies and the technologies have different strategic payout to different organization units at different points in time. While it is superficially attractive and orderly to conceive planning all technologies for all business units to the same level of detail and time horizon, in reality this is an inappropriate goal.

4. IS planning must be tailored to the realities of the corporate style of doing business. Importance and status of the IS managers, geographic placement of IS in relation to general management, corporate culture and management style, and organizational size and complexity all influence how IS planning can be best done.

5. The planning process must be considerably broader in the range of technologies it covers than just data processing. It must deal with the technologies of electronic communications, data processing, office automation, stand-alone minis, and so forth, both separately and in an integrated fashion.

Chapter 6 □ IS Management Control

Chapter \ Manageable Trend	Strategic Impact	DP/TP/OA	Organization Learning	Make/Buy	Life Cycle	GM/ User/ IS
IS Technology Organization Issues **Chapter 3**		●	●			●
Organizational Issues in IS Development **Chapter 4**	●		●	●		●
Information Systems Planning **Chapter 5**	●		●			●
IS Management Control **Chapter 6**	●		●	●		●
A Portfolio Approach to Information Systems Development **Chapter 7**	●				●	●
Operations Management **Chapter 8**	●			●	●	●
Multinational IS Issues **Chapter 9**		●				●
The IS Business **Chapter 10**	●		●	●		●

INTRODUCTION

The IS management control system is a critical network which integrates the information services activities with the rest of the firm's operations. Whereas the project management system *guides* the life cycle of individual projects (which often last more than a year) and the planning process takes a multiyear view in assimilating technologies and systems to match the company's evolving needs and strategies, the IS management control system focuses primarily on guiding the entirety of the information services department on a year-to-year basis. The management control system builds on the output of the planning process to develop a portfolio of projects, hardware/software enhancements and additions, facilities plans, and staffing levels for the year. It then monitors their progress, raising red flags for action when appropriate. The broad objectives an effective IS management control system must meet include the following:

1. Facilitate appropriate communication between the user and deliverer of IS services and provide motivational incentives for them to work together on a day-to-day, month-to-month basis. The management control system must encourage users and IS to act in the best interests of the organization as a whole. It must motivate users to use IS resources appropriately and help them balance investments in this area against those in other areas.
2. Encourage the effective utilization of the IS department's resources, and ensure that users are educated on the potential of existing and evolving technology. In so doing, it must guide the transfer of technology consistent with strategic needs.
3. It must provide the means for efficient management of IS resources and give necessary information for investment decisions. This requires development of both standards of performance measures and the means to evaluate performance against those measures to ensure productivity is being achieved. It should help facilitate make-or-buy decisions.

Early IS management control systems tended to be very cost focused, relying heavily, for example, upon ROI evaluations of capital investments. These proved workable in situations where the technology was installed on a cost displacement justification basis. However, in firms where the computer was a competitive wedge (CAD/CAM, or industrial robotics today) or the technology was pervasively influencing the industry structure of operations, such as in banking and financial services, focus on cost analysis and displacement alone was not an appropriate metric, and development of additional management control techniques has been necessary. For example, a large metropolitan bank several years ago instituted an expensive, complex chargeout system to improve user awareness of costs. Poorly thought out in broad context, the system generated a surge in demand for "cheap" minicomputers, triggered an overall decline in quality of central IS support, and ultimately created market image and sales difficulties for the bank as a whole. Recently, the system was abandoned.

Four special inputs now appear to be critical to the specific structuring of an appropriate IS management control system for an organization. These are:

1. The control system must be adapted to a very different software and operations technology in the 1980s then was present in the 1970s. An important part of this adaptation is development of appropriate sensitivity to the mix of phases of IS technologies in the company. The more mature technologies must be managed and controlled in a tighter, more efficient way than ones in an early start-up phase which need protective treatment appropriate to a research development activity.
2. Specific aspects of the corporate environment influence the appropriate IS Management Control System. Key issues here include IS sophistica-

tion of users, geographic dispersion of the organization, stability of the management team, the firm's overall size and structure, nature of relationship between line and staff departments, etc. These items influence what is workable.

3. The general architecture of the organization's overall corporate management control system and the philosophy underlying it.

4. The perceived strategic significance of IS both in relation to the thrust of its applications portfolio and the role played by currently automated systems.

IS TECHNOLOGY EVOLUTION AND MANAGEMENT CONTROL

Software Issues. The management control problem posed by software development has become more complex because an increasing percentage of DP software support is for maintenance while most OA is bought. This has meant that necessary operational changes to keep the business running have become intermixed with a stream of small, long-term, service-improving capital investments. These two streams are not easily decomposable in many organizations; consequently inadequate controls on operating expense maintenance have developed in many organizations. These controls are often inappropriately applied to stimulate or choke off systems enhancements that are really capital investments.

A second software issue is posed by outside software sourcing. As the percentage of development money devoted to outside software acquisition grows, management control systems designed for an environment where all sourcing was done internally may be inappropriate for environments now dominated by software and make/buy alternatives.

Operations Issues. For IS operations, management control is complex because of the difficulty in measuring and allocating costs in a way which will encourage appropriate behavior in a situation where short-term costs are relatively fixed, and there is considerable volatility in the mix of uses of the IS resource. The operations cost control problem has been further complicated by the cost behavior of IS technology over time. Technical change has created a world where the replacement for a previous computer generally has 4 to 10 times more capacity than the existing one while costing somewhat less than the original one's purchase price. This has created an interesting control issue.

Should the cost per unit of IS processing be lower in the early years (to reflect the lower load factor) so that it can be held flat over the life of the gear, while permitting full (but not excessive) recovery of costs? Conversely, as utilization grows over the years, should the cost per unit of IS processing to the user decline?

An example of coping with this is provided by a large insurance company which replaced an IBM 370/158 several years ago with an Amdahl V5, gaining four times the computing capacity at 15 percent less cost. Because the machine, after conversion, was loaded to barely 30 percent capacity, the managers were faced with the choice of spreading all the present costs on to their current users or forecasting future costs (assuming future volume activity) and setting a three-year average which would recover costs at the period's end. The first approach would have covered expenses from the start but, through its higher prices, would inhibit the initiation of useful work that was economically justified long term. Consequently, they chose the three-year average cost as the price basis to encourage use and to pass on the immediate productivity improvement to their current users. The unabsorbed costs were directly closed to corporate overhead.

The selection of a particular financial structure varies with the firm's experience with technology. Many organizations' current control architecture gives complete management to the user for office automation, while giving the same authority to IS for communications. This leaves traditional DP as the focus for negotiation. As we have noted, however, these are so interrelated as to make this former control architecture highly suspect. A critical contemporary problem is to ensure that these controls evolve forward to meet this new technical environment. For example, a large industrial organization was given free OA support to stimulate users while simultaneously charging for its traditional data base time-sharing decision support system. Very quickly they discovered that users started creating their own data bases on the micro OA equipment which both limited their OA experimentation and underutilized the time-sharing, thereby undercutting the firm's objectives. Our discussion of control structure, while recognizing these issues, does not attempt to definitely resolve it.

Corporate Culture Forces on the Control System

The User Growth in Influence.   A major stimulant to growth is IS usage has been the emergence of a group of experienced IS users familiar with how to solve problems with IS technology. After 20 years, it is clear that effective applications by users generate additional ideas for use on their part. This is desirable and healthy, provided a control system exists to encourage appropriate appraisal of the new use in terms of its potential costs and benefits to the organization. The absence of such a control system may result in explosive growth (often unprofitable and poorly managed) with new capacity required every one or two years or, alternatively, little growth with frustrated users obtaining necessary services surreptitiously (and more expensively).

Both events cause confidence in the IS department and its management control system to erode. The problem is further complicated by the fact that many of the new generation of user demands pose more difficulty in benefit articulation than in costs of provision. Repeatedly, we uncover situations where the control system has caused the hard cost of implementation numbers of an application to attain undue weight against the soft, but often very strategic, management benefits.

The preceding discussion suggests a paradoxical aspect of controlling information services; namely that, while the area is technologically complex, most of the critical success factors for its effective and efficient use are *highly* human dependent and, thus stated, pose very familiar management control challenges from a corporate perspective. A complicating element is, since both technology and user sophistication are continually changing, the types of applications to be done are changing. Many individuals are sufficiently set in their ways (reinforced by a control approach) that they find change difficult to implement and attempt to resist it. A by-product is that often the user perceptions of the change agent department (IS) are unnecessarily poor. For example, all sorts of spurious effects are attributed by the users to the introduction of a change to new computer systems, word processors, etc. In addition to technology and user learning, hidden forces of change also exist in external items, such as new tax laws, and in internal strategic items such as adding customers or products, moving offices, and modifying the organization. Recognition and appropriate implementation of these changes can be facilitated by a well-designed management control system.

The Geographic and Organizational Structure Influences. Other important control aspects relate to the organization's geographic dispersion and size. As the number of business sites grow and staff levels increase, often substantial changes are needed in organization structure, corporate management control, and IS management control. Informal personnel supervision and control which fits the more limited setting will fall apart in the larger and more dispersed ones. Similarly, the nature of relationships between line and staff departments within the company, in general, influences what relationship between the IS department and its users can be reasonably expected to evolve and thus the type of IS management control which is appropriate.

The organization structure of the firm plays an important role in the IS management control architecture. Firms which have a strong functional organization with central services function maintained as unallocated cost centers often find it appropriate to keep IS as an unallocated cost center. On the other hand, firms which are heavily decentralized into profit or investment centers, or which have a tradition of charging out for corporate services, are quickly propelled down the path of charging for corporate IS activities and often will move as far as setting it up as a profit or investment center. Over time, it becomes increasingly difficult to manage with good results an IS organization where the control architecture is sharply different from that present in the rest of the firm.

Corporate Planning and Control Process

In concept, the process of an appropriate IS planning and management control system should be similar to the corporate planning and control system. Ideally, in both cases there should be a multiyear plan linked appropriately to the overall business strategy which is also linked to a budget process that allows the responsible managers to negotiate an operating budget. As such, IS planning/budgeting should be compatible with overall business planning/budgeting. However, if business planning primarily includes an annual budget with periodic follow-up of performance during the year, a very difficult environment exists for IS management control. This is because the project life-cycle implementation of any sizable change can easily take two or more years from beginning to end, including as much as a year to formulate, select, and refine the appropriate design approach.

Thus, an IS organization often must maintain at least a three-year view of its activities to ensure the resources are available to meet these demands. In many cases, this extends the IS planning horizon beyond the organization's planning horizon. To be useful, these IS project plans must systematically and precisely identify alternative steps for providing necessary service. For example, to upgrade reservation service in a large hotel chain, the IS department, in concert with key hotel managers, had to project the type of service the hotels would need four years out. This was necessary in order to select the correct terminals and provide an orderly transition from the present situation to the new one over a 30-month period. A key bottleneck in this massive, one-time, 600-terminal installation was the total lack of a corporate planning and control approach which extended more than a year into the future.

This combination of short corporate horizons, long IS time horizons, and technical innovation generates conflict within the firm concerning management control that can only be resolved by repeated judgments over time. These conflicts pose two major clusters of managerial issues:

First, how congruent/similar should the management control architecture and process of information services be to that present in other parts of the organization? Where differences do exist, how can this dissonance be best managed, and should they be allowed to exist long term? Secondly, how can the tension between sound control and timely innovation be best balanced? Control typically depends on measuring costs against budgets, actual achievements versus promised, and evaluation of investments against returns. Innovation involves risk taking, gaining trial experience with emerging technologies, relying on faith, and at times moving forward despite a lack of clear objectives. A portfolio excessively balanced in either direction poses grave risks. (As will be discussed in Chapter 7, different companies will appropriately balance their portfolios quite differently.)

Strategic Impact of IS on the Congruence of IS Business Controls

An important input on how closely the IS control system should be matched to the business planning/control process is the strategic importance of IS for the next three years. If very strategic for the firm to achieve its goals, then development of a close linkage between corporate planning and control and IS planning and control is important, and differences between the two will cause great difficulty. Additionally, investment decisions and key product development innovations must be subject to periodic top management review.

The control system for these strategic environments must encourage value-based innovations even in the face of the reality that perhaps as few as one out of three will produce payoff. Often, in this situation the key control challenge is to encourage the generation, evaluation, and management of multiple and unplanned sources of suggestions for new services. Several now defunct brokerage houses and soon-to-be merged banks were unable to do this.

If IS is not strategically core to the business but is more a factory or support-type effort, congruency of links to the rest of the business planning and control activities are not as critical. IS can more appropriately develop an independent planning/control process to deal with its need to manage a changing user demand with an evolving technology.

A factory environment, for example, must emphasize efficiency controls, while a turnaround should focus upon effective utilization of new technology.

Summary

The theme of the above discussion is that to achieve appropriate results, the specific approach to IS management control must vary widely by organization because of its specific context, and also over time, as the context evolves on one or more of the dimensions discussed above. The rest of the chapter describes the key factors, beyond these contextual items, which influence selection of different forms of control architecture (financial), control process (financial), nonfinancial controls, and audit.

Our treatment of IS management control divides it into three parts. Each part is briefly defined here and discussed in depth later in the chapter.

1. Control Architecture. Should the IS function be set up as a cost center (unallocated), cost center (allocated), profit center, or an investment center or residual income center? Further, if costs are allocated from the IS function to the users, should the transfer price be market based, cost based, cost plus, split level, or negotiated? Each of these alternatives generates quite different behavior and motivation and are fundamental decisions which once made are not lightly changed. Finally, what nonfinancial measurements should be designed to facilitate effective use of IS.

2. Control Process (Financial and Nonfinancial). What form of developing action plans is most appropriate? Typically, this is represented by the annual budget and drives both operations and project development. Particular attention will be given here to the issues surrounding zero-based budgeting. What form of periodic reporting instruments and exception reporting tools (against budget targets) during the year are appropriate? As opposed to architectural issues, these are changed much more frequently.

3. Audit Function. Issues here include ensuring that an IS audit function exists, that it is focused on appropriate problems, and that it has suitable staff.

CONTROL ARCHITECTURE

Unallocated Cost Center

Establishment of the information services department as an *unallocated cost center* is a widely used approach and has many advantages associated with it. As an essentially free resource to the users, it stimulates a number of user requests and creates a climate which is conducive to encouraging user experimentation. This is particularly good for technologies which are in phase 1 or 2 of their assimilation into the firm. The lack of red tape makes it easier for the IS department to sell its services. All the controversy and acrimony over the IS chargeout process is avoided since no chargeout system exists. Further, very low expenditures need to be made on development and operations of IS accounting procedures. In aggregate, these factors make this a good alternative for situations where a small IS budget is present. Innovation is critical in settings where financial resource allocation is not a high-tension activity.

A large western bank has been introducing electronic mail and word processing for two years as an unallocated cost center. Their intent is to build a network and establish standard procedures. They see the value in the short run of encouraging a growing network as outweighing the cost savings from a standard systems development.

On the other hand, significant problems exist when IS is treated as an unallocated cost center. With no financial pressure being placed on the user,

IS can quickly be perceived as a free resource where each user should be sure to get their piece of the action. This can rapidly generate a series of irresponsible user requests for service which may be difficult to turn down. Further, in a situation where staff or financial resources are short, the absence of this chargeout framework increases the possibility of excessive politicization around IS resource allocation decisions. The unallocated cost center insulates the IS department from competitive pressures and external measures of performance, permitting the hiding of operational inefficiencies. Further, this approach fits the management control structure of some firms poorly (i.e., firms which have a strong tradition of charging out corporate staff services to users). Finally, this approach poses particular problems for organizations where IS charges are perceived to be both large and strategic. In combination, these pressures explain why, although many firms start with an unallocated cost center approach, they often evolve forward to another approach, at least for their more mature technologies and more mature users.

One approach widely followed is to keep IS as an unallocated cost center but inform users through memos of what their development and operations charges would have been if a chargeout system was in place. Without raising the friction associated with chargeout procedures (described below), this approach stimulates awareness by users that they are not using a free resource of the corporation, and gives them a feel for the general magnitude of their charges. The approach is often adopted as a way station when a firm is moving IS from an unallocated cost center to some other organizational form. Unfortunately, however, a memo about a charge does not have the same bite as the actual assignment of the charge.

Allocated Cost Center and Chargeout

The approach of establishing the information services department as an *allocated cost center* has the immediate virtue of helping to stimulate honesty in user requests from a corporate perspective. This approach fits rather well the later phases of technology assimilation where the usefulness of the technology has been widely communicated within the firm. While it opens up a debate as to what cost is, it avoids controversy about whether an internal service department should be perceived as a profit-making entity. This approach particularly fits environments which have a strong tradition of corporate services charges.

Inevitably, however, the allocated cost center introduces a series of complexities and frictions, since such a system necessarily has arbitrary elements in it. The following paragraphs suggest some of the practical problems which come from allocating IS department costs to users (irrespective of whether in a cost center or some other approach). The first problem is that the IS charges will be compared to IS charges prepared both by other companies in the same industry and by outside service organizations. This opens the possibility of generating clearly misleading and invidious conclusions. The words *misleading* and *invidious* are related because the prices prepared by other organizations often have one or more of the following characteristics:

1. The service being priced out is being treated as a by-product rather than as a joint costing problem.
2. IS is being treated under a different management control architectural scheme from that present in the company which is making the evaluation. Thus the comparison of costs is highly misleading.
3. An independent IS services firm or an in-house operation selling services to outside customers may deliberately produce an artificially low price as a way of buying market share, over a short-term horizon. Thus, their prices may be perceived as fair market when, in fact, they are nothing of the sort.

Consequently, since the prices produced by other companies are not the result of an efficient market, there is substantial possibility that comparing them to our prices may produce misleading data for management decisions.

Another issue of concern is that unless carefully managed, the chargeout system tends to discourage phase 1 and phase 2 research projects. These activities must be carefully segregated and managed in a different way than projects utilizing the more mature technologies. It is unnecessary in our view that 100 percent of IS costs be charged to the users. Segregating as much as 15 percent to 25 percent as a separately managed R&D function to be included in corporate overhead is a sound strategy. This is particularly important in the technology of the 1980s to ensure that artificial and inappropriate incentives are not stimulating inappropriately the installation of mini/microcomputers. Repeatedly, minicomputer systems have looked good to the user when their estimated costs were compared with the full cost charges of a central IS installation. From the corporate perspective, however, when an incremental analysis of costs is done, a quite different picture may emerge.

On a more technical note today, in the majority of companies which are charging out IS costs, two major concepts underlie the chargeout process. The first concept is that the chargeout system for IS operations costs is based on a very complex formula (based on use of computer technology by an application) which spreads the costs in a supposedly equitable fashion to the ultimate users. Featuring terms such as EXCPU's, the concept is that each user should bear computer costs in relation to his pro-rata use of the underlying resource. The second concept is that the chargeout system ensures that *all* costs of the activity are passed out to consumers of the service. Not infrequently, this involves zeroing out all IS costs each month and certainly by year end.

Rigorous application of these concepts have led to a number of unsatisfactory consequences from the user's perspective. Most important, the charges are absolutely *unintelligible* and *unpredictable* to the end user. Clothed in technical jargon and highly impacted by whether it has been a heavy or light month in the IS department, there is no way for the user to predict or control them short of disengaging from the IS activity (hence the explosion of stand-alone minis).

Not infrequently the charges are highly *unstable*. The same application, processing the same amount of data, run at the same time of the week or month will cost very different amounts depending on what else happens to be scheduled in the IS department during the month. In addition, if all unallocated costs are closed to the users at the end of the year, they may be hit with an entirely unwelcome and unanticipated surprise, generating considerable hostility.

Further, the charges tend to be *artificially high* in relation to incremental costs. As mentioned earlier, this can cause considerable friction with the users and encourage examination of alternatives which optimize short-term cost behavior at the expense of the long-term strategic interests of the firm.

Additionally, in both operations and development, this approach makes no attempt to segregate IS efficiency variances out and hold IS uniquely responsible for them. Rather, all efficiency variances are directly assigned to the ultimate users, creating additional friction and allegations of IS irresponsibility and mismangement. Finally, administration of a chargeout system of this type not infrequently turns out to be very expensive.

The combination of these factors have generated chargeout systems which do not satisfactorily meet the needs of many organizations. We believe this is a direct result of the technical and accounting foundations of the system. We believe that, for most situations, technology and accounting are the wrong disciplines to bring to the problem and that the task can be better approached as a problem in applied social psychology. What type of behavior do you want to trigger on the part of the IS organization and the users? What incentives can be provided to them to assure that, as they move to meet their individual goals, they are simultaneously moving more or less in a goal-congruent fashion with the overall interests of the corporation?[1] The design of such a system is a very complex task requiring trade-offs along multiple dimensions. As needs of the corporation change, the structures of the chargeout system will also appropriately change. Critical issues to be dealt with include:

1. Should the system be designed to encourage use of IS services (or components thereof) or should it set high hurdles for potential investments? The answer for phase 1 and phase 2 technology projects will be different from that for phase 3 and phase 4 technology projects.

---

[1] Robert N. Anthony and James S. Reece, *Accounting: Text and Cases*, 6th ed. (Richard D. Irwin, 1979), pp. 778–79.

2. Should the system encourage IS to adopt an efficiency or an effectiveness focus? The answer here may evolve over time.
3. Should the system provide a tilt in favor of use of IS department resources or encourage outside IS service sourcing decisions?
4. What steps must be taken to ensure that the system is congruent with the general control architecture in the organization, or if not congruent, ensuring that this deviation is acceptable?

While the answers to these questions will dictate different solutions for different settings, some generalizations spring out—which fit most settings and represent the next step in the evolution of a chargeout system. First of all, for an IS chargeout system to be effective in this environment, it is critical that it be understandable by the users. The corollary of understandability is that the system be simple. Repeatedly, evidence suggests that a chargeout system for IS operations which is a gross distortion of the underlying electronics but which the user can understand is vastly preferable to a technically accurate system which no one can understand (even taking into account the games some programmers will play to reduce costs). Partial motivation and goal congruence is better than none. In this context, systems which are based on an agreed-upon standard cost/unit are better than those which allocate all costs to whoever happened to use the system. Even better (and the clear trend today) is to design these standards not in IS resource units but in items which are user-understandable transactions (e.g., so much per paycheck, so much per order line, so much per inquiry).

A second desirable characteristic is that the IS operations chargeout system should be *perceived* as being fair and reasonable on all sides. In an absolute technical sense, it doesn't have to be fair. It is enough that all involved believe that it is a fair and reasonable system. In this vein the IS operations chargeout system should produce replicable results. A job processing the same amount of transactions at 10 A.M. on Tuesday morning should cost the same thing week after week. When it doesn't, an air of skepticism sets in which undermines the system's credibility.

A third desirable characteristic of an IS operations chargeout system is that it should separate IS efficiency-related issues from user utilization of the system. IS should be held responsible for its inefficiencies. Clearly, closing at month- or year-end any over- or under-absorbed cost variances to the user usually accomplishes no useful purpose (other than raising emotional temperatures). After appropriate analysis of the causes for the variance it is appropriate to close it directly to corporate overhead.

The issues involved in charging for IS maintenance and systems development are fundamentally different from those of IS operations and must be decoupled and dealt with separately. For development and maintenance expenditures of any size a professional contract must be prepared between IS and the users in advance of major work (as though it were a relationship with an outside software company). Elements of a good contract include:

1. Estimates of the job costs are prepared by IS, and IS is held responsible for all costs in excess of this.
2. Procedures are established for re-estimating and, if necessary, killing the job if changes in job scope occur.
3. If a job is bid on a time and materials basis (very frequent in the software industry), a clear understanding must be developed in advance with the user as to what represents such a change in scope that the contract should be reviewed.

In this context, of course, for many systems, such as data base systems, the most challenging (sometimes impossible) task is to identify the definable user (or group thereof) to write the contract with. Further, if the contract is written with one group of users and others subsequently join, are they charged at incremental cost, full cost, or full cost plus (because they have none of the development risks and are buying into a sure thing)? There are neither easy nor general-purpose answers to these questions.

The following paragraphs describe how a recently studied company approached the tasks. This company provides computer services to 14 user groups, many of which have very similar needs. Operations expenses were spread in the following ways:

1. Every time a piece of data was inputted or extracted on a CRT, a standard charge was levied on the user, irrespective of the type of processing system involved. This was understandable by the user.
2. Since all costs from the modems out (terminal, line, modem) could be directly associated with a user in a completely understandable fashion, these charges were passed directly to the end user.
3. All report and other paper costs were charged to the user on a standard cost/ton basis, irrespective of the complexity of the system which generated them.
4. All over- or under-recovered variances were analyzed for indications of IS efficiency and then closed directly to a corporate overhead account bypassing the users.

With respect to maintenance and development cost, the following procedures were used:

1. Items budgeted for less than 40 hours were charged directly to the users at a standard rate/hour times number of hours spent.
2. Projects budgeted to take more than 40 hours were estimated by the IS organization. If the estimate was acceptable to the user, work would be done. Any variances, in relation to budget, were debited or credited to the IS organization, with the user being billed only budget.
3. A process of job re-estimating was created to handle potential changes in job specification, with the users being given the option of accepting the new costs, using the old specifications, or aborting the job.

4. Research and development projects were budgeted separately by the IS organization. IS was accountable to corporate for the costs of these jobs and the users were not charged for them.

The combination of these items over a several year period did a remarkable job of defusing the tensions in user/IS relationships, enabling them to work together more easily.

Profit Center

A third, frequently discussed and used method of management control is the establishment of the IS department as a profit center. Advocates of this approach note that this puts the inside service on the same footing as an outside one and brings the pressures of the marketplace to bear on it. Consequently, it puts pressures on the IS function to hold costs down by stressing efficiency and to market itself more aggressively inside the company. This structure hastens the emergence of the IS marketing function which, if well managed, will improve user relationships. Further, excess IS capacity tends to be promptly dealt with by IS management, with their being willing to run more risks on the user service side. It also encourages sales of services by the IS department to outside firms. This later, however, has often turned out to be a mixed blessing. Often priced as incremental sales (rather than on a full-cost basis), not only are these sales unprofitable, but many IS departments, excited by the volatile *hard* outside dollars as opposed to the captive *soft* inside ones, begin to give preferential treatment to these outside customers, with a resulting erosion of treatment to inside users.

Establishing IS as a profit center, however, has other problems. First, a significant amount of concern often is raised inside the firm whether it is appropriate for an inside *service* department to establish itself as a profit center, particularly when it does not sell any products outside the company. "Profits come from outside sales, not service department practices" is the dominant complaint. The problem is further complicated by the fact that because of geography, shared data files, and privacy and security reasons, many users do not have a legitimate alternative of going outside. Therefore, the argument that the profit center is subject to normal market forces is widely perceived by many users to be a spurious one.

Setting up the IS activity as a profit center, at least in the short run, leads to higher user costs because a profit figure is added on to the user costs. Not only can this create user hostility, but in many settings, it prevents the user from having legitimate full-cost data from the corporation for external pricing decisions. In summary, the combination of these issues must be addressed before an organization precipitously moves to the installation of a profit center approach. A deceptively intriguing approach on the surface, underneath it has many pitfalls.

Investment Center

Many of the issues involved in establishing the IS activity as an investment center, or residual income center (a profit center where a carrying charge for net assets employed is subtracted from the profit figure for both budget and actual performance), are similar to those involved in the establishment of IS as a profit center. The critical reason for moving in this direction (as opposed to a profit center), of course, is to make the IS department fully responsible for the assets employed and force them to make appropriate trade-offs of investment versus additional profits. In a nonstrategic support role this may work well. This must be managed very sensitively because it produces strong IS motivations to delay capacity expansion and run close to the margin on service. It must also be monitored very closely because it is easy to make a good short-term residual income through serious erosion in service levels. Another problem is that almost no one worries about software as an asset for these purposes but focuses only on hardware. This can result in serious misunderstanding about the real assets of the company and the amount of maintenance necessary to service them.

In general, if IS is to be held responsible for the profit/net asset trade-off, it is better to do it on a residual income than on a ROI basis. This is because residual income has every unit of a company thinking in the same way about the attractiveness of new investment. When return on investment is used, one result is that high ROI units are reluctant to make investments which would be to the overall benefit of the firm. Similarly, low ROI units are willing to make some marginal investments, which would improve their ROI but are not in the best interest of the company.

An additional advantage of IS being a stand-alone investment or residual income center is that it can be perceived as being fully organizationally neutral, instead of being the captive of a particular business unit. Several years ago a multibank holding company found it attractive for this reason to spin the IS activity out of the lead bank and put it as a stand-alone unit (measured on residual income) in the holding company. Over the years, the quality of the relationships of the other member banks with the IS department improved markedly as a result of this move which has allowed the department to be perceived as independent.

Transfer Pricing. When an IS activity is set up as a profit, investment, or residual income center, establishment of the IS transfer price becomes a critical issue. There are at least four different conceptual ways of approaching it, each with specific strengths and weaknesses (the issues involved are very similar in nature to those found in transfer pricing situations in general).

For the purpose of this discussion, we will assume that IS operations is being priced in end user transaction terms (i.e. so much per paycheck, so much per invoice line, etc.), while for IS development and maintenance a fixed price contract is being written. Obviously, as described in our earlier discussion on chargeout issues, there are many other ways to approach these items. We believe, however, these assumptions are useful in order to introduce the different cluster of issues described in these paragraphs. These include:

Cost-Based Price.   Assuming a full-cost method is used, this method has the advantage of producing the lowest cost from the user's perspective and is thus most likely to produce minimal user complaints. In this setting, establishing IS as a profit center is largely similar to making it a cost center since profits can only be earned on internal sales by generating positive efficiency variances (obviously sales outside the company can be priced to generate a profit). This approach does not permit one to sidestep the previously mentioned issue as to what constitutes cost and how it should be determined (joint versus by-product, etc.)

A variant of this approach is a cost-plus basis. On the positive side, this makes IS generate profits and at the same time provides an understandable number for users to deal with. On the negative side, the users raise both the narrow issue of capriciousness in how the "plus" was selected and the broader issue of the general inappropriateness of an internal service department earning profits.

Market-Based Price.   A key alternative, this method is used in many companies, particularly as the availability of outside services has grown. Its implementation however, poses several problems similar to creating profit centers. The first is the near impossibility in many settings of finding comparable products and services to establish the market. Unique data bases or process control systems are examples of items where it is impossible to find them. Even so-called standardized services such as payroll and accounting turn out to have so many special ramifications and alternative designs as to make identification of a market price very elusive. Also, suppliers of IS services treat some IS products as a by-product. Still other organizations calculate prices for in-house use; they make no attempt at rigor but only attempt to achieve ballpark figures. To use these figures as market price surrogates is to invite difficulty.

Split-Level.   This approach is designed to satisfy simultaneously the motivational needs of the IS department and the key users. As long as a single transfer price is used, it is impossible to come up with a price which will simultaneously allow IS to feel that it is earning a fair profit and the users to be given prices which will permit them to manage aggregate costs on behalf of the company's overall interests. The pain can be spread around but in the end it is reallocation of a finite amount of pain as opposed to its elimination. Split-level transfer pricing in IS works as follows:

1. The users are charged items either at direct or full cost, depending on the company's overall management control philosophy.
2. The IS department is allocated revenue on a standard cost of services delivered, plus a standard fixed markup (or at a market price if a good one happens to exist). Improvements in actual profits vis-à-vis plan come either from selling more services than planned or from gaining unanticipated cost efficiencies.
3. The difference between the revenue of the IS department and the cost figure charged to the user is posted to an overhead expense account, which on a monthly basis is closed to corporate overhead.

This method at least in theory allows both the IS department and users to be simultaneously motivated to behave in the best overall corporate interest. Users are given appropriate economic trade-offs to consider, while IS is provided incentives both to operate efficiently and sell extra services. This has worked satisfactorily in a number of settings and has dramatically changed the tenor and quality of relationships where the accounting system now permits them to work together instead of against each other. Its Achilles heel is that careful attention must be paid to the establishment of the cost target to ensure that the IS group is being asked to stretch enough and is not building in excess slack into its budget. Also, its implementation involves some additional accounting work.

Negotiated. This is quite difficult to execute in the IS business environment because the two parties often bring quite different strengths to the negotiating table. For example, systems which interface directly with other systems or which share proprietary data bases must be run by the central IS department, hence the negotiating positions of the two parties cannot be considered equal.

Summary

In aggregate, there are a wide variety of potential IS control architectures. No one represents a perfect general-purpose solution. The challenge is to pick the one which fits well enough the company's general management control culture, present user/IS relationships, and current state of IS sophistication. The typical firm has approached these issues in an evolutionary fashion rather than being able to get it "right" the first time.

CONTROL PROCESS (FINANCIAL AND NONFINANCIAL)

The foundation of the IS management control process is the budgeting system. Put together under a very complex set of trade-offs and interlocked with the corporate budgeting process, its first objective is to provide a mechanism for appropriately allocating scarce financial resources. While the planning effort sets the broad framework for the IS activity, the budgeting process ensures that fine-tuning in relation to staffing, hardware, and resource levels takes place. A second important objective of budgeting is to set a dialogue in motion to ensure that organizational consensus is reached on the specific goals and possible short-term achievements of the IS activity. This is particularly important in organizations where the planning process is not well formed. Finally, the budget establishes a framework around which an early warning system for negative deviations can be built. Without a budget, it is difficult to spot deviations in a deteriorating cost situation in time to take appropriate corrective action.

The budget system must involve senior management, IS management, and user groups. Its key outputs include the establishing of planned service levels and costs of central operations, the amount of internal development and maintenance support to be implemented, and the amount and form of external services to be acquired. The planned central IS department service levels and their associated costs must flow from review of existing services and the approved application development portfolio as well as user desires for new services and the degree of available purchased service. In addition, these planned service levels must take into account long-term systems maintenance needs. This ensures that appropriate controls are in place on purchased services (software and hardware, such as minis), as opposed to being focused only on the activities of the central IS department.

The dialogue between users and the IS department on their forecast of needs/usage for the budget year helps generate an understanding of the IS department's goals and constraints which iteratively leads to a better IS plan as well as to clarification of what the user intends to provide. To ensure this happens, for example, a leading chemical company asks both the user and the IS department to develop two budgets, one for the same amount of dollars and head count as last year and one for 10 percent more dollars and 2 percent more head count. Typically, the IS department's proposals involve an expansion of central services while the users involve an expansion of distributed services. To ensure communication, the main description of key items are all in user terms, such as the number of personnel records and types of pension planning support, with all the jargon relating to technical support issues being confined to appendixes. Both groups are asked in this process to rank services of critical importance as well as identify those that are of lower priority or which are likely to be superseded. A senior management group then spends one day reviewing a joint presentation which "scopes" the budget in terms of probable levels of expenditure and develops a tentative ranking of priority. This meeting allows senior management to provide overall direction to guide the final budget negotiations between the two groups. The priorities coming out of these discussions are then consolidated by the IS manager for final approval. This modified, zero-based budgeting approach is judged to have provided good results in this setting.

The budget must establish benchmark dates for project progress, clarify type and timing of technical changeovers, and identify needed levels and mixes of personnel as well as fix spending levels. A further mission is identifying key milestones and completion dates and tying them to the budget to ensure that periodic review and early detection of variance from plan can take place. Budgeting the key staff head count and levels is a particularly important management decision. A major cause for project overruns and delays in many situations is lack of talent available in a timely manner to support multiple projects. Shortage of personnel must be dealt with realistically in fitting projects together. This, of course, needs to be done not just in the budget process but periodically through the year as well.

An important benefit of involving both users and suppliers in the budget is the joint educational process. On the one hand, it helps the IS department to truly understand the particular needs of each business and to assess their real needs for IS support vis-à-vis other programs. On the other hand, it helps the users develop an awareness of what is possible with available technology and to better define their potential needs. For example, in one financial institution the budget process is used heavily as a stimulus for innovation. During budget preparation, both user and IS take many trips to other installations and receive debriefing from their hardware/software suppliers to generate thinking on potential new banking services. Over a several-year period this has significantly improved the relationship between the two groups.

Zero-Based Budgeting

One of the dangers of the budgeting process is that it can become too routinized and incorporate successive layers of fat in the discretionary costs. An effective tool for separating out this fat in many organizations has been zero-based budgeting. Although called zero-based budgeting (ZBB), in practice most firms don't do real zero-based budgeting because building a department's budget up from scratch would be prohibitively expensive. Rather, each staff (as opposed to line) department begins by taking a 15 to 20 percent reduction in budget from the previous year and then identifies the services it can deliver for this amount of money which would best support the organization. This is called the base increment. The staff department then identifies in descending priority a series of discretionary increments of services, each with a price tag attached to it. (If it gets more money, here is how it will be spent, and here are the benefits.) This base increment and the associated sequence of prioritized discretionary increments then ascend through the various levels in the organization. At each level they are reviewed for appropriateness and blended with increments from other departments. Finally, at the very top of the organization, the overall list of priorities are reviewed, and a line is drawn through the sheet of prioritized discretionary increments. Items above the line are funded and those below the line are not funded. All departments do not have equally favorable outcomes in this process. A department whose mission is perceived to be vital in the coming year might have its budget increased by 51 percent, while two other departments whose mission is decreasing in perceived significance might have their budgets decreased.

At its heart, therefore, ZBB is a reallocation process for expenditures on the margin, not an aggregate budget reduction tool. Under ZBB it is perfectly appropriate for discretionary expenditures to rise in aggregate. This process has turned out to be very appropriate for the discretionary level IS staff departments such as technical support, development, and planning. It is not so appropriate for manufacturing departments whose staffing is driven by the physical volume of work passing through it, such as computer operations, data entry, or maintenance.

Zero-based budgeting is attractive to IS organizations (particularly when it is also being done elsewhere in the firm) in the first place because it forces careful examination of all expenditures and should identify redundant or obsolete services. All too often in companies realistic budgeting starts with last year's budget and attempts are then made to add extra items to it. Unfortunately, however, staffing and expenditure levels which made sense at one point in time may have been obsolesced by later developments. Zero-based budgeting is an important discipline for ensuring that the layers of fat are exposed and peeled away.

Often ZBB's most important benefit is that it is a sharp change from the past. People are forced to budget in a very different way, with the positive by-product being that old ways of thinking are challenged and creativity is stimulated.

The theory behind ZBB is conceptually clean and sound. However, resolving the many problems of practical administration has been the key to whether it has been successful in specific situations. As the subsequent paragraphs will discuss, these problems are real and failure to resolve them has turned ZBB into a very expensive game in some organizations.

First, effective ZBB is heavily dependent on good top-down communication within the corporation during planning. This is because ZBB is fundamentally a bottoms-up process. If a clear understanding of corporate mission and department goals is not communicated to the department head who prepares the initial ZBB materials, the formation of the base package and discretionary increments may be so flawed as to prevent effective review and action on priorities of the package increments when it reaches senior level.

Further, since the priorities of different increments are reviewed in the organization chain of command, it is not until very late in the review process that a general management input is provided to the reviewers. By that time, often, so much detail is present that it is hard for management to gain the perspective needed to spot trends and meaningfully influence overall direction. Additionally, because the ranking process works up the organization hierarchy, there is a substantial possibility of gamesmanship in the establishment of priorities.

It is important to recognize that the ZBB process takes place independently of the personnel system. Consequently, a series of adjustments between different programs of activities may be suggested which turn out to be undoable from a personnel staffing viewpoint. People are not infinitely retrainable, and simultaneous layoffs and hirings often have their hidden pitfalls, if indeed they are possible.

Critical to successful ZBB is the establishment of integrity in the base increment. In reality, the process of reviewing the priority of the discretionary increments is often so time-consuming that inadequate attention is paid to the base increment's contents. Consequently, it becomes an attractive hiding place for a department's pet projects which cannot stand the light of day.

Zero-based budgeting in its full-blown form is very time-consuming and expensive. During a company turnaround year it is very useful and can produce a significant series of benefits by finding layers of fat and stimulating creative ideas as to how they should be dealt with. Often, however, the same payoff is not present in immediately subsequent years and a number of firms have moved to doing it only every three to four years (or conversely only a few departments each year). Finally, ZBB with its one-year departmental focus runs directly contrary to the thrust of multiyear programs (which cut across a number of departments) and therefore poses dangers through bringing a nonintegrated short-term focus to the overall IS function. Related to this is the problem of how to develop a satisfactory approach for projects and service relationships between departments, where the service being offered is relatively low priority to the generating department but very high priority to the receiving department.

In combination, these factors have tended to make ZBB a more useful ad hoc tool for the technical services and development groups than to the IS operations groups. The red tape and complexity associated with it makes it more attractive to utilize on an every-three-to-four-year basis than annually. To get payoff from it, however, requires that careful attention be paid to multiple administrative dimensions. Unassailable in logic, in reality it can be very frail.

Periodic Reporting

Effective monitoring of the department's financial performance requires a variety of tools, most of which are common to other settings. These normally include a series of reports which highlight actual performance versus plan on a monthly basis with variances. Often this includes the generation of exception reports. Design and operation of these systems is rather routine. Relatively routine, obvious issues present in them include the following. Are budget targets readjusted during the year through a forecasting mechanism? If so, is the key performance target actual versus budget, or actual versus forecast? Are budgets modified for seasonal factors or are they prepared on a basis of one-twelfth of the annual expense each month?

The IS financial reporting task is complicated by the fact that an IS organization requires a matrix cost reporting system as it grows in size. One side of the matrix is represented by the IS department structure and the need to track costs and variances by IS organizational unit; the other side of the matrix involves keeping track of costs and variances by programs or projects. An issue that will not be discussed in this book, other than its identification, is whether budget numbers and actual results should be reported in nominal dollars or in inflation-adjusted dollars. Obviously, today this is an issue of major importance for corporate management control systems in general.

Nonfinancial Reporting Process

At least in an operational sense, the nonfinancial controls are of more importance than financial ones in assuring management that the day-to-day and month-to-month aspects of the IS function remain on target. Critical items here include preparation of regular six-month surveys of user attitudes toward the adequacy of the type of IS support with which they are being provided. Not only do such surveys identify problems, but they provide a benchmark against which progress can be measured over time. Their distribution to the users for filling out also clearly communicates to them that IS is concerned about user perception of service. Clearly, the problems surfacing in such a survey need to be acted on promptly if the survey is to be an effective control.

Another important set of controls are those relating to staff. Reports which monitor personnel turnover trends over time provide a critical early insight into the problems of this notoriously unstable group. These data allow timely action to be taken on items such as sensitivity of leadership, adequacy of salary levels, and working climate conditions. In the same vein, development of formal training plans and periodic measurement of progress toward their implementation is an important management tool in both ensuring a professionally relevant group and maintaining morale.

In relation to IS operations, reports and other procedures for generating absolute measures of operational service levels are very important. These include data on items such as trends in network uptime, ability to meet schedules on batch jobs, average transaction response time by type of system, number of mis-sends and other operational errors, and a customer complaint log. Critical to the effectiveness of these systems is not just that they be set up but that they be maintained and adhered to on a constant basis. It is easy to allow quality control errors to creep in and show better performance than is actually present. Those issues are discussed further in Chapter 8, with a particular emphasis on the fact that all dimensions of service cannot be simultaneously optimized. Additionally, reliable records concerning installed equipment and its location is important infrastructure data. Lack of sound fact-based registers of equipment opens the possibility of excess equipment, and inadequate and excessive payments of bills.

In relation to systems development the reports on development projects (in terms of elapsed time and work-months expended vis-à-vis budget) are a critical early warning system in assessing overall performance. The type of data needed and appropriately available varies widely by company. The company's maturity in dealing with IS technology, the relative strategic role of IS development and operations, and the corporation's general approach to managerial control also influence both the form and detail with which these issues are approached.

IS AUDIT FUNCTION[2]

This department provides a vital check and balance on the IS activity as it moves to meet cost and service goals. Located as a part of the office of the general auditor, the elements of its basic missions are threefold. The first is to ensure that appropriate standards for the IS development and operations functions have been developed and installed consistent with the control architecture. With both technology and the organization's familiarity with it changing, development of these standards is not a one-time job but requires continuous effort.

The second mission is to ensure that these standards are being adhered to by the various operating units. This includes both regular progress reviews and the conduct of surprise audits. These audits should reduce exposure to fraud and loss. Ensuring adherence to these standards should help reduce operations errors and omissions and increase user confidence and satisfaction. These audits also act as a prod towards improving operating efficiency.

The third mission is to be actively involved in both the systems' design and maintenance functions to ensure that systems are designed to be easily auditable and that maintenance changes do not create unintended problems. This clearly compromises the supposedly independent mission of the auditor, but is a necessary accommodation to the real world. Such involve-

---

[2] This is an introductory discussion to emphasize the role and importance of auditing. For a fuller treatment see B. Allen, "Embezzler's Guide to the Computer," *Harvard Business Review* (July–August 1975).

ment helps ensure the smooth running of the final system. Successful execution of all three missions help to reduce the amount of outside assistance needed by the firm.

These apparently straightforward tasks, however, have turned out to be very hard to implement in the real world. The three main causes of this IS auditing difficulty are the following. The first and most important block is the difficulty in recruiting necessary staff skills. Operating at the intersection of two disciplines (IS and auditing), good practice demands thorough mastery of both. In fact, because IS auditing frequently turns out to be a dead-end career path, staff members who can be retained often are sufficiently deficient in both disciplines to be ineligible as practitioners in either. Better salaries and visibly attractive career paths are essential precondition steps to reverse this situation.

Second, the art of IS auditing continually lags behind the challenges posed by new technologies. Today, understanding methodologies for controlling batch systems for computers is not very relevant for a world dominated by complex operating systems, networks, and online technologies. Managing catch-up for these lags poses a key IS auditing challenge for the foreseeable future.

Third, there has been an unevenness of senior management support for IS auditing due in part to the lack of formally defined requirements from an outside authority. Support for a strong IS auditing function tends to be very episodic, with periods of strong interest following either a conspicuous internal or conspicuous external failure. (This interest, however, tends to erode rapidly as time passes and the calamity is over.)

The IS auditing function at this time has a poorly defined role in most organizations. It is typically part of the internal auditing organization and often does not report to senior management. This is a function that deserves serious consideration by senior management.

SUMMARY

Many of these issues are clearly similar to the general issues of management control which face an organization. Several dimensions, however, do make it especially interesting. The first is posed by the rapid changes in the underlying technology and the long time span required for users to adapt to new technologies. The phase 1 and phase 2 technologies require a commitment to R&D and user learning which is in direct conflict with the chargeout techniques appropriate for the phase 3 and phase 4 technologies. It is very easy for an organization to become too uniform in its control system and try to standardize, in order to use systems "efficiently", and as a by-product stamp out appropriate innovation. In most organizations today, different divisions (which are at separate stages of learning and using varying mixes of technologies) require quite different control approaches. Further, as organizational learning occurs, different types of control approaches become appropriate. Thus quite apart from any breakthroughs in the general cluster of IS control notions, their practice in an organization undergoes a continual process of evolution. In most organizations there is continuing change in what constitutes good IS control practice.

As IS technologies bury themselves deeper into the fabric of an organization's operation the penalties of uneven performance of their technology may come to have very severe consequences for the organization as a whole. As a company (department or system) evolves from turnaround to factory to support very different control philosophies become appropriate.

When these comments are added to the issues, discussed at the beginning of the chapter concerning the changing corporate environment and evolving corporate planning and control processes (in a world shifting from make to buy in software), the full complexity of the IS management control problem is apparent. Different organizations must adopt quite different control approaches, which must evolve over time to deal with their changing corporate environment, changing strategic role of IS technologies, and changing IS technologies.

Chapter \ Manageable Trend	Strategic Impact	DP/TP/OA	Organization Learning	Make/Buy	Life Cycle	GM/User/IS
IS Technology Organization Issues **Chapter 3**		●	●			●
Organizational Issues in IS Development **Chapter 4**	●		●	●		●
Information Systems Planning **Chapter 5**	●		●			●
IS Management Control **Chapter 6**	●		●	●		●
A Portfolio Approach to Information Systems Development **Chapter 7**	●				●	●
Operations Management **Chapter 8**	●			●	●	●
Multinational IS Issues **Chapter 9**		●				●
The IS Business **Chapter 10**	●		●	●		●

A major industrial products company discovers one and a half months before the installation date for a computer system that a $15 million effort to convert from one manufacturer to another is in trouble, and installation must be delayed a year. Eighteen months later, the changeover has still not taken place.

A large consumer products company budgets $250,000 for a new computer-based personnel information system to be ready in nine months. Two years later, $2.5 million has been spent, and an estimated $3.6 million more is needed to complete the job. The company has to stop the project.

A sizable financial institution slips $1.5 million over budget and 12 months behind on the development of programs for a new financial systems package, vital for the day-to-day functioning of one of its major operating groups. Once the system is finally installed, average transaction response times are much longer than expected.

A Midwest mail-order house found nine months after it had installed a state-of-the-art office automation system for $900,000 that 50 percent of the terminals were unused and 90 percent of the work was simple word processing. Further, the communications system was incompatible with the main data processing, and system support was unobtainable. They returned the system.

Stories from the stage 1 and stage 2 days of the late 1960s and early 1970s?[1] No! All these events took place in 1980 in Fortune 500 companies. (We could have selected equally dramatic examples from overseas.) Although it is almost too embarrassing to admit, the day of the big disaster on a major information systems project has not passed. Given business's more than 20 years of IS experience, the question is, Why?

An analysis of these cases and firsthand acquaintance with a number of IS projects in the past 10 years suggest three serious deficiencies in practice that involve both general management and IS management. The first two are the failure to assess the individual project risk and the failure to consider the aggregate risk of the portfolio of projects. The third is the lack of recognition that different projects require different managerial approaches.

These aspects of the IS project management and development process are so important that we have chosen to deal with them in a separate chapter. Chapter 8 discusses project management further in terms of how different corporate cultures and perceived strategic relevance of the technology influences how control over different pieces of the project management life cycle should be balanced between IS and the user. Since many projects have multiyear life cycles, these project management issues have to be dealt with separately from those of the management control system with its calendar-year focus as discussed in Chapter 6.

ELEMENTS OF PROJECT RISK

The typical project feasibility study covers exhaustively such topics as financial benefits, qualitative benefits, implementation costs, target milestones and completion dates, and necessary staffing levels. In precise, crisp terms the developers of these estimates provide voluminous supporting documentation. Only rarely, however, do they deal frankly with the risk of slippage in time, cost overrun, technical shortfall, or outright failure. Rather, they deny the existence of such possibilities by ignoring them. They assume the appropriate human skills, controls, and so on that will ensure success.

[1] Richard L. Nolan and Cyrus F. Gibson, "Managing the Four Stages of EDP Growth," *Harvard Business Review,* (January–February 1974), p. 76.

Consequences of Risk.   By risk we are suggesting exposure to such consequences as:

1.   Failure to obtain all, or even any, or the anticipated benefits.
2.   Costs of implementation that is much greater than expected.
3.   Time for implementation that is much greater than expected.
4.   Technical performance of resulting systems that turns out to be significantly below estimate.
5.   Incompatibility of the system with the selected hardware and software.

These kinds of risk in practical situations, of course, are not independent of each other; rather, they are closely related. In discussing risk, we are assuming that the manager has brought appropriate methods and approaches to bear on the project (mismanagement is obviously another element of risk). Risk, in definition here, is what remains after application of proper tools.

In our discussion, we are also not implying a correlation between *risk* and *bad*. These words represent entirely different concepts, and the link between the two normally is that higher-risk projects must yield higher benefits to compensate for the increased downside exposure.

Dimensions Influencing Inherent Risk.   At least three important dimensions influence the risk inherent in a project:

1.   Project Size.   The larger it is in dollar expense, staffing levels, elapsed time, and number of departments affected by the project, the greater the risk. Multimillion-dollar projects obviously carry more risk than $50,000 projects and also, in general, affect the company more if the risk is realized. A related concern is the size of the project relative to the normal size of a systems development group's projects. The implicit risk is usually lower on a $1 million project of a department whose average undertaking costs $2 million to $3 million than on a $250,000 project of a department that has never ventured a project costing more than $50,000.

2.   Experience with the Technology.   Because of the greater likelihood of unexpected technical problems, project risk increases as the familiarity of the project team and IS organization with the hardware, operating systems, data base handler, and project application language decreases. Phase 1 and phase 2 technology projects are intrinsically more risky for a company than phase 3 and phase 4 technology projects. A project that has a slight risk for a leading-edge, large systems development group may have a very high risk for a smaller, less technically advanced group. Yet the latter group can reduce risk through purchase of outside skills for an undertaking involving technology that is in general commercial use.

3.   Project Structure.   In some projects, the very nature of the task defines completely, from the moment of conceptualization, the outputs. We classify such schemes as highly structured. They carry much less risk than those whose outputs are more subject to the manager's judgment and hence are vulnerable to change. The outputs of highly structured projects are fixed and not subject to change during the life of the project.

An insurance company automating preparation of its agents' rate book is an example of such a highly structured project. At the project's beginning, planners reached total agreement on the product lines to be included, the layout of each page, and the process of generating each number. Throughout the life of the project, there was no need to alter these decisions. Consequently the team organized to reach a stable, fixed output rather than to cope with a potentially mobile target.

Quite the opposite was true in the personnel information project we mentioned at the beginning of the chapter, which was a low-structure project. In that situation, the users could not reach a consensus on what the outputs should be, and these decisions shifted almost weekly, crippling progress.

PROJECT CATEGORIES AND DEGREE OF RISK

Exhibit 7–1, by combining the various dimensions of risk, identifies eight distinct project categories, each carrying a different degree of risk. Even at this gross intuitive level, such a classification is useful to separate projects for quite different types of management review. IS organizations have used it successfully to distinguish the relative risk for their own understanding and as a basis for communicating these notions of risk to users and senior corporate executives.

A legitimate concern is how to ensure that different people viewing the same project will come to the same rough assessment of its risks. While the best way to assess this is still uncertain, several companies have made significant progress in addressing the problem.

ASSESSING RISK IN INDIVIDUAL PROJECTS

Exhibit 7–2 presents, *in part,* a method one large company developed for measuring risk: a list of 42 questions about a project, which the project manager answers both prior to senior management's approval of the proposal and several times during its implementation.

This company developed the questions after carefully analyzing its experience with successful and unsuccessful projects. We include some of them as an example of how to bridge concepts and practice. No analytic framework lies behind these questions, and they may not be appropriate for

EXHIBIT 7-1 □ Effect of Degree of Structure, Company-Relative Technology, and Size on Project Risk

	High structure	Low structure
Low company-relative technology	Large size— low risk	Large size— low risk (very susceptible to mismanagement)
	Small size— very low risk	Small size— very low risk (very susceptible to mismanagement)
High company-relative technology	Large size— medium risk	Large size— very high risk
	Small size— medium-low risk	Small size— high risk

all companies; however, they represent a good starting point, and several other large companies have used them.

Both the project leader and the key user answer these questions. Differences in the answers are then reconciled. (Obviously, the questionnaire provides data that are no better than the quality of thinking that goes into the answers.)

These questions not only highlight the risks but also suggest alternative ways of conceiving of and managing the project. If the initial aggregate risk score seems high, analysis of the answers may suggest ways of lessening the risk through reduced scope, lower-level technology, multiple phases, and so on. Thus managers should not consider risk as a static descriptor; rather, its presence should encourage better approaches to project management. Numbers 5 and 6 under the section on structure are particularly good examples of questions that could trigger changes.

The higher the score, the higher must be the level of approval. Only the executive committee in this company approves very risky projects. Such an

EXHIBIT 7-2 □ Risk Assessment Questionnaire (sample from a total of 42 questions)

Size risk assessment		*Weight*
1. Total development man-hours for system*		**5**
100 to 3,000	Low—1	
3,000 to 15,000	Medium—2	
15,000 to 30,000	Medium—3	
More than 30,000	High—4	
2. What is estimated project implementation time?		**4**
12 months or less	Low—1	
13 months to 24 months	Medium—2	
More than 24 months	High—3	
3. Number of departments (other than IS) involved with system		**4**
One	Low—1	
Two	Medium—2	
Three or more	High—3	

Structure risk assessment		*Weight*
1. If replacement system is proposed, what percentage of existing functions are replaced on a one-to-one basis?		**5**
0% to 25%	High—3	
25% to 50%	Medium—2	
50% to 100%	Low—1	
2. What is severity of procedural changes in user department caused by proposed system?		**5**
Low—1		
Medium—2		
High—3		
3. Does user organization have to change structurally to meet requirements of new system?		**5**
No	—0	
Minimal	Low—1	
Somewhat	Medium—2	
Major	High—3	

Structure risk assessment		Weight
4. What is general attitude of user?		**5**
Poor—anti data-processing solution	High—3	
Fair—sometimes reluctance	Medium—2	
Good—understands value of DP solution	—0	
5. How committed is upper-level user management to system?		**5**
Somewhat reluctant, or unknown	High—3	
Adequate	Medium—2	
Extremely enthusiastic	Low—1	
6. Has a joint data processing/user team been established?		**5**
No	High—3	
Part-time user representative appointed	Low—1	
Full-time user representative appointed	—0	

Technology risk assessment		Weight
1. Which of the hardware is new to the company?†		**5**
None	—0	
CPU	High—3	
Peripheral and/or additional storage	High—3	
Terminals	High—3	
Mini or micro	High—3	
2. Is the system software (nonoperating system) new to IS project team?†		**5**
No	—0	
Programming language	High—3	
Data base	High—3	
Data communications	High—3	
Other—specify	High—3	
3. How knowledgeable is user in area of IS?		**5**
First exposure	High—3	
Previous exposure but limited knowledge	Medium—2	
High degree of capability	Low—1	

EXHIBIT 7–2 *(concluded)*

Technology risk assessment		*Weight*
4. How knowledgeable is user representative in proposed application area?		**5**
Limited	High—3	
Understands concept but no experience	Medium—2	
Has been involved in prior implementation efforts	Low—1	
5. How knowledgeable is IS team in proposed application area?		**5**
Limited	High—3	
Understands concept but no experience	Medium—2	
Has been involved in prior implementation efforts	Low—1	

Note: Since the questions vary in importance, the company assigned weights to them subjectively. The numerical answer to the questions is multiplied by the question weight to calculate the question's contribution to the project's risk. The numbers are then added together to produce a risk score number for the project. Projects with risk scores within 10 points of each other are indistinguishable, but those separated by 100 points or more are very different to even the casual observer.
* Time to develop includes systems design, programming, testing, and installation.
† This question is scored by multiplying the sum of the numbers attached to the positive response by the weight.
Source: This questionnaire is adapted from the Dallas Tire case, no. 9-180-006 (Boston, Mass.: Harvard Business School Case Services, 1980).

approach ensures that top managers are aware of significant hazards and are making appropriate risk/strategic-benefit trade-offs. Managers should ask questions such as the following:

1. Are the benefits great enough to offset the risks?
2. Can the affected parts of the organization survive if the project fails?
3. Have the planners considered appropriate alternatives?

On a periodic basis, these questions are answered again during the undertaking to reveal any major changes. If all is going well, the risk continuously declines during implementation as the size of the remaining task dwindles and familiarity with the technology grows.

Answers to the questions provide a common understanding among senior, IS, and user managers as to a project's relative risk. Often the fiascoes occur when senior managers believe a project has low risk and IS managers know it has high risk. In such cases, IS managers may not admit their assessment because they fear that the senior executives will not tolerate this kind of uncertainty in data processing and will cancel a project of potential benefit to the organization.

PORTFOLIO RISK PROFILE

In addition to determining relative risk for single projects, a company should develop an aggregate risk profile of the portfolio of systems and programming projects. While there is no such thing as a correct risk profile in the abstract, there are appropriate risk profiles for different types of companies and strategies. For example, in an industry where IS is strategic (such as banking and insurance), managers should be concerned when there are no high-risk projects. In such a case, the company may be leaving a product or service gap for competition to step into. On the other hand, a portfolio loaded with high-risk projects suggests that the company may be vulnerable to operational disruptions when projects are not completed as planned.

Conversely in support companies heavy investment in high-risk projects may not be appropriate. However, often even those companies should have some technologically exciting ventures to ensure familiarity with leading-edge technology and to maintain staff morale and interest. This thinking suggests that the aggregate risk profiles of the portfolios of two companies could legitimately differ. Exhibit 7–3 shows in more detail the issues that

EXHIBIT 7–3 □ Factors that Influence Risk Profile of Project Portfolio

	Portfolio low-risk focus	Portfolio high-risk focus
Stability of IS development group	Low	High
Perceived quality of IS development group by insiders	Low	High
IS critical to delivery of current corporate services	No	Yes
IS important decision support aid	No	Yes
Experienced IS systems development group	No	Yes
Major IS fiascoes in last two years	Yes	No
New IS management team	Yes	No
IS perceived critical to delivery of future corporate services	No	Yes
IS perceived critical to future decision support aids	No	Yes
Company perceived as backward in use of IS	No	Yes

influence IS toward or away from high-risk efforts (the risk profile should include projects that will come from outside software houses as well as those of the internal systems development group). In short, the aggregate impact of IS on corporate strategy is an important determinant of the appropriate amount of risk to undertake.

In summary, it is both possible and useful to talk about project risk during the feasibility study stage. The discussion of risk can be helpful both for those working on the individual project and for the department as a whole. Not only can this systematic analysis reduce the number of failures, but equally important, its power as a communication link helps IS managers and senior executives reach agreement on the risks to be taken in line with corporate goals.

CONTINGENCY APPROACH TO PROJECT MANAGEMENT (BY PROJECT TYPE)

Now the organization faces the difficult problem of project operations. Much of the literature and conventional wisdom about project management suggest that there is a single right way of doing it. A similar theme holds that managers should apply uniformly to all such ventures an appropriate cluster of tools, project management methods, and organizational linkages.

While there may indeed be a general-purpose set of tools, the contribution each device can make to planning and controlling the project varies widely according to the project's characteristics. Further, the means of involving the user—through steering committees, representation on the team, or as leader (not DP or IS professional)—should also vary by project type. In short, there is no universally correct way to run all projects.

Management Tools. The general methods (tools) for managing projects are of four principal types:

1. *External integration* tools include organizational and other communication devices that link the project team's work to the users at both the managerial and the lower levels.
2. *Internal integration* devices ensure that the team operates as an integrated unit.
3. *Formal planning* tools help to structure the sequence of tasks in advance and to estimate the time, money, and technical resources the team will need to execute them.
4. *Formal control* mechanisms help managers evaluate progress and spot potential discrepancies so that corrective action can be taken.

Exhibit 7–4 gives examples of the tools in each category commonly used by companies. The next paragraphs suggest how the degree of structure and the company-relative technology influence the selection of items from the four categories.

EXHIBIT 7-4 □ Tools of Project Management

External integration tools	Internal integration tools
Selection of user as project manager	Selection of experienced DP professional to lead team
Creation of user steering committee	Selection of manager to lead team
Frequent and in-depth meetings of this committee	Frequent team meetings
User-managed change control process	Regular preparation and distribution of minutes within team on key design evolution decision
Frequent and detailed distribution of project team minutes to key users	
Selection of users as team members	Regular technical status reviews
Formal user specification approval process	Managed low turnover of team members
Progress reports prepared for corporate steering committee	Selection of high percentage of team members with significant previous work relationships
Users responsible for education and installation of system	Participation of team members in goal setting and deadline establishment
Users manage decision on key action dates	Outside technical assistance
Formal planning tools	Formal control tools
PERT, critical path, etc. networking	Periodic formal status reports versus plan
Milestone phases selection	Change control disciplines
Systems specification standards	Regular milestone presentation meetings
Feasibility study specifications	Deviations from plan
Project approval processes	
Project postaudit procedures	

High Structure–Low Technology

Projects that are highly structured and that present familiar technical problems are not only the lower-risk projects but are also the easiest to manage (see Exhibit 7–1). They are also the least common. High structure implies that the outputs are very well defined by the nature of the task, and the possibility of the users changing their minds as to what these outputs should be is essentially nonexistent. Consequently, the leaders do not have to develop extensive administrative processes in order to get a diverse group of users both to agree to a design structure and to keep to that structure. Such external integration devices as inclusion of analysts in user departments, heavy representation of users on the design team, formal approval of the design team by users, and formal approval by users of design specifications are cumbersome and unnecessary for this type of undertaking. Other integrating devices, such as training users in how to operate the system, remain important.

The system's concept and design stage, however, are stable. At the same time, since the technology involved is familiar to the company, the project can proceed with a high percentage of persons having only average technical backgrounds and experience. The leader does not need strong IS skills. This type of project readily gives opportunity to the department's junior managers, who can gain experience that may lead to more ambitious tasks in the future.

Project life-cycle planning concepts, with their focus on defining tasks and budgeting resources against them, force the team to develop a thorough and detailed plan (exposing areas of soft thinking in the process). Such projects are likely to meet the resulting milestone dates and keep within the target budget. Moreover, the usual control techniques for measuring progress against dates and budgets provide very reliable data for spotting discrepancies and building a desirable tension into the design team to work harder to avoid slippage.

An example of this type of highly structured project is the agent's rate book project mentioned earlier. A portfolio of which 90 percent comprises this type of project will produce little excitement for senior and user managers. It also requires a much more limited set of skills for the IS organization than might be needed for companies whose portfolios have a quite different mixture of projects.

High Structure–High Technology

These projects, vastly more complex than the first kind, involve some significant modifications from the practice outlined in project management handbooks. A good example of this type is the conversion of systems from one computer manufacturer to another with no enhancements (which is of course, easier said than done). Another example of this kind of project is the conversion of a set of manual procedures onto a minicomputer with the objective only of doing the same functions more quickly.

The normal mechanisms for liaison with users are not crucial here (though they are in the next type of project), because the outputs are so well defined by the nature of the undertaking that both the development of specifications and the need to deal with systems changes from users are sharply lower. Liaison with users is nevertheless important for two reasons: (1) To ensure coordination on any changes in input-output or other manual procedure changes necessary for project success and (2) to deal with any systems restructuring that must follow from shortcomings in the project's technology.

It is not uncommon in this kind of project to discover during implementation that the technology is inadequate, forcing a long postponement while new technology is chosen or vital features pruned in order to make the task

fit the available technology. In one such situation, a major industrial products company had to convert some computerized order-entry procedures
to a manual basis so that the rest of an integrated materials management
system could be shifted to already-purchased, new hardware.

Such technological shortcomings were also the main difficulty in the
financial institution described at the start of this chapter. In such a case,
where system performance is much poorer than expected, user involvement
is important both to prevent demoralization and to help implement either an
alternative approach (less ambitious in design) or a mutual agreement to end
the project.

The skills that lead to success in this type of project, however, are the
same as for effective administration of projects involving any kind of technical complexity. The leader needs this experience (preferably, but not necessarily, in an IS environment) as well as administrative experience, unless the
project is not very large. The leader must also be effective in relating to
technicians. From talking to the project team at various times, the ideal
manager will anticipate difficulties before the technicians understand that
they have a problem. In dealing with larger projects in this category, the
manager's ability to establish and maintain teamwork through meetings, a
record of all key design decisions, and subproject conferences is vital.

Project life-cycle planning methods, such as PERT (program evaluation
and review technique) and critical path, identify tasks and suitable completion dates. Their predictive value is much more limited here, however, than
in the preceding category. The team will not understand key elements of the
technology in advance, and seemingly minor bugs in such projects have a
curious way of becoming major financial drains.

In one company, roughly once an hour an online banking system generated garbage across the CRT screen. Although simply hitting a release key
erased this screen of zeroes and x's, four months and more than $200,000
went into eliminating the so-called ghost screen. The solution lay in uncov-
ering a complex interaction of hardware features, operating system functions, and application traffic patterns. Correction of the problem ultimately
required the vendor to redesign several chips. Formal control mechanisms
have limits in monitoring the progress of such projects.

In summary, technical leadership and internal integration are the keys in
this type of project, and external integration plays a distinctly secondary
role. Formal planning and control tools give more subjective than concrete
projections, and the great danger is that neither IS managers nor high-level
executives will recognize this. They may believe they have precise planning
and close control when, in fact, they have neither.

Low Structure–Low Technology

When these projects are intelligently managed, they have low risk. Over
and over, however, such projects fail because of inadequate direction. In

this respect they differ from the first type of project, where more ordinary managerial skills could ensure success. The key to operating this kind of project lies in an effective effort to involve the users.

Developing substantial user support for *only one* of the thousands of design options and keeping the users committed to that design are critical. Essential aspects of this process include the following:

1. A user either as project leader or as the number 2 person on the team.
2. A user steering committee to evaluate the design.
3. An effort to break the project into a sequence of very small and discrete subprojects.
4. Formal user review and approval on all key project specifications.
5. Distribution of minutes of all key design meetings to users.
6. Strong efforts to keep at least chief subproject time schedules. Low managerial and staff turnover in the user areas are vital (since a consensus on approach with the predecessor of a user manager is of dubious value).

The personnel information debacle we mentioned at the start of this chapter is an example of what can happen when this process does not take place. Soon after work started, the director of human resources decided that his senior staff's participation in the design was a waste of their time, and he made sure none of them was involved.

Instead of immediately killing the undertaking, the IS manager attempted to continue work under the leadership of one of his technically oriented staff who had little experience dealing with the human resources department. Bombarded by pressures from the human resources staff that he did not understand, the project manager allowed the systems design to expand to include more and more detail of doubtful merit until the system collapsed. The changing design made much of the programming obsolete. Tough, pragmatic leadership from users in the design stages would have made all the difference in the outcome.

The importance of user leadership increases once the design is final. Almost inevitably, at that stage users will produce some version of "I have been thinking . . ." Unless the desired changes are of critical strategic significance to the user (a judgment best made by a responsible, user-oriented project manager), the requests must be diverted and postponed until they can be considered in some formal change control process.

Unless the process is rigorously controlled (a problem intensified by the near impossibility of distinguishing between the economies of a proposed alternative and those implicit in the original design), users will make change after change, and the project will evolve rapidly to a state of permanent deferral, with completion always six months in the future.

If the project is well integrated with the user departments, the formal planning tools will be very useful in structuring tasks and helping to remove any remaining uncertainty. The target completion dates will be firm as long as the systems target remains fixed. Similarly, the formal control devices afford clear insight into progress to date, flagging both advances and slippages. If integration with user departments is weak, use of these tools will produce an entirely unwarranted feeling of confidence. By definition, the problems of technology management are usually less difficult in this type of project than in the high technology ventures, and a staff with a normal mixture of technical backgrounds should be adequate.

In fact, in almost every respect, management of this type of project differs from the previous two. The key to success is close, aggressive management of external integration supplemented by formal planning and control tools. Leadership must flow from the user rather than from the technical side.

Low Structure–High Technology

Because these projects are complex and carry high risk, their leaders need technical experience and knowledge of, and ability to communicate with, users. The same intensive effort toward external integration described in the previous class of projects is necessary here. Total commitment on the part of users to a particular set of design specifications is critical, and again they must agree to *one* out of the many thousands of options.

Unfortunately, however, an option desirable from the user's perspective may turn out to be infeasible in the selected hardware–software system. In the last several years, such situations have occurred particularly with stand-alone minicomputer systems designs, and they commonly lead either to significant restructuring of the project or elimination of it altogether. Consequently, users should be well represented at both the policy and the operations levels.

At the same time, technical considerations make strong technical leadership and internal project integration vital. This kind of effort requires the most experienced project leaders, and they will need wholehearted support from the users. In approving such a project, managers must face the question whether it can or should be divided into a series of much smaller problems or use less innovative technology.

While formal planning and control tools can be useful here, at the early stages they contribute little to reducing overall uncertainty and to highlighting all problems. The planning tools do allow the manager to structure the sequence of tasks. Unfortunately, in this type of project new tasks crop up with monotonous regularity, and tasks that appear simple and small suddenly become complex and protracted. Time, cost, and resulting technical performance turn out to be almost impossible to predict simultaneously. In the Apollo moon project, for example, technical performance achievement was key, and cost and time simply fell out. In the private sector, all too often this is an unacceptable outcome.

RELATIVE CONTRIBUTION OF MANAGEMENT TOOLS

Exhibit 7-5 shows the relative contribution that each of the four groups of project management tools makes to ensure maximum possibility of project success, given a project's inherent risk. It reveals that managers need quite different styles and approaches to manage the different types of projects effectively. Although the framework could be made more complex by including more dimensions, that would only confirm this primary conclusion.

EXHIBIT 7-5 □ **Relative Contribution of Tools to Ensuring Project Success**

Project type	Project description	External integration	Internal integration	Formal planning	Formal control
I	High structure, low technology; large	Low	Medium	High	High
II	High structure, low technology; small	Low	Low	Medium	High
III	High structure, high technology; large	Low	High	Medium	Medium
IV	High structure, high technology; small	Low	High	Low	Low
V	Low structure, low technology; large	High	Medium	High	High
VI	Low structure, low technology; small	High	Low	Medium	High
VII	Low structure, high technology; large	High	High	Low+	Low+
VIII	Low structure, high technology; small	High	High	Low	Low

SUMMARY

The usual corporate handbook on project management, with its unidimensional approach, fails to deal with the realities of the task facing today's managers, particularly those dealing with information services. The right approach flows from the project rather than the other way around.

The need to deal with the corporate culture within which both IS and project management operate further complicates the problems. Use of formal project planning and control tools is much more likely to produce successful results in a highly formal environment than in one where the prevailing culture is more personal and informal. Similarly, the selection and effective use of integrating mechanisms is very much a function of the corporate culture.

Thus the type of company culture further complicates our suggestions as to how different types of projects should be managed. (Too many former IS managers have made the fatal assumption that they were in an ideal position to reform corporate culture from their position!)

The past decade has brought new challenges to IS project management, and experience has indicated better ways to think about the management process. Our conclusions, then, are threefold:

1. We will continue to experience major disappointments as we push into new fields. Today, however, the dimensions of risk can be identified in advance and a decision made whether to proceed. If we proceed, we will sometimes fail.
2. The work of the systems development department in aggregate may be thought of as a portfolio. Other authors have discussed what the appropriate components of that portfolio should be at a particular point in time. The aggregate risk profile of that portfolio, however, is a critical (though often overlooked) strategic decision.
3. Project management in the IS field is complex and multidimensional. Different types of projects require different clusters of management tools if they are to succeed.

Chapter 8 □ Operations Management

Chapter / Manageable Trend	Strategic Impact	DP/TP/OA	Organization Learning	Make/Buy	Life Cycle	GM/ User/ IS
IS Technology Organization Issues **Chapter 3**		●	●			●
Organizational Issues in IS Development **Chapter 4**	●		●	●		●
Information Systems Planning **Chapter 5**	●		●			●
IS Management Control **Chapter 6**	●		●	●		●
A Portfolio Approach to Information Systems Development **Chapter 7**	●				●	●
Operations Management **Chapter 8**	●			●	●	●
Multinational IS Issues **Chapter 9**		●				●
The IS Business **Chapter 10**	●		●	●		●

A major North American manufacturing company has a brand new $3.5 million underground operations center protected by four guards, nine TV cameras, and multiple levels of access security. The chief executive officer personally approved and supervised its construction. At the same time, the critical application being run in the center, an online order system, is 13 years old. Under tight head-count control, imposed by senior management, the systems and programming staff had decreased by nearly 35 percent over the previous four years and were barely able to implement necessary maintenance work, let alone major systems enhancements of new projects. Senior IS management was deeply concerned about the unbalanced allocation of resources between invisible required maintenance and visible facilities.

After years of debate, a major bank reluctantly built a second data center, 50 miles away from the primary data center. The source of debate had focused on whether a 7 percent increase in costs was a good trade-off vis-à-vis the extra security against disaster provided by the second data center. This bank currently has over 4,000 online terminals and is deeply dependent on the smooth, uninterrupted, 24-hour-a-day operation of IS services to meet its daily operating performance targets.

The chief executive officer of an industrial products concern discovered that the delay in year-end financial closing was not due to reduced emphasis on close control of financial accounting but to unexpected work and personnel problems in the computer systems department. Increased use of an online query system (and associated problems) to provide salesmen and customers detailed delivery and cost information had absorbed all available system support personnel to keep this vital system operational. No time had been left to revise the accounting system for changes in the new tax law before year-end closing.

The director of IS of a major engineering firm is pondering whether to break apart and totally reconfigure his operations center. At present, a single large computer supports the company's batch and online system. Workloads are quite erratic, and in the past year, long response-time delays on the online systems, combined with batch schedules, has put him under considerable user pressure to be more responsive.

Unusual problems? Hardly! Historically, the glamorous part of the IS function has been the technology orientation of systems development and technical support functions, with maintenance and operations occupying a distinctly backseat role. For the purposes of this chapter, we will define *operations* to include the running of IS hardware, data input, equipment scheduling, and work forces associated therewith. We have also chosen in this chapter to deal with the issues relating to the impact on the systems life cycle by the change in software make-or-buy decisions to outside sourcing. While this could have been covered in Chapter 7, the *operational* implication of this shift seemed so important that we choose to deal with it in its entirety here.

Both the type and amount of management resources devoted to operations activities and the sophistication of management practices within the operations center have often been inadequate for their growing and changing mission inside the company. The following aspects of changing technology are now triggering major changes in the way these activities are managed:

CHANGING OPERATIONS ENVIRONMENT

The explosion of online technology applications and increased sophistication in operating systems in the past decade has taken what originally was a batch, job-shop environment with heavy human control and turned it first into a process manufacturing shop and at present into a largely self-scheduled and monitored 24-hour-a-day utility. This change in manufacturing work flow has triggered a total rethinking of both what is appropriate scheduling and what is the definition of adequate service levels.

An increased recognition that there is no such thing as an ideal standard IS operations management control system, or set of performance metrics. The trade-off between quality of service, response time of online systems, handling of unexpected jobs, total cost, and ability to meet published schedules on batch systems appropriately varies from one organization to another.

Different IS operations environments must strike different balances between efficiency (low-cost producer) and effectiveness (flexibility) in responding to unplanned, uneven flow of requests. IS operations cannot be *all things* simultaneously to *all people* but must operate on a set of priorities and trade-offs that stem from corporate strategy. Implementation of this has sparked the reorganization of some large IS operations into a series of focused, single service-oriented groups, each of which can be managed to quite different user service objectives.

The types of staffing needed are changing. Many formerly appropriate employees are unsuited now for the new tasks. These problems have been complicated by the unionization of this function in many parts of the globe.

Continued change in the IS technology. This initiates the normal problems of change and new operating procedures, while offering potential benefits of lower cost and new capabilities.

The major shift toward more outside sourcing in IS processing and software sourcing decisions. This requires changes in the procedures of both the operations and development functions of IS if they are to be handled responsibly.

These issues are similar to those involved in running a manufacturing facility characterized by the words, *highly volatile technology, specialized labor, serving dynamic markets,* and *changing industry structure.* Consequently, much of the analysis in this chapter draws on work done in manufacturing management, particularly as it relates to balancing efficiency–effectiveness trade-offs.

A key question stemming from this manufacturing analogy is how focused should the department be. Should it subdivide itself into sets of stand-alone services or be organized as a general-purpose IS service. The example at the beginning of the chapter, of the late closing of the books versus providing online service for query, provided a stimulus within the company to review how operations were responding to the demands of new services. The company's review produced a conclusion similar to Skinner's plea for a focused factory.[1] They perceived it as being impossible for a single unit to adequately respond to such very different user needs; consequently, to address the problem, the IS development and maintenance group was reorganized into four independent systems groups, each of which operated independently of the others but reported to a common boss (the manager of IS).

One group was to support the online query systems with goals to provide 10-second response, one-day change implementation, and all data refreshed hourly. The second systems/customer group was devoted to the general ledger accounting system. Their goals were to keep the software up to date for month-end closing schedule work so as to not interfere with other systems, ensure the quality and reliability of accounting data, and operate to close the books five days after the end of the last working day of the month. The third group was to be responsible for all material management systems. Their objectives were to ensure all production control persons were well trained to use the system, to provide updated data overnight, and to maintain and operation of the system in a manner consistent with material policies on inventory and customer delivery. The fourth group was to work with the systems supporting new-product development. They were responsible for identifying system requirements of new products, maintaining the availability of the capacity simulator for planning new-product developments, establishing data standards and new data files in existing systems for approved new products, and developing and performing analyses on new products as directed by the vice president of product development. Each focused group included at least one user and two to three systems professionals. All worked full time on their respective services with the exception of the new-product group which had spurts of work as new products hit the market and lulls after the market settled down. This structure has produced happier customers and significantly better percentages of service as well as increased employee morale.

Historically, the evolution of IS systems has developed a series of services and products running out of an integrated IS operations unit. As noted above, some firms have reorganized IS development and construction to be more responsive to user needs. For example, several organizations shifted application programmers (e.g., construction) to users, allowing maintenance and operations to be decentralized around the local system. As IS's monopoly of system construction and make/buy decision erodes to more and greater user control, the result is fragmentation of the factory into a series of focused services (e.g., a word processing system for customer mailing). For some users and applications this may be very effective. For other users, however, their services may be dependent upon an integrated set of data, in which case severe coordination problems can be created. The chal-

---

[1] Wickham Skinner, "The Focused Factory," *Harvard Business Review* (May–June 1974).

lenge is to identify where focus in operations (either within the central unit or by distributing to the user) is appropriate and then execute it in a way which provides the necessary thrust. Implementation of this will be discussed further in the section on production planning and control.

To build on this manufacturing strategy theme, and develop an appropriate range of make-buy plans, our operations management discussion is organized around the following topics:

Development of an operations strategy.

Technology planning.

Measuring and managing capacity.

Managing the IS operations work force.

Production planning and control.

Security.

DEVELOPING AN OPERATIONS STRATEGY

As noted earlier, the management team of an IS operations activity is trying to stay on top of a utility that is radically changing its production system, customer base, and role within the company. Eight years ago, the manager and his staff were monopolists running a job shop where the key issues were scheduling (with substantial human inputs), ensuring telecommunications were adequate, managing a large blue-collar staff, and planning capacity and staffing levels for future workloads of similar characteristics. Today, they are operating an information utility providing a 24-hour/7-day-a-week service that must cope cost effectively with uncertain short-term and long-term user demand; manage a far higher skilled, more professional work force; and evaluate competing services, both internal and external, which in many cases offer the potential to solve problems cheaper and more comprehensively. Key issues for the IS operations manager are still staff, capacity, and telecommunications. Prominent additions to this list, however, are: appropriate assessment, assimilation and integration of software and services emanating from outside the corporation.

Senior management must assess both the quality of IS operations support and, depending on how critical it is to the overall strategic mission of the corporation, involve themselves appropriately. The central question both senior and IS management must address is whether IS operations as organized now effectively supports the firm.

In this context, we see the key issues an operations strategy must address as follows:

1. Ensuring that each phase of a system's life cycle appropriately address the critical long-term operating needs of the system.

2. Ensuring that the internal/external sourcing decisions are carefully thought through as to both their outcome and who should primarily influence the outcome with respect to operational characteristics.
3. Resolving the extent to which IS operations should be managed as a single entity or broken down into a series of perhaps more costly but more focused subunits which provide more customized user service than is possible from a monolithic facility.

The following paragraphs discuss these items in more detail.

System Design and Operations

A review of IS operations organization must start with an assessment of the first phase of the systems life cycle, the design phase, because the key operations decisions for a system are often made early in the design phase and, unless identified as such and handled appropriately at that phase, can cause great difficulty. Proper operations input to the systems design phase is complicated by the fact that the IS operations department is a victim of history. Past decisions have shaped today's operating environment, which influences the art of the possible in both today's operating environment, and in today's design decisions.

Both user operational personnel and IS operational personnel need to be involved in the early design phase to get their viewpoint of need across—as well as to be educated on the reality of the existing situation. This IS operations involvement not only ensures the operational integrity of the new system design but ensures that other existing systems are not adversely impacted operationally during the design and implementation stages of the new system and that the conversion plan from the old to the new is satisfactory. These issues are particularly important to review for externally sourced software, since interfacing issues are complex.

Externally Sourced Services—Pressures and Challenges

The recent shift in software construction, from a situation where the bulk of energy was devoted to in-house software construction managed by IS staff to today's position where there is a greater reliance on purchased software and service, is not surprising. The supply of cheap hardware is growing dramatically. However, the human resources to develop software for it have remained relatively constant and have thus shrunk significantly in relation to demand. Neither user-oriented programming languages nor programming efficiency aids have been able to fully address the problem of resource shortage. Consequently, significant increases in prices for skilled people have occurred. Appropriately, a large market has developed for software firms which can develop reliable products at significantly lower user cost by spreading these costs over multiple users. This industry started with software vendors developing complex technical software to support the operation of computers (operating systems, data base handlers, inquiry languages, etc.). This vendor software evolution has now evolved downstream to products such as standard user-oriented software services, including payroll and accounting packages, as well as report writers and procedural languages. This trend has caused the in-house system construction phase to be eliminated (or drastically shortened) in many office automation and data processing activities. The design phase continues to focus on careful definition of business operational needs (but often to guide a package selection). The system implementation phase's challenge is to understand the purchased service's key characteristics so as to train individuals to its operational use. Finally, systems maintenance involves ensuring that the vendor is prepared to be responsive to long-term needs.

These purchased systems generate special problems for IS operations management as noted below. These problems are particularly sticky where the user has full authority to purchase and operate the new service, while the IS operations department must maintain and operate other services and, at the same time, ensure that they are compatible where necessary with the new service. This loss of operations monopoly control poses three key challenges to IS operations management:

1. How to maintain existing services while building appropriate and necessary data bridges to the new ones.
2. How to evolve the IS operations organization from a primary integrated system of data processing to a series of services which are better focused on the specific needs of different users.
3. How to develop user understanding of both their real operational responsibility over the systems under their control and how to interface effectively with corporate IS.

Individual skill levels and perspectives of IS operations management further complicate resolving these problems. Many IS operations departments are run by individuals accustomed to exercising monopoly control over operations while sharing control with users over selection and implementation of maintenance changes. These individuals must now learn to adapt to new ways of operations. Evidence of failure to adapt is provided by the many organizations which, because of senior management frustration over IS's unresponsiveness, have delegated total authority for purchased services acquisition and operation to users.

IS operations must assume roles which include reviewing designs in the *design* phase to ensure that they are compatible with existing services; auditing documentation preparation in the *construction* phase to ensure long-term maintainability; ensuring essential services are still being provided during the *implementation* phase; appraising whether necessary skills are in the organization (IS and/or user) to assure effective operation in the *opera-*

tions phase, etc. The degree to which senior management needs to get involved in reviewing this depends on whether existing and planned services are critical for the organization to meet its day-to-day operating objectives (i.e., is the company at the bottom of the "factory" or "strategic" boxes?).

Service Sourcing—Decision Authority

Senior management must provide guidance as to where the company should be moving on the dimension of software/processing service sourcing decisions, and whether the user or IS should have a primary voice in these decisions.

This sourcing decision can occur in all phases of the information service life cycle, from design to maintenance, and for all three IS technologies of communications, data processing, and office automation. In practice, most of these decisions will involve at least some IS input and user involvement, particularly in the design and implementation phases; however, at the extremes, either group may be willing to take total responsibility.

Further, each phase of the project life cycle is in a state of transition in terms of options, both as to where in the organization the service sourcing decision should be made, whether the service should be sourced in-house or externally, and what internal work should be done by IS versus the user. For example, in the design phase in many organizations, the in-house users are developing more *make* capacity (decision support systems and user programming), therefore becoming less dependent on IS or an outside supplier (with the risk to the organization that it may lose operational control over key systems). Similarly, some office managers are personally purchasing and installing completely designed support systems.

What is being constructed is also changing—no one (outside the vendor) builds internal computer operating systems any more, and only a few construct data base systems software. A shrinking percentage of data processing applications are consequently being designed and constructed by IS staff, with an even smaller percentage of office automation systems software being designed and constructed inside the firm.

Implementation is changing from being almost the exclusive domain of IS to a situation where the user often has control over local department micro-based systems, and either IS or user may have the primary relationship with an outside software vendor. Operations has moved from an exclusive IS-controlled activity to one where service bureaus and user-controlled minis and micros have considerably altered the picture. Maintenance in some of the newer technologies can be done more by the users.

The nature of the application is important in selecting primary decision-making responsibility. On the one hand, implementation and operation of a customized new decision support system in a bank can be completely under the control of the portfolio manager fresh from school, because it requires neither two-way interaction with the organization's data files nor the controls implicit in day-to-day transaction processing. An office automation system implementation effort, on the other hand, may require significant IS professional support in user training to ensure that potential operating problems are avoided.

Different firms have chosen rationally to locate in quite different positions the sourcing decision for different phases of the systems life cycle for different IS technologies. Our concern here is twofold:

1. This is an important strategic decision and should be addressed explicitly rather than be left to chance.
2. The transitional nature of the information services industry makes it hard to be specific as to a long-term sourcing policy that a firm should implement for any phase of the system's life cycle or any IS technology. The dynamics of change defy either simplistic or long-term solutions.

Within these general caveats, however, we find that discussion on the location of decision-making power should flow primarily around the OA and DP technologies. Communications decisions have such a pervasive influence on the ability to distribute data and other information that they demand a strong central IS policy and decision-making role. In the two other technologies, however, although either the IS department or user may have the prime authority to decide, continuous consultation with each other is strongly encouraged.

Examples of Different Organization Approaches to Life-Cycle Control

Three comparative examples are presented of how six firms have allocated decision responsibility for each phase of the product life cycle, and how these vary by make-or-buy.

Exhibit 8–1 compares the IS sourcing decisions for two organizations where IS plays a role of *strategic significance.* The one which emphasizes central IS decision power is a bank, and the other which emphasized decentralized decision power is a multidivision consumer product firm. Both desire to maintain control over their integration of systems activity and develop expertise inside their firms while simultaneously gaining experience in purchasing services and reducing software costs. The bank, however, feels the integrated nature of its business and customer relationships are such that it must maintain central control of data and develop central standards compatible with its overall mode of operations. The consumer product firm, on the other hand, has traditionally decentralized profit responsibility along with all staff support to each division and felt that integrated data files were neither critical to its operation nor appropriate to its management philosophy and

EXHIBIT 8-1 □ Systems Are Strategic to Company—Two Organizational Strategies

Bank

	Technology	Life-cycle phases to be bought	Life-cycle phases to be made
User responsibility	Communications		I*
	Data processing	D C O M	D* I* O*
	Office automation	D C M	D I* O*
IS responsibility	Communications	D C O M	D I*
	Data processing	D C M	D* I* O* M
	Office automation	D C M	I* O* M

Consumer product firm

	Technology	Life-cycle phases to be bought	Life-cycle phases to be made
User responsibility	Communications	C* O M	D* I*
	Data processing	C*	D I
	Office automation	D C I M	D I O
IS responsibility	Communications	C*	D* I*
	Data processing	C*	O M
	Office automation		

D - Design
C - Construct
I - Install
O - Operate
M - Maintain

Note: A letter appearing on same line twice means some aspects of phase are bought and others made.
*Indicates joint responsibility for phase by user and IS.

structure. Although the consumer product firm has a central DP department, all development is done by divisional staff. Each company reached its decision only after careful consideration of all elements, although obviously different structures emerged. Of particular interest is that the IS-dominated bank felt more need for joint efforts in implementation than the user-oriented consumer products divisions.

Exhibit 8–2 compares two organizations where IS, although large, was perceived to be relatively *strategically unimportant*. Both are choosing to buy more than make in order to reduce their professional work force (which they are understandably having trouble recruiting). One, a nationwide men's clothing chain with a strong inventory control and accounting system, decided to continue having IS control the development of systems although shifting their construction from primarily make to a strong buy orientation. In particular, they have been trying to buy more complete services. They were much concerned about how to avoid the danger of operational disruption. The other, an automobile parts distributor with four large warehouses in different states, decided to allow local general managers to purchase services.

The auto parts company assumed their small central staff would assist but wanted to develop local expertise in purchasing information services, as they did with purchasing for their main product lines. The IS department designed the communications system and spun off the former central DP and OA into one of the warehouse IS groups. A one-man corporate IS department now manages corporate communications and audits performance of the division's IS group. This company felt that each warehouse taking control of its operation was compatible with its managerial philosophy. Conversely, the men's clothing chain central IS department merged OA and DP into one vendor's system which included communications capability. They are now in the process of implementing this system in all stores.

A final example (Exhibit 8–3) compares two firms that *split equally responsibility* for acquiring services between the users and IS staff. The machine tool company felt that, because of the rapid developments in CAD/CAM, they should buy their software in light of their particularly good experience with a specific vendor's bill of material processor. The large chemical company, on the other hand, felt it must do most development inside, as they had several unique process control systems they wanted to link to their management systems. The exhibit shows the resulting structure where users are in control of OA and IS is in control of communications. Design and DP systems is split between the two. Both firms felt operational review required central coordination.

These examples emphasize the range of possible organization and control structures for each phase of the systems life cycle. Clearly, the final decision rests on the nature of the business, with each organization intending to have some user and IS involvement in design/construction/implemen-

EXHIBIT 8-2 □ Systems Are Nonstrategic to Company—Two Organizational Strategies

Clothing chain

	Technology	Life-cycle phases to be bought	Life-cycle phases to be made
User responsibility	Communications		I*
	Data processing	D C I O M	D* I*
	Office automation	D C I O M	D* I* O
IS responsibility	Communications	D C I O M	D I*
	Data processing	D C I O M	D* I*
	Office automation	D C I M	D* I*

Auto parts distributor

	Technology	Life-cycle phases to be bought	Life-cycle phases to be made
User responsibility	Communications	D C I O M	D* I*
	Data processing	D C I M	D I O
	Office automation	D C I M	D* I*
IS responsibility	Communications		D* I*
	Data processing		
	Office automation		

D - Design
C - Construct
I - Install
O - Operate
M - Maintain

Note: A letter appearing on same line twice means some aspects of phase are bought and others made.
*Indicates joint responsibility for phase by user and IS.

EXHIBIT 8-3 □ Systems Strategic to Company (shared user-IS control)—Two Organizational Strategies

Machine tool company

	Technology	Life-cycle phases to be bought	Life-cycle phases to be made
User responsibility	Communications	C	D* I*
	Data processing	D* C* M*	I* O*
	Office automation	D*	I O
IS responsibility	Communications	O M	D* I*
	Data processing	D* C* M*	I* O* M
	Office automation	D* C M	

Chemical company

	Technology	Life-cycle phases to be bought	Life-cycle phases to be made
User responsibility	Communications		D* C I
	Data processing	C* M*	D* I* O*
	Office automation	C M	D I O
IS responsibility	Communications	C O M	D*
	Data processing	C* M*	D* C I* O* M
	Office automation		

D - Design
C - Construct
I - Install
O - Operate
M - Maintain

Note: A letter appearing on same line twice means some aspects of phase are bought and others made.
*Indicates joint responsibility for phase by user and IS.

tation phases in both internally developed and purchased systems. The scope and balance of this decision, however, varies widely. The machine tool company felt that its large backlog of maintenance would preclude many inside developments, particularly since it believed its location would make recruitment of more programmers very difficult. The bank, conversely, was actively recruiting systems personnel because it felt their design needs were expanding rapidly and that even withdrawing from internal construction efforts would not free up adequate resources for maintaining key systems. In an urban market, they felt they had to, and could, compete for a substantial increase in staff resources.

TECHNOLOGY PLANNING

The technology planning for operations involves an ongoing audit for potential obsolescence and opportunities. The technology planning scope and effort associated with this audit depends upon the nature of the business and state of IS. For a bank, it should be across many technologies and be very extensive; a mail-order business may concentrate on OA technology, whereas a wholesale distributor may just focus on DP and TP technologies. The audit should compare the means of providing IS today with the potential available two or three years from now and, to be effective, must involve very high caliber, imaginative staff. (Outside technical consulting can be very effective here.) This potential must be based on technological forecasting. If a company is trying to differentiate itself from competition by application of these technologies, the resources focused on this technological planning should be quite extensive. If a firm is trying to just stay even, and the IS activity is seen primarily as support, comparison of their operations with their competitors or "leaders" in particular fields may be sufficient. A few firms periodically solicit bids from different vendors on the service they are providing to ensure their IS department is fully up-to-date. For example, a large insurance company, whose IS department is dominated by technology of one vendor, annually asks a competitor of the vendor to bid an alternative system, even though they do not perceive a need for change. As a result of these bids, in the recent past they switched to another vendor's minicomputers and on still another occasion installed a large machine purchased from a different vendor.

The objective of the audit is to determine, relative to available and announced systems, how cost effective and adequate for growth are the existing installed technologies. Such an audit should generate an updated priority list of technologies to be considered as replacements. This lead time is critical because technology replacement or additions planned two years in advance cause a small fraction of the disruption of those planned only six months in advance. This technological planning should sponsor external testing, field trips, education, and pilot studies as vehicles for obtaining an understanding of emerging technologies, in order to better define the architecture of the future information service.

A useful approach to this technology audit is to categorize the applications portfolio of operations systems by their age since development, or last total rewrite. Exhibit 8–4 identifies the four major eras of the information systems industry and the characteristics of applications and technology of each era. The hardware and software technology of each era was quite different and led to totally different systems design. If a significant percentage of IS systems running today was designed in an earlier era this is normally a strong tip-off to major opportunities for reduced maintenance and improved operational efficiency through a major redesign and rewrite.[2] A large financial service firm recently performed such an audit and discovered 40 percent of their systems and 75 percent of their systems effort were devoted to maintaining an accounting-like system constructed in the second era. The purchase of a general ledger package, four months of development, and a period of parallel runs permitted 28,000 lines of COBOL code to be scrapped and freed up almost half of their maintenance effort.

The identification and implementation of new technology can be transparent to the user when it involves hardware replacement or new systems which use existing hardware more effectively. Other replacement technology may impact users by providing different or improved service such as report writers for data bases or new terminals, but are basically supporting them rather than changing their basic operations style. Some are so integrated with user habits that it is important to obtain user leadership in the implementation. Each implementation situation requires a careful plan to ensure service is not interrupted and relevant individuals understand how to operate with the new service. Exhibit 8–5 illustrates the tensions and forces which must be managed.

When IS planning maintains an appraisal of user readiness and an inventory of use of existing technology, and an appropriate assessment of where technology is going, a program of new technology can be developed rather easily for each entity. For example, a large consumer products company has a very strong IS technology planning group. As part of their activity, they maintain for each division and function an updated log of services in use and an assessment of current problems. They are currently in the midst of a program of introducing OA which includes a large portfolio of different applications in a pilot division. Their detailed program for this division is scheduled over 24 months. This program includes benchmarks and reviews to evaluate both benefits and operating problems and progress. This pilot testing provides a useful vehicle to stimulate broader organizational aware-

---

[2] Martin Busch, "Penny-Wise—Pound Foolish," *Harvard Business Review* (July–August 1981).

EXHIBIT 8-4 □ Major Eras of Information Systems

	Industry	Technology	Hardware	Software	Portfolio
1955– Shake out era	Data processing firms Analog engineering firms	Vacuum tube to transistor Many memory types to core mag tape as secondary storage card-archival	Central logic memory Small peripheral in/out	Machine language to assembler language Start of operating system	Clerical replacements Computation improvements Accounting and engineering applications
1962– Data-processing-market formation era	IBM + several equal computer marketers	Transistor to integrated circuits Core dominates memory Disk emerges as secondary storage Tape archival	Growth of large central systems Huge tape files	Multiprogramming Multiprocessing Operating systems Start of time-sharing and virtual COBOL/FORTRAN/BASIC	Operational control Reservation systems Completion of clerical automation Mathematical programming
1970– Computer market era	IBM + fewer equal competitors + Minicomputer manufacturers	Integrated circuit to LSI MOS memories Huge disks as secondary storage Tape archival Satellites	Linking systems Several remote terminals Mag card typewriters Stand-alone mini computer Store and forward communications	Growth of special-purpose systems (e.g., newspaper) Remote online data base Communication controller	Simulation to planning models Marketing systems Financial portfolios Personnel systems
1978– Information market era	IBM + ATT + DEC Xerox + several other	LSI to V³SI Huge disk Laser Optical light pipes	Linked large systems Distributed systems	Large data base Report writer Fail soft systems Communication system	Decision support systems CAD/CAM Office automation Electronic mail

EXHIBIT 8-5 □

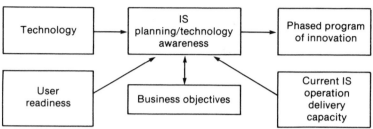

ness of the opportunities and operational issues associated with this technology and permits better planning for full-scale implementation in the other divisions. This approach has proven to be an effective means of marketing new IS technology to many organizational units. The art of technology planning is building a process to move from the raw technical idea to an informal awareness of its operational implications before widespread installations. The failure to build this bridge is a primary cause of implementation trouble.

MANAGING CAPACITY

The less one knows about computer hardware/software technology, the more certain one is as to what capacity is. In reality, the different hardware/software elements tend to interact in such a complex way that the diagnosis of bottlenecks and proper long-term planning of capacity is a very important task requiring a high order of skill to execute. Key elements of the changing capacity decision include the following items:

1. Capacity comes in much smaller, less expensive increments than a decade ago. This has created an asymmetric reward structure for capacity overages versus underages in many organizations. For these firms, a shortage of capacity in critical operating periods is very expensive, while conversely, the cost of extra capacity is very low. For these organizations, carrying excess capacity is a sound decision.

2. The approach of a capacity crunch comes with devastating suddenness. One large financial institution operated with few difficulties during a six-month period with a 77 percent load on the CPU during peak demand. Senior management refused to listen to IS management, which warned that they were on the edge of a crisis, and would not permit IS management to place an order for additional equipment. During the next six months, the introduction of two new minor systems and steady growth in transaction volumes brought CPU load during peak periods to 83 percent. This was accompanied by a dramatic increase in online systems response time, a

steady stream of missed schedules on the batch systems, and twice key delivery times of items to an industry clearinghouse were missed. The move from a satisfactory to a thoroughly unsatisfactory situation does not creep up on an organization but can arrive dramatically to the untutored eye.

3. There has been an explosion of diagnostic tools, such as hardware and software monitors, to assist in the identification of these problems. These tools are only analytical devices, and they are no better than the quality of the analyst using them and the detailed forecast of future demands to be placed on the systems. This has led to a significant growth in both the number and quality of technical analysts in a firm's operations group in situations where operations plays a vital role.

4. A dramatic increase has taken place in the number of suppliers of equipment to be hooked on to a computer configuration. This is reducing the number of firms totally committed to one vendor's gear. Additional features, coupled with attractive prices of specialist manufacturing, pushed many firms in the direction of proliferation. This phenomenon, when combined with the integration of telecommunications and office automation, has made the task of capacity planning more complex as well as increased the exposure to refereeing vendor disputes when their network goes down.

5. Complex trade-offs have to be made in innovation (with both its risks and economic opportunities) versus conservatism (with perhaps higher operating costs but more reliability). Companies where *significant* (in terms of overall company profitability) cost reductions are offered by this technology, or where significant strategic competitive advantage may stem from the operation of this technology, should appropriately be more adventuresome than other firms where this is not true. Similarly, firms which have great dependence on the smooth operation of existing systems must be more careful about the introduction of new technology into a network where unanticipated interaction with existing systems could cause great difficulty in ensuring reliable operation of key parts of the organization.

6. The cost and disruption caused by change often outweighs the advantages associated with a particular technology and it becomes attractive to skip a generation of change. This has to be looked at carefully on two grounds:

a. The system design practices of the 1960s and early 1970s were quite different from those being employed today. Some firms, anxious to postpone investment, have stayed too long with these systems and exposed themselves to great operational risk by trying to implement massive change in an impossibly short period of time, with disastrous results. Software is, in every sense, like a building—it depreciates. Unfortunately, industry accounting practices do not recognize this; consequently, it is very easy to get into difficulty through excessive, apparently innocent, postponement.

b. Some changes are critical if the firm is to be competitive, while others are nice but cannot legitimately be considered essential. Investments in this later category are clearly eligible for postponement.

7.   As an increasing set of investments are made in the products of small software and hardware vendors, another cluster of important issues is brought to the surface. These issues relate to vendor viability and product maintainability over the past 15 years. There has been a high mortality rate among these suppliers. In evaluating hardware vendors, the issues are: If they go under, is there an acceptable alternative? Is it easy to keep existing systems going both short term and long term? What are the likely costs of these alternatives? In evaluating software vendors, the issue is: If the vendor goes out of business, has the contract provided for our having access to source programs and documentation? An additional area of complexity is their posture toward program maintenance, both as to the type of error correction and systems enhancement change which may be expected and as to the cost-charging policy for these items. As noted earlier, it is critical that experienced operations thinking be involved in these negotiations. All too often, very unhappy outcomes have ensued when either the user or the systems and programming department acquired software without under-standing the long-term operating implications of the decision.

8.   Finally, a hidden set of capacity decisions focus on the acquisition of appropriate backup infrastructure items, such as power, chilled water, and adequate building strength for the weight of the equipment. The importance of availability and reliability of these items are easily often underassessed. For example, recently the temperature in a large metropolitan data center suddenly went from 78 degrees to 90 degrees in a two-hour period, shutting down the entire operation. A frantic investigation finally uncovered the fact that, three floors down, a plumber had mistakenly cut off a valve essential to the provision of chilled water to the operations room.

These points suggest clearly that not only is capacity planning a very complex subject but it requires as much administrative thinking as technical thinking. In the 1980s, for most organizations, we are not talking about building a new factory but rather implementing a continuous program of renovation and modernization on the factory floor while keeping the assembly line in full production. This is a formidable and, unfortunately, often seriously underestimated task.

MANAGING THE WORK FORCE

The personnel issues in the operations function have changed significantly in the past few years. Most dramatic has been the major reduction in data input and preparation departments. The introduction of online data entry has not only changed the type of tasks to be done (keypunching, key verification, job-logging procedures, etc.) but has permitted much of this work to be transferred to the department which originated the transaction, often to the person who first initiates the transaction. A desirable trend in terms of locating control firmly with the person most interested, in many settings this has been exceptionally hard to implement with users turning out to be less enthusiastic than anticipated about taking over this accountability. In general, however, the large centralized data entry departments are fading and will continue to fade into history.

At the same time, the jobs in the computer operation section are being significantly altered:

1. Data base handling jobs are being steadily automated. The mounting of tapes and disks are being reduced in frequency. Some firms have even successfully automated the entire tape library function. Further, as CRTs have exploded in popularity, the amount of paper handling has been reduced.
2. Former manual expediting and scheduling functions have been built into the basic operating system, eliminating a class of jobs.
3. In the more sophisticated shops, many of the economies indicated in items 1 and 2, which are possible, have already been achieved. A point of diminishing returns has been reached in this area and the past economies gained are not a prologue to the future here.
4. The establishment of work performance standards in this environment has become a less feasible and useful task. As the data input function disappears and as the machine schedules itself rather than being paced by the operator's performance, the family of time-and-motion performance standards of the 1960s has become largely irrelevant for the 1980s. Inevitably, performance evaluation of individuals has become more subjective.

These factors clearly indicate that the composition of the operations work force has changed dramatically. The blue-collar component is significantly reduced, with a large number of new, highly educated technologists and production planners being needed instead. The issue is further complicated by the continuous change taking place in technology, which requires that both types of staff must upgrade their skills if they are to be relevant for future needs.

In this environment, career path planning is a particular challenge. At present, for the professionals, three major avenues are available. Those who have technical aptitude tend to move to positions either in technical support or in systems development. A very common exit point for a console operator is as a maintenance programmer. As a result of operations experience, he has developed a keen sensitivity to the thorough testing of systems changes. The second avenue is a position as a manager in operations, particularly in large shops where there are a multitude of management positions ranging from shift supervisors to operations managers, which are mostly filled through internal promotions. Finally, in banks and insurance companies in particular, there have been a number of promotions out of IS operations into other operations positions in the firm. This represents, particularly in the manufacturing sector, a neglected avenue of opportunity. All of these promotion paths, if given the proper attention, make the operations environment an attractive place to work and prevent it from becoming ossified and therefore unresponsive to change.

The introduction of the trade union movement in this department has been relatively infrequent in the U.S. environment. It has been quite frequent in Europe and in portions of western Canada. In many settings organizing this department gives the union great leverage because a strike by a small number of individuals can virtually paralyze an organization. In the past several years, strikes of small numbers of computer operations staff in the United Kingdom's Inland Revenue Service have caused enormous disruptions in its day-to-day operations. In thinking about the potential impact of being unionized, the following points are important:

1. The number of blue-collar jobs easily susceptible to being organized has been dropping. A convincing argument can be made that shops were more vulnerable to being organized in the technology of the past generation than the current generation. One reason some companies have embraced the new technology is to eliminate this unionization exposure through job elimination.

2. The creation of multiple data centers in diverse locations makes the firm less vulnerable to a strike in any one location. Reducing this vulnerability has been a factor (although generally not the dominating one) in some moves toward distributed processing.

3. The inflexibilities of work-to-rule in this type of manufacturing organization are enormous. The dynamics of technical change in necessary functions and jobs make this a particularly poor time from the firm's point of view to be organized. As technology stabilizes, the inefficiencies resulting from premature organization will be less a matter of concern.

Selection of Operations Manager and Staff. Another area of significance is the selection of the IS operations manager, and his or her key staff. There are several important factors which generate different skill needs for different environments.

1. *Size* is the most important dimension. As an IS activity grows in numbers of staff, the complexity of the management task significantly increases, requiring many more managerial skills at the top.

2. *Criticality of IS operations Unit.* Firms which are heavily dependent on IS operations ("factory" or "strategic") are forced to devote a higher

caliber professional resource to this area. The penalties to the company of uneven quality of support are clearly heavier and more effort must be made to avoid them.

3. *Technical sophistication of shop.* A shop heavily devoted to batch-type operations, with a relatively routine nondynamic hardware/software configuration, requires less investment in leading-edge management than a shop with a rapidly changing, leading-edge environment. The latter situation requires staff who can lead, effectively, efforts in upgrading operating systems, etc.

These factors suggest clearly the impossibility of defining a general-purpose operations manager. Not only do different environments require different skills, but over time the requirements in an individual unit shift. The overall trend, however, in the last decade is to demand an ever high quality of manager. Increasingly, the former tape handler or console operator of 15 years ago has proven inadequate for handling this job.

Human Issues in Managing the Work Force. Finally, there are a series of long-term human issues which must be dealt with in managing the work force effectively. These include:

1. Recognition that the problem of staff availability and quality is a long-term challenge for IS operations. Intensified efforts in an environment of decreasing entrants to the total work force are needed to attract quality individuals to the IS operations group. Career paths and salary levels require continuous reappraisal. For "factory" and "strategic" companies, IS operations can no longer be treated as a stepchild to the development group.

2. There is a critical need for IS operations to develop appropriate links to both the users and the development group. The linkage to development focuses on ensuring that appropriate standards are in place so that new systems and enhancements are both operable (without the development staff being present or on call) and that no unintended interaction take place with other programs and data files. The establishment of an IS operations quality assurance function is an increasingly common way to deal with this. The user linkage is critical to ensure that when operating problems occur, the user knows who in IS operations can solve them. Finally, it is important that development and operations have their respective roles vis-à-vis one another clearly defined and separate, so that a minimum of confusion exists in the user's mind when he or she has a problem as to where to go for the solution.

3. Not only does a long-term IS staff development plan need to be generated, but a specific training program must be prepared and executed for staff.

4. Quality-of-work-life issues need to be addressed continuously. This includes items such as flexible time, three-day (12 hours at a time) work-

weeks, and shift rotation. There is no clear right answer to these issues, but rather a continuous reassessment must occur.

PRODUCTION PLANNING AND CONTROL

Operations production planning is complicated by the fact that a multitude of goals are possible for an IS operations function. Among the most common ones are the following:

Ensure a high-quality, zero-defect operation. All transactions will be handled correctly, no reports lost or missent, etc.

All long-term job schedules will be met (or at least within some standard).

The system will be responsive to handling unanticipated, unscheduled jobs, processing them within x minutes or hours of receipt, providing they do not consume more than 1 percent of the resource.

Average reponse time on terminals for key applications during first shift will be x seconds. Only 1 percent of transactions will require more than y seconds.

"Day-to-day" operating costs will not exceed the given levels.

Capital expenditure for IS equipment will not exceed the budgeted levels.

Resolving Priorities. It is important to recognize that, by and large, these are mutually conflicting goals and all cannot be optimized simultaneously. For companies where IS operations support is critical to achievement of corporate missions ("factory" and "strategic"), resolution of these priorities requires senior management guidance. In environments where it is less critical, they can be sorted out at a lower level. In our judgment, failure to explicitly sort out the priorities in an appropriate manner (that is, widespread concurrence and understanding of the trade-offs to be made has been gained) has been a primary source of the poor regard in which some operations units have been held. Their task has been an impossible one.

The sorting out of these priorities immediately gives insight into how to address two other items.

1. Organization of capacity. The relative desirability of a *single integrated computer* configuration or a series of modular units either within a single data center or multiple data centers (assuming the nature of the workload is such that you have a choice) is an important strategic decision. Setting up modular units (plants within a plant at some cost) will allow specialized delivery service to be implemented for different types of applications and users. These multiple factories also allow for simpler operating systems in addition to allowing quite different types of performance measures and management styles be implemented for each. This focused factory concept has been too often neglected in IS operations.

2. *Ensuring consistent operating policies are in place.* Uncoordinated management specialists, each trying to optimize his or her own function, may create a thoroughly inconsistent and ineffective environment. In one large insurance company, the following policies were simultaneously operational:

a. An operator wage-and-incentive system, based on meeting all long-term schedules, and minimizing job setup time.

b. A production control system which gave priority to quick turnaround, small-batch jobs meeting certain technical characteristics.

c. A quality control system which focused on zero defects and ensuring that no reruns would have to take place.

d. A management control system which rewarded both low operating budgets and low variances from the operating budgets. Among other things, this control incentive had helped to push the company toward a very constrained facilities layout to minimize costs.

While individually each of the policies could have made sense, collectively they were totally inconsistent and had created both tension and friction within the IS operations group and a very uneven perception of service on the part of key users.

Job Shop versus Process Manufacturing. The conflicting needs posed by job shop operation versus process manufacturing operation causes significant tensions and confusion, because they each pose quite different production planning problems. The job shop (the predominant IS environment in 1970) involves the processing of multiple discrete jobs, each of which uses different amounts of computing capacity. Many of these jobs require different routing paths through the operation center (Inforex, check sorting, bursting, etc.), as well as within the computer.

Quality control in the job shop involves ensuring that key production deadlines are not missed, jobs and outputs are not lost, incorrect data is not processed, reports are not missent to the wrong locations, and so forth. Production scheduling is a complex task divided between a production control department and the computer's operating system. The production control department identifies desired target times for completing job processing, prepares schedules and establishes priorities for work stations outside the computer department control, prepares necessary job setup instructions, and determines relative job priority. The computer operating system then does the detailed allocation of the computer resource to each job (balancing its relative priority against efficient use of the system) and shepherds it through to completion. The production control department normally has both an expediting function, for squeezing short rush jobs through the system, and a tracing function, to allow them to answer user questions about the status of different jobs. Human expediting is an important part of ensuring that this happens.

In addition, since a job is moved from work station to work station, careful attention is paid to overall facilities layout to minimize congestion and confusion while ensuring staff resources are efficiently utilized. Within limits, machine downtime and rerun problems can be effectively hidden from the customer (assuming there is some excess capacity). In the job shop environment it is possible to identify precisely what jobs are to be run, assess closely the volume of transactions to be processed, predict the amount of time each job would take, and write a detailed production schedule. The week's production schedule can be formalized in some detail in advance and posted on a board in a GANTT chart or some similar type of format. Long-term production planning involves forecasting increases in business volume, hence transaction levels, and identifying major new applications and their potential requirements. Both of these turn out to be relatively cut-and-dried. Finally, throughout the day, tactical decisions as to how to juggle the schedule have to be made on items such as unexpected machine downtime, extra reruns, and the occurrence of more or fewer transactions than planned for in programs such as order entry. Other complicating items include submission of unplanned small jobs or programmer test shots. These changes are made by both production schedulers and machine operators. Production planning, in this environment is not only well structured but has a high amount of predictive power associated with it and can be fine-tuned with considerable human input.

Process manufacturing, or utility operation (most online systems), poses very different problems. It involves the continuous processing and flow of transactional work through a finite resource. The arrival of work in the IS environment takes place in an unscheduled intermittent fashion, with a variety of queues to hold it during periods of excess demand. Substantial control has been lost over the timing of the utilization of the computing configuration. It is difficult to forecast the number of transactions coming from dispersed users in half-hour periods. Forecasting becomes more probabilistic and the definition of service levels in terms of response time performance becomes more complex. A lot of terminal use turns out to be less transaction driven and more user-inquiry driven. In this regard, substantial organizational learning takes place and more individuals find it attractive to use terminals in ways they could not conceive of in advance. This significantly complicates the task of capacity planning.

Quality control in process manufacturing involves ensuring that an acceptable pattern of response time exists during the day, and ensuring that an acceptable level of systems downtime and machine downtime is maintained, etc. In general, much higher absolute levels of service are required than in the job shop, because failures are absolutely visible and cause great emotional problems. Day-to-day production scheduling outside the operating system priority-setting mechanism is not an important issue. Transaction-volume forecasting, capacity planning, and bottleneck analysis, however, are very important items. It takes only a very small increase in volume over planned levels when the IS computing resource is near capacity to go from satisfactory to intolerable response times. Human expediting is not necessary.

In 1982 the problem is complicated because, in most organizations, it is not an either/or situation but rather a mix of both types of processing occurring simultaneously. In general, the move from a heavily batch world to an extensive online environment that still handles batch work has resulted in the following changes:

There has been a pronounced shift in the number and type of staff working in IS operations. There has been a sharp decrease in the number of blue-collar workers (tape handlers, console operators, disk pack mounters, etc.), and an increase in the number of high-salary process engineers (i.e., tech support people). Not only has the maintenance and fine-tuning of the operating system become much more complex, but the payoff resulting from capacity fine-tuning has become more important and is having to take place on a more continuous basis than in the past.

There has been a move away from very detailed human production scheduling to a more macro approach, where analyzing and attempting to manage the patterns across the hours and work shifts of a week becomes the major role of a production control group. Individual production job expediters and schedulers have become much less numerous and important.

Hot-line troubleshooting advice on an instantaneous basis has become important. The immediate transparency of the operating systems glitches, and the frustration of one minute downtime to users doing operating tasks has increased the importance of this integration.

Much tighter quality control checks are needed, both on systems modifications and on the introduction of new systems, to protect against their unintentional impact on other systems running simultaneously. Similarly, the problems of introducing poorly tested new technology have become much more severe.

User priority rules built into the operating system have been established, so that in times of peak utilization the resource is allocated in accordance with some corporate priorities. Since many of the users are inputting data at locations physically remote from the operation center, these rules must be built into the operating system. The heavy loads posed by unexpected volumes of online transaction and inquiries make it difficult to meet batch-run schedules, unless their priorities are carefully built into the operating systems.

The combination of these factors means that the human scheduling on an hour-to-hour basis is much less important than in the past and that considerable attention must be devoted to the architecture of the priority system inside the basic operating system. Long-term scheduling and planning of IS is harder because of uneven and sometimes unpredictable organizational learning about the utilization of this technology. (In one bank the use of an online portfolio management system grew fourfold over a two-year period as, successively, individual trust officers became comfortable with working with this new management tool.) Even though new applications can be identified in advance, the growth in their use cannot be predicted in the same way as for transaction processing systems.

In many settings, this transition in management focus has not taken place smoothly but has been quite troubled, both because of resistance to change and lack of explicit definition as to how corporate goals have changed.

Strategic Impact of IS Operations. The type of management focus brought to the IS operation function depends on IS operation's role in the firm. IS operations in the "support" and "turnaround" categories can appropriately be dominated by cost-efficiency thinking. Deadlines, while attractive to meet, are not absolutely critical to the organization's success. Quality control, while important on the error dimension, can be dealt with in a slightly relaxed way. It is appropriate to take more risks on the capacity dimension for both job shop and process type IS operations in order to reduce the financial investment. Less formal and expensive backup arrangements are also appropriate. Finally, corners can safely be cut in user-complaint response mechanisms.

The "factory"-type operation poses very different challenges. Integrally woven into the ongoing fabric of the company's operations, quality in accuracy, response time, and schedule meeting is absolutely critical. Appropriate capacity to meet various contingencies is critical because severe competitive damage may occur otherwise. The issue of capacity not only needs to be managed more carefully, but usually more reserve capacity for contingencies needs to be acquired. New operating systems and hardware enhancements must be very carefully evaluated and managed to avoid the danger of downtime and the financial damage associated therewith. These factors in a budget crunch cause the company to make changes more carefully here than in organizations less dependent on the service.

The "strategic" operation, while facing all the issues of the "factory," has several other facets. Capacity planning is more complicated because it involves major new services instead of just extrapolation of old services with new volume forecasts. A stronger liaison needs to be maintained with the users to deal with the potential service discontinuities that will be associated with both new technology and new families of applications. These factors suggest that more slack needs to be left in both capacity and budget to protect vital corporate interests.

Implementing Production Control and Measurement. The above factors clearly suggest the need for an evolutionary and adaptive control and reporting structure. The same indexes, standards, and controls that fit one organization at a particular point in time will not meet other organizations' needs over an extended period of time as both the technology and the organization evolve toward an online system, and perhaps a "factory" organization.

Within the appropriate goals for the operations department, there is a critical need to identify both performance indexes and standards of performance. Actual data can then be compared against these standards. These indexes will normally include the following types of items:

Cost performance: aggregate performance versus standard for different types of IS services.

Staff turnover rates.

Average and worst 5 percent response times for different services.

Quality of service indicators such as amount of system downtime by services.

Number of user complaints by service.

Number of misrouted reports and incorrect outputs.

Growth in usage of services, for example, word processing, electronic mail, peak hours, computer utilization, etc.

Surveys focusing on user satisfaction with service.

While the underlying detail may be quite voluminous, this data, including trends, should be summarizable on a one- to two-page report each week or month. This quantitative data provides a framework within which qualitative assessments of performance can then take place.

SECURITY

One of the emotional topics surrounding IS operations is how much security is needed to protect the site and how much actually exists. We will not dwell at length on this as it is a complex subject that bears mentioning here only to call attention to the nature and importance of the problem. Exhaustively covered in other sources, we define the breadth of the issue by noting the following points.

1. Perfect security is unachievable at any price. The question for an organization is to understand, for its particular mission and geography, where the point of diminishing returns is located. Different units in the

organization or different systems may have distinctly different requirements in this regard.

2. Large organizations, where the activity is fundamental to the very functioning and existence of the firm, will appropriately think about this differently. The large firm where IS operations is fundamental to corporate success will be strongly motivated toward multiple remote centers. Duplicate data files, telecommunications expense, duplicate staff and office space, all make this an expensive (although necessary) way of organizing. These firms have come to the conclusion that if they do not back themselves up no one else will.

3. Smaller organizations, where this activity is critical, have found it attractive to go to something like the SUNGUARD solution, where a consortium of 80 users have funded the construction and equipping of an empty data center. If any one incurs a major disaster, this site is then available for them to use.

4. For organizations where the IS operation is less critical, appropriate steps may include arranging backup with another organization. (It always sounds better in theory than it is in reality.) Another alternative is to prepare a warehouse site with appropriate wiring, air conditioning, etc. (In a real emergency, locating and installing the computer is the easiest thing to do. It is the location and installation of all other items that consume the time.)

5. Within a single site, a number of steps can be taken to improve security. Listed below are some of the most common, each of which has a different cost associated with it.

    a. Limiting physical access procedures to the computer room. This can vary from simple buzzers to isolated diving-chamber entrances.

    b. Surrounding the data center with chain-link fences, automatic alarms, and dogs. Access to inner areas monitored by guards using remote TV cameras.

    c. Uninterrupted power supply, including banks of batteries and stand-alone generators.

    d. Complex access codes to deny file- and system-entry to all but the most qualified personnel.

    e. Significant number of files stored off-site and updated with a higher level of frequency.

    f. Installation of a Halon inert gas system to protect installation in case of fire.

    g. Systematic rotation of people through jobs, enforcement of mandatory vacations (no entry to building during the vacation), and physical separation of development and operations staff.

This is merely an illustrative list and in no sense is intended to be comprehensive.

SUMMARY

IS operations management is a very complex and evolutionary field. In part, this problem comes with changing technology obsolescing existing manufacturing processes and controls, in part from technology's impact on how best to implement the system life cycle, and in part from the changing profile of the work force. In thinking this area through, it appears the major insights come from applying the broad insights gained—in the fields of management of technological change and manufacturing—to this very special type of high technology factory. Most large firms now know how to schedule and control multiprocessing batch computer systems working on numerical data from decentralized input stations. Building upon this base to include word processing, electronic mail, and a host of more decentralized IS activities is a challenging growth opportunity. The critical resource for success in operations is the acquisition and retention of knowledgeable people to operate, maintain, and evolve IS services.

Chapter 9 □ Multinational IS Issues

Chapter \ Manageable Trend	Strategic Impact	DP/TP/OA	Organization Learning	Make/Buy	Life Cycle	GM/ User/ IS
IS Technology Organization Issues **Chapter 3**		●	●			●
Organizational Issues in IS Development **Chapter 4**	●		●	●		●
Information Systems Planning **Chapter 5**	●		●			●
IS Management Control **Chapter 6**	●		●	●		●
A Portfolio Approach to Information Systems Development **Chapter 7**	●				●	●
Operations Management **Chapter 8**	●			●	●	●
Multinational IS Issues **Chapter 9**		●				●
The IS Business **Chapter 10**	●		●	●		●

The head of multinational IS (MIS) of a major European research company's central IS activity suddenly discovered that subsidiaries in three of their largest countries had recently ordered medium-sized computers and were planning to move their work from the corporate IS department to installations in their countries (reducing the workload in corporate IS's data center by 45 percent). The reasons cited for this were better control over day-to-day operations, more responsive service, and lower costs. Located in a country with a high-cost, tight labor pool, the IS head was unsure how to assess the risks this posed to his operation and the company as a whole.

The head of corporate IS of a large pharmaceutical company recently held a three-day international meeting of the 15 IS heads of the company's major foreign subsidiaries. A major unresolved problem at the meeting was what should the relationship of corporate IS be to the more than 50 smaller foreign subsidiaries which also had computing equipment. Historically, the department had responded to requests for assistance (5 to 8 per year) but had not gone beyond that. The head of corporate IS was increasingly uncertain whether this was an appropriate level of involvement.

The chief financial officer of a major Singapore company in early 1981 ordered 13 APPLE II computers in his controller's department to stimulate awareness of how modern financial analysis could help the company. Five months later, with the experiment a great success, he found himself overwhelmed with requests for system support. The company not only lacked the staff to provide the support but even in the two- to three-year planning horizon were unlikely to be able to acquire it in the local market at any price.

These stories are the tip of a major, largely unreported, unstudied IS story; namely, that the management of multinational IS support for a company is very complex and its issues go well beyond legislation relating to transborder information flows. These issues have become more significant in the past decade as the post–World War II explosion of the numbers and scope of multinationals has continued. This growth has sparked the need for development and expansion of management systems to permit appropriate coordination of geographically distant business activities. In the past, investigation of this area has tended to fall between two schools. On the one hand, it has appeared to be so specialized and technical that the scholars of international business have tended to ignore it. On the other hand, those writing about management of information systems have tended to be highly national in their orientation and have tended to slide past the issues in this area of IS technology application.

We see this area as representing a major management challenge today, as well as one where the resolution of issues is likely to be even more significant in the coming years. Managing the forces driving transition in IS (described as six trends in Chapter 2) is confounded by the diversity of country infrastructure (for example, Germany vis-à-vis Sri Lanka), as well as prior discussed variations in corporate manufacturing and distribution technologies, current scope of IS activity, and relative sophistication in IS application. Building on our concepts of strategic relevance, culture, contingent planning, and managing diffusion of technology, we will focus on international aspects that impinge on IS.

This chapter is organized as follows: The first section deals with some important country characteristics which influence the type of IS support appropriate for a firm's operations in the country. The second section talks about specific IS environmental issues which influence how a firm can develop IS support in a specific country. The third section deals with company-specific issues which influence how it should think about IS development overseas. The final part suggests the types of policies that firms have adopted for dealing with these issues and discusses the factors which make them more or less appropriate in different settings.

COUNTRY DIVERSITY

There are a number of important factors inherent in a country's culture, government, and economy which influence what IS applications make sense, how they should be implemented, and what is the appropriate type of corporate guidance from an IS activity located in another country. The more important of these factors include the following:

Sociopolitical. The obvious factors of industrial maturity and the form of government are particularly important in considering the use of information services technology. Emerging countries with high birth rates have views and opportunities far different from those of mature industrial states with shrinking labor populations. Further, mature societies have stable bureaucracies which allow the necessary continuity for development of communications systems.

Language. Common languages of Western origin provide a sound means for technical communications and relevant documentation. However, this is lacking if the local language is not Latin-based. This is especially true for discussions of a technical nature, because, frequently, senior managers of the subsidiary are fluent in the parent company language, but lower-level managers and staff technicians lack this fluency. This tends to be true even in companies such as N. V. Philips (the large Dutch electronics company), which has made a major effort to develop English as a company-wide language.)

Local Constraints. A whole network of local cultural facets exist which make it difficult to develop coordinated systems and an orderly process of technology transfer. Union agreements, timing of holidays, government tax regulations, and customs procedures all force major modifications of software, for applications such as accounting, and personnel from one country to another. Further, different holidays, different working hours, etc. make coordination of reporting and data gathering an ongoing evolutionary process. Also important are issues relating to geography and demographics. For example, a large phonograph record company has found it attractive to have centralized order entry and warehouse management for Paris, which serves retailers around the country. It fit the structure of the French distribution system. In Germany, however, they were driven to establish multiple factories, distribution points, and a quite different order entry system to service the market. The German structure was a rational response to the realities of German geography and prevailing distribution patterns. Unfortunately, this also meant that the software and procedures appropriate for the French subsidiary were inappropriate for the German situation.

Economic. A mature industrial economy normally has a pool of well-trained, procedurally oriented individuals who typically get high wages relative to world standards. This incentive to replace clerical people is complemented by the limited availability of talent, and it is a sensible economic decision. In cultures with low-wage rates, often dependent on one or two main raw material exports for currency, there is typically a lack of both talent and economic incentive. The true need is to develop a reliable source of available information (a noneconomic decision). Implementing this, however, may move against both economic and cultural norms.

Currency Exchange. Organizing international data centers is complicated by both currency restrictions and volatility in exchange rates. The latter may mean that a location initially cost effective for providing service to neighboring countries may suddenly become quite cost ineffective. For example, several Swiss data centers which were very cost competitive in the early 1970s were very noncompetitive in the late 1970s as a result of the heavy appreciation of the Swiss franc, even against currencies like the German mark.

Autonomy. Another point of importance is the universal drive for autonomy and feelings of nationalism. The normal drive for autonomy in units within a single country is intensified by differences in language and culture as one deals with international subsidiaries. In general, a larger integration effort is needed to appropriately coordinate foreign subsidiaries than is needed with domestic ones (with not necessarily better results). The difficulties in this task increase not only with the distance of the subsidiary from corporate headquarters but also as the relative economic importance of the subsidiary drops.

National Infrastructure. The availability of utilities and a transportation system are often important constraints on feasible alternatives. On the other hand, their absence also serves as an opportunity for emerging technology. For example, to overcome the unpredictable transportation and communication systems, one South American distributor developed a private microwave tower network to link the records of a remote satellite depot with the central warehouses. This system enabled him to obtain a significant competitive edge which led to rapid growth.

All of the above factors make international coordination of IS activities, in general, more complicated than domestic coordination of domestic IS activities. Often development of special staff and organizational approaches are needed if these issues are to be effectively handled.

COUNTRY/IS ENVIRONMENT

In addition to the above more general issues, there are some very specific IS issues, which make the coordination and transfer of IS technology particularly challenging from one country to another. In part these are due to the long lead times to build effective systems and in part due to the changing nature of the technology. The more important of these include the following:

Availability of IS Professional Staff.   While inadequate availability of systems and programming resources is a general worldwide problem it is much worse in some settings than others. For example, in 1981, Singapore had only 1,000 analysts and programmers vis-à-vis a need for over 6,500. Further, as fast as people develop these skills in English-speaking countries, they become targets for recruiters from the high-wage, highly industrialized countries. This has been a particular problem in the Philippines in the past several years.

When an attempt is made to supplement local staff with individuals from headquarters, the results are not always uniformly satisfactory. An initial outburst of productivity by the expatriates and effective transfer of technology at a later phase often leads to resentment by the local staff (whose salaries and benefits are usually much lower) and broken career paths on the part of the expatriates, who find they have become both technically and managerially obsolete when they return to corporate headquarters. Management of this reentry problem of IS expatriates, in general, has been quite inadequate.

Central Telecommunications.   The price and quality of telecommunication support varies widely from one country to another. On both dimensions, the United States sets the standard. In many European countries, the tariffs will run an order of magnitude higher than those in the United States. In addition, in many countries, lead times to get extra land lines, terminals, and so forth from date of order can stretch to years instead of weeks. Variances in line capacity, costs, and up-time performance mean that profitable online applications are either cost ineffective or fail to meet adequate up-time or reliability standards in other countries. Also, communication quality, availability, and cost varies widely from one country to another.

Country/National IS Strategy.   In some countries, development of a local computer manufacturing and software industry is a key national priority item (France, Germany, and the United Kingdom, for example). In these situations, subsidiaries of foreign companies often find it attractive to buy the products of the local manufacturer as part of being a good citizen and building credit for later dealing with the government. This may create a legitimate local need to deviate from corporate hardware/software standards. A related issue is that some countries (such as India and Nigeria) require that computer vendors sell a majority share of their local subsidiary to local shareholders if they are to do business in the country. Some vendors (such as IBM) have preferred to withdraw from a market rather than to enter into such an arrangement. Again, this may force a deviation in those countries from corporate-mandated IS standards. Finally, concern may exist about whether the country exporting the hardware will continue to be a reliable supplier in a world of turbulent national, and shifting foreign, policies. For example, a number of South African companies, uneasy about the ability to get a sustained flow of products from one country, have moved to hedge their bets on potential disruptions of equipment delivery by dealing with several countries.

General Level of IS Sophistication.   The speed and ease with which one can either start or grow an IS activity is linked to the general level of IS activity in the country. A firm located in a country with a substantial base of installed information systems, and with a base of well-trained mobile labor, can grow more rapidly and effectively than where none of these preconditions exist. The countries with a limited base of installed information systems require substantially more expatriate labor to implement IS work. This is accompanied by greater effort and time to educate users concerning the idiosyncrasies of IS and how best to interface with it. The staff mobility factor is particularly important to investigate carefully because both bonding arrangements and cultural norms add real rigidities into what on the surface appears to be a satisfactory labor supply situation.

Size of Local Market.   The size of the local market influences the number of vendors who can compete for service in it. This means that, in smaller markets, a company's preferred international supplier may not have a presence. Further, the quality of service support often varies widely from one setting to another, with vendors who provide good support in one country turning out to be inadequate in another. Another important issue is the availability and quality of local software and consulting companies (or subsidiaries of large international ones). A thriving competent local information services industry can do much to offset other differences in local support and availability of staff.

Data Export Control.   A topic which has received significant publicity in the past three to four years has been the specter of legislation to reduce dramatically the amount of information relating to people and finances which can be transmitted electronically across national boundaries. One factor is increased governmental prescription concerning the types of tele-processing services that may be offered by suppliers. This involves both establishment of technical standards and type of nonlocally manufactured equipment which can be used. Another factor is growth of interest in regulation concerning the type of data (including quality and security standards) which should be permitted to be sent abroad. It is perceived that not only is privacy of individuals threatened but unacceptable security and quality controls exist over these data, raising the threat of substantial accidental danger to the individual. The potential scope of this legislation, and the procedures for effectively monitoring compliance with it, are very speculative at present. Our guess is that, when the dust settles, its practical impact on a firm's operations may be limited, although some modifications in procedures will have to be made to accommodate specific country problems.

Technological Awareness. One of the great management problems is that awareness of contemporary technology spreads very rapidly around the globe because key IS magazines and journals have international distribution. The authors have had as spirited discussions about the pros and cons of various data base management systems in Beijing (although none are there) as in New York. This awareness poses real problems in terms of orderly application development in less sophisticated countries, because subsidiaries often tend to push technologies which they neither really understand, need, nor are capable of managing.

Trade Union Environment. In the past five years, particularly in Europe and western Canada, there have been substantial successful efforts to organize IS departments. As mentioned in Chapter 8, in 1980 and 1981, for example, there were serious and successful strikes of the U.K.'s Inland Revenue Service's computer operations staff which substantially interrupted its operations. This has caused some companies to do a better job of distributing their IS activities, to minimize both the possibility of labor action and the disruption which flows from it. It has also become a factor in picking appropriate locations for regional data centers to support activities in several countries.

Border Opportunities. In periods of fluctuating exchange rates, significant discontinuities often appear in vendor prices for the same equipment in different countries. In 1980, for example, there was a period where a 15 to 20 percent savings could be achieved by buying equipment in Italy for use in Switzerland, as opposed to a direct purchase in Switzerland.

The practical implication of these factors is to restrain severely the degree to which standard policies and controls can be placed on diverse international activities. There are a large number of legitimate reasons for diversity.

The problem is complicated by the fact that considerable *local* know-how must be brought to the decisions. Rigid policy on many of these issues cannot be dictated from corporate headquarters, often located a vast distance from the operating management.

COMPANY AND IS REQUIREMENTS

Within the context of the different country cultures and current state of the IS profession in different countries, a number of factors exist inside a company which influence how far it must move to manage the transfer of IS technology, and how actively it should attempt to centrally control international IS activity. By definition, more control must be delegated locally because of the above-mentioned issues than are delegated in a domestic environment. However, important opportunities exist for technology transfer, and potentially important information service limitations will occur if these issues are not managed. The more important company-specific factors include the following:

Nature of Firm's Business. Some firms' businesses demand that key data files be managed centrally to be immediately accessible to all units of the firm around the globe or on a short delayed access basis. Airline reservation files for international air carriers require such access. A Pan American agent in Boston confirming a flight segment from Tokyo to Hong Kong needs up-to-the-minute access to the flight's loading to make a valid commitment, while other agents around the globe need to know that seat is no longer available for sale. Failure to have this information poses risks of significant loss of market share as customers perceive the firm to be both unreliable and uncompetitive. For example, a major shipping company has to maintain a file, updated every 24 hours, as to where its containers are around the globe, what their status is, and their availability for future commitment by regional officers in 20 countries. The absence of this data would lead to their making undoable commitments, subsequently presenting an unreliable image to present and potential customers. Other firms require integration and online updating of only some of their files. For example, a major European electronics firm attempts to provide for its European managers up-to-date online access to various key operational files on items such as production schedules, order status, and so forth. This is done for its network of 20 plus factories to manage an integrated logistics system. No such integration, however, is attempted for either their key marketing or accounting data, which are essentially processed on a batch basis and organized by country. While it is technically possible to develop such integration, they see at present no operational or marketing advantage in doing so.

Still other firms require essentially no integration of data and each country can be managed on a stand-alone basis. A major U.S. conglomerate, for example, manages each division on a stand-alone basis. Eight of its divisions have operations in the United Kingdom and, by corporate policy, they have no formal interaction with each other in IS or any other operational matters (a single tax specialist who files a joint tax return for them is the sole linking specialist). The general perception of the company's staff is that this is an appropriate way to operate and nothing of significance is being lost. These examples suggest the impossibility of general-purpose prescriptions as to organization of multinational IS activities.

Strategic Impact of IS. Firms where the IS activity is at the strategic heart of the company need tighter corporate overview of the area to ensure that new technology (and hence new ways of operating) is rapidly introduced to the outlying areas in an efficient way. One of the U.S.'s largest international banks, for example has a group of over 100 staff at corporate headquarters to both develop software for their international branches and to coordinate the orderly dissemination of this software—thus technology—to their key countries. The successful use of this technology is felt to be too critical to the firm's ultimate success for it to be managed without technical coordination and senior management perspective. At the other extreme is a reasonably large manufacturer of chemicals where the general perception is that IS technology is playing an important but distinctly support role. At least twice a year, the head of the European IS unit and the head of corporate IS exchange visits and share perceptions with each other. The general consensus is that there is not enough payoff to warrant further coordination.

Corporate Organization. As the firm grows in international activity, it adopts different structures, each of which requires quite different levels of international IS support and coordination. In the earliest phase of an export division, there are only limited numbers of staff overseas, who require little if any local IS processing and support. As the activity grows in size, it tends to be reorganized as an *international* division with an increasing number of marketing, accounting, and manufacturing staff located abroad. At this stage, there may be an increasing need of local IS support. At its full-blown level, this may involve regional headquarters in Europe, the Far East, and Latin America, for example, to coordinate the activities of the diverse countries. This structure can become very complex for a company to coordinate where there are not only vertical relationships of some form between corporate IS and the country IS activities, but where cross-border marketing and manufacturing integration requirements create the need for relationships between the country IS units. The best form of this coordination, of course, will vary widely from one organization to another. One multibillion dollar pharmaceutical firm, recently studied, was discovered to have very close links between corporate IS and its major country IS units (defined as those which had budgets in excess of $5 million). None of its major country IS unit managers, however, either know the names of their contemporaries or had visited any of the other locations. Since there was little cross-border product flow, and none planned in the near future, this did not appear to represent a significant problem.

At the most complex, we have firms organized in a matrix fashion, where there is a corporate IS activity, divisional IS activities (which may or may not be located at corporate headquarters), and country IS activities, where balancing of relationships is a major challenge. This may be further complicated by divisions having substantial vertical supplier relationships with each other and substantial integration of activities across national borders. Clearly, the policies that work for the international divisions are likely to be too simplistic for this latter situation.

Company Technical and Control Characteristics. An important input to the type of IS control that will work is the general level of functional control present in the company overall. Companies with a strong tradition of central functional control find it both appropriate and relatively easy to implement line IS control worldwide. For example, a major manufacturer of farm equipment for years has implemented very strong management and operational control over its worldwide manufacturing and marketing functions. Consequently, they found considerable acceptance by the organization of similar controls for the IS organization. Today, the majority of software which runs their overseas plants has been developed and is being maintained by the corporate IS headquarters group.

At the other extreme is a multibillion-dollar conglomerate of some 30 divisions whose corporate staff is approximately 100 people, who are involved mostly in financial and legal work associated with acquisitions and divestures. This company's philosophy has been total decentralization of operating decisions to the divisions, and corporate headcount is deliberately controlled to prevent meddling. At present there is a two-person corporate IS group who work on only very broad policy and consulting issues. In this organization environment, effective execution of even this role is very challenging and it would be very difficult to visualize its effective expansion.

Another element of significance is the technology base of the company. High technology companies which have a tradition of spearheading technical change from a central research and engineering laboratory and ensuring its dissemination around the globe have had success in processing a similar approach with IS. A receptivity to technical change exists, and a base of experience concerning the problems associated with technical change exists. Firms without this experience in their management teams not only have had more difficulty assimilating IS technology in general but have had more problems in transplanting IS technology developed in one location to another setting.

A final point of relevance here is the corporate size. Smaller organizations, because of the limited and specialized nature of their application, find transfer of IS packages and expertise to be particularly complex. As the scope of the operation increases, it appears to become easier to find common applications and to facilitate transfer of technology.

Effects of Geography and Size of Companies. Of potential benefit is the possibility of using the company's location in different time zones to creatively take advantage of excess capacity on the firm's large computers during the second and third shifts. The savings in hardware and staff in some cases have substantially exceeded the additional telecommunications expense. One manufacturing firm located on the East Coast of the United States uses the time between 1 A.M. and 9 A.M. to process much of the manufacturing load of its European subsidiaries. Daytime hours, 9 to 5 P.M., are primarily devoted to supporting its U.S. operations, and the early evening hours to handling the work of its Far Eastern subsidiaries. Obviously, because of data transmission costs, there are limits as to the extent that this can go on.

The number and relative size of foreign operations are important inputs to evolving appropriate policies. Large subsidiaries provide an opportunity for effective coordination on both technical issues and staff rotation. A large U.S. automotive company recently picked its new IS head from France. As the relative economic significance of the foreign unit drops, the intensity of the relationship between corporate IS and the local unit appropriately lessens. Less opportunity exists for both technical coordination and meaningful staff transfers. As will be discussed below, different policies and relationships need to be established for units of different sizes.

Economic Analysis. The relevant economies of hardware/software investment overruns need to be monitored carefully on two dimensions. First, vendors often adopt different pricing strategies within countries, and what may be an attractive or unattractive investment in the home country of the parent company may not be uniformly true in all parts of the globe. Related to this, and more serious, are the problems and discontinuities caused by fluctuating currency exchange rates, which can substantially change the economics of equipment/staff trade-offs inside a country. Fortunately for U.S. companies, recent changes in regulation FASB-8 have eliminated some of the artificial accounting considerations as to whether it is better to buy or lease computing equipment.

Other Considerations. Several other considerations in a firm's environment exist which also influence the resolution of IS coordination policy. Is there substantial rotation of staff between international locations? If this takes place, it is marginally more attractive to have common reporting systems and operating procedures in place in each subsidiary to ease the assimilation of the transfers? Does the firm's operating and financial requirement essentially demand up-to-the-week reporting of overseas financial results? Where this is not needed, consolidation of smaller overseas operations on a one-month delayed time basis is attractive.

MULTINATIONAL IS POLICY ISSUES

As the preceding sections identify, there appropriately exists great diversity in the policies used to coordinate and manage international IS activities between companies, and from one country to another. This section identifies the most common types of policies and relationships and briefly focuses on some of the key issues associated with their selection and implementation.

The scope of these policies and the size of the effort to be focused on their implementation are influenced by the nature of the business (central control needed or not needed), corporate culture relating to corporate-mandated policies, strategic impact of IS technologies, and so forth.

Communication and Data Management Standards. The opportunity to transmit data electronically between countries for file updating and processing purposes has created the need for some form of corporate international data dictionary. Too often this need is not addressed, leading to both clumsy systems designs and incorrect outputs. Where data should be stored, the form in which it should be stored, and how it should be updated are all items which require centrally managed policy (operating, of course, within the framework of what is legally permissible).

Similarly, centrally guided coordination on communication technology acquisition is needed. At present, communication flexibility and cost varies widely from country to country and is shifting rapidly. For example, in 1981 seven countries opened their communication systems to satellite inputs. Western Europe is in the process of developing a packet switched network which operates independently of "normal" communication. Effective anticipation of these changes requires a corporate view and broad design of telecommunications over a decade, to meet growth and changing business needs. It must be specific in terms of service levels needed and appropriate technologies. This plan requires both capable technical inputs and careful management review. An important by-product of the plan is to provide guidance for corporate negotiation and lobbying efforts on relevant items of national legislation and policies regarding the form, availability, and cost of telecommunication.

Central Hardware Concurrence or Approval. The objective of a central policy is to ensure that obvious mistakes in vendor viability are avoided and potential economies of scale in purchasing decisions are achieved. Other benefits are the additional support leverage which can be achieved by being perceived to be an important customer, the reduction of potential interface problems between national systems, and enhancement of portability of software between countries). Practical factors which require sensitive interpretation and execution of this policy include the following items:

Lack of awareness at corporate headquarters of the vendor's support and servicing problems in the local country.

Desire of the local subsidiary to exercise its autonomy and control of its operations in a *timely* way. The Korean subsidiary of a large bank recently wanted to buy a $25,000 word processing system. The gaining of concurrence took six months to pass through three locations and involved one senior vice president and two executive vice presidents before the process was completed. It was generally felt that, whatever benefits standardization might have achieved for the bank in this situation, they were more than offset by the cost and time of the approval process.

Need to maintain good government relationships locally. This may involve such items as patronizing the local vendors, not moving to eliminate certain types of staff, and using the government-controlled teleprocessing network.

Level and skill of people at corporate headquarters in setting appropriate policy in both technical and managerial dimensions. A technically weak corporate staff dealing with large well-managed foreign subsidiaries must operate quite differently from a large, technically gifted central staff dealing with many small, rather unsophisticated subsidiaries.

Central Software Standards and Feasibility Study Approval.   This policy's objective is to ensure that software is written in both a maintainable and secure way so that the company's long-term operational position is not jeopardized. A second objective is to ensure that potential applications are evaluated in a consistent and professional fashion. The problems, if any, with this policy revolve around both the level of effort and potential erosion of corporate culture. Implementation of such standards can be expensive and time-consuming in relation to the potential benefits. The art is to be flexible in relation to small investments while sifting out for closer review the ones where there is real operational exposure. Implementation of this approach requires more sensitivity than many staffs are capable of.

A second problem with this policy is that in many decentralized companies it is directly counter to the prevailing management control system and the location of other operating decisions. The significance of this objection is partially offset by the size and relative strategic impact of the investment. Relatively small, distinctly support investments in these decentralized organizations clearly should be resolved in the local country. Large strategic investments, however, are often appropriate for central review in these organizations, even taking time delays and cost overruns into account.

Central Software Development. In the name of efficiency, reduced costs, and standard operating procedures worldwide, repeatedly firms have attempted to develop software centrally or at some designated country subsidiary for installation in other country subsidiaries. The success of this approach has been definitely mixed. Companies which have a well-established pattern of technology transfer, strong functional control over subsidiaries, substantial numbers of expatriates working in the overseas subsidiaries, and where some homogeneity exists in manufacturing, accounting, and distribution practices have had considerable success with this. The success has also been assisted by very intensive marketing and liaison activities of the IS unit assigned responsibility for the package's development and installation. Repeatedly, however, when these preconditions have not been present, installation has turned into a troubled situation. Most commonly cited reasons for the failure include:

"The developers of the system didn't understand local need well enough. Major functions were left out, and the package required extensive and expensive enhancements."

"The package was adequate, but the efforts needed to train people to put data in and properly handle outputs were significantly underestimated or mishandled. This was complicated by extensive language difficulties and insensitivity to existing local procedures."

"The system evolution and maintenance involved a dependence on central staff which was not sustainable in the long run. We needed more flexibility and timeliness of response than was possible."

"Costs were totally underestimated by more than an order of magnitude. The overrun on the basic package was bad enough but the fat was really in the fire when it came to estimating installation costs."

In our judgment, these statements emanate directly from the above structural factors. In reality, an outside software house, with its marketing orientation and existence outside of the family, often can do a better job of selling standard software than an in-house IS unit in a decentralized environment.

IS Communications. Investments in improving communications between the various national IS units, while expensive, have paid big benefits. Devices which have proven useful include the following:

An annual or biannual conference of the IS directors and their key staff in the major international subsidiaries. For organizations in the "turnaround" or "strategic" categories, these meetings ought to take place at least as frequently as meetings of international controllers. The smaller countries (IS budgets under $1 million) will probably not generate enough profitable opportunities to warrant inclusion in this conference or to have a separate one. The agenda of the conference needs to have a blend of formal planned activities such as technical briefing, application briefings, and company directives, together with substantial blocks of unplanned time. The informal exchanges of ideas, initiation of joint projects, and sharing of mutual problems are among the most important activities of a successful conference.

A regular program of visits of corporate IS personnel to the national organizations (as well as national IS personnel coming to corporate). These visits should take place at planned intervals rather than just around an operational crisis or technical problem. Obviously, on balance, less contact should take place with the smaller units than with the larger ones.

Preparation and circulation of a monthly or bimonthly newsletter to communicate staffing shifts, new technical insights, major projects completion, experience with software packages, vendors, and so forth.

Organization of joint education programs where possible. This may involve either the acquisition and/or creation of audiovisual-based materials to be distributed around the world. A large oil company recently supplemented communication of a radically different IS organization structure with the preparation of a special film, complete with soundtrack in five different languages.

The fundamental issue is to build a stronger sense of organizational identity between the national IS units by encouraging the development of better links between national IS units, rather than have the only links between a country's IS unit and the parent company's IS unit.

Staff Planning. A very important, if difficult to administer, way of addressing the issue of communications is through rotation of staff between the country IS units and corporate IS. Key advantages which stem from this include the following:

Better awareness in corporate IS of the problems and issues in the overseas IS units. The corollary of this is that the local IS units have a much better perspective on the goals and thinking at corporate headquarters as a result of one of their members having spent a tour of duty there.

More flexibility in managing career paths and matching positions with individual development needs. Particularly, in a crowded corporate IS department, an overseas assignment can provide an attractive opportunity.

Efficient dispersion of technical know-how throughout the organization.

Practical problems on the negative side of staff rotation include the following:

Career paths of individuals moving from corporate headquarters to less IS-developed portions of the globe have frequently been very unsatisfactory. The individuals bring leading-edge expertise to the overseas installation and have a major positive impact for several years. Upon returning to corporate headquarters, they find themselves totally obsolete in terms of the contemporary technologies being used, and also on occasion have been dropped out of the normal progression stream through oversight.

Assignment of individuals overseas is not only expensive in terms of moving allowances and cost-of-living differentials but it also raises a myriad of potential personal problems. These problems, normally of a family nature, make the success of an international transfer more speculative than a domestic one.

Transfers from corporate to smaller overseas locations may cause substantial resentment and feelings of incipient nationalism to arise. "Why aren't our people good enough?" Appropriate language skills and efforts on the part of the transferred executive, control over the number of transfers, and local promotions plus the clearly visible opportunity for local staff to be transferred to corporate does much to temper these problems.

On balance, appropriately managed within reasonable limits, the positives far outweigh the negatives.

Consulting Services. Major potential payoff exists from a central IS group providing consulting services on both technical and managerial matters to foreign subsidiaries. In many cases, corporate headquarters is not only located in a technically sophisticated country but its IS activities are bigger in scope than those of individual foreign installations. Among other things, this means:

Corporate IS is more aware of leading-edge hardware/software technology and has had firsthand experience with its potential strengths and weaknesses. Communication of this know-how can be of significance.

Corporate IS is more likely to have experience with large project management systems and other management methods. Communication of this expertise can be of value.

In both of these examples, the communication must be done with some sensitivity, as the art is to move the company forward at an appropriate pace. Movement through the stages of management practices or through the phases of technology assimilation can be speeded up and smoothed. It is very hard, however, to skip either a stage or a phase. All too often, the corporate group pushes too fast in a culturally insensitive fashion, creating substantial problems.

As an organization becomes more IS intensive, effective IS auditing becomes increasingly important to ensure that the organization is not exposed to excessive and unnecessary risks. As mentioned in Chapter 6 on management control, IS auditing is still a rapidly evolving profession which faces a real shortage of staff. The problem is far worse outside the U.S. and Europe. Accordingly, the corporate audit group of a multinational is frequently forced to undertake major responsibility both for conducting international IS audits and for helping to develop national IS audit staff and capabilities.

Central IS Processing Support. The extent to which it makes sense to push IS toward a central hub or linked international network is absolutely dependent on both a firm's type of industry and those particular dimensions along which it chooses to compete. At one extreme is the airline industry where significant competitive disadvantage comes from being unable to confirm seats on a global basis (hence most international airlines are driven to establish such a network—originally as an offensive weapon and now as a defensive one). At the other extreme is a company running a network of paper converting operations where transportation costs severely limit how far away from a plant orders can be profitably shipped. Consequently, it manages order entry and factory management on a strictly national basis with little interchange of data between countries.

Technology Appraisal Program. The development of an international appraisal plan can serve as a useful means to maintaining a perspective and coordination of the IS overseas effort. An example is a U.S.-based multinational company that had a long history of European operations and discovered that the Far East and South America were posing increasingly complicated information problems. A three-year program was initiated by general management to bring the overseas operation under control. The first step was to appraise the state of IS technology and its potential business in each country. This was done by corporate IS management. This appraisal was followed by a discussion, at the annual meeting of company executives, of a proposed set of policies, and where appropriate, action programs. The appraisal was conducted by a three-person IS technical team with multilingual abilities. Originally scheduled on a one-time basis in only 11 countries, the effort was considered so successful it was reorganized as an established audit function. The team learned to appraise locally available technology and to guide local managements' attention to judging its potential. This required a minimum of a week and often two weeks in the field, typically in two trips. The first visit appraised existing services, and generally raised a series of questions which could be effectively pursued by the on-site management as the audit expanded to include:

1. Government restriction.
2. Quality and quantity of available human skills.
3. Present and planned communications services.
4. Generation of alternatives to the present means of service.
5. Economic analysis of at least three standard alternatives, including:
   a. Expansion of present system.
   b. Transfer of all or portions of IS work to a neighboring country.
   c. Transfer of all or portions of IS work to regional headquarters.

The enthusiasm of local managers for this review was not consistent and in several countries long delays occurred between the first and second set of meetings. However, in 7 of the original 11, the appraisals succeeded in generating appropriate change through a better understanding of the potential impact of uncertainties, such as changing import duties, insight into planned market introduction of new technologies by U.S. suppliers, and a new satellite communications alternative. This organized appraisal significantly increased both awareness and comfort among senior management concerning IS. It resulted in the conversion of the activity into an ongoing effort and the addition of several more members to the team.

SUMMARY

International IS development must be actively managed if major long-term difficulties are not to emerge both within and between country IS activities. This is complicated, since as discussed earlier, foreign assimilation of IS technology must be more heavily influenced by local conditions than the current absolute state of the technology. Resolving these local situations is much more complex than simply keeping abreast of technology, thus a long view is required to succeed. For some firms, however, success offers the potential for a significant competitive edge.

Chapter 10 □ The IS Business

Chapter \ Manageable Trend	Strategic Impact	DP/TP/OA	Organization Learning	Make/Buy	Life Cycle	GM/ User/ IS
IS Technology Organization Issues **Chapter 3**	●		●			●
Organizational Issues in IS Development **Chapter 4**	●		●	●		●
Information Systems Planning **Chapter 5**	●		●			●
IS Management Control **Chapter 6**	●		●	●		●
A Portfolio Approach to Information Systems Development **Chapter 7**	●				●	●
Operations Management **Chapter 8**	●			●	●	●
Multinational IS Issues **Chapter 9**		●				●
The IS Business **Chapter 10**	●		●	●		●

INTRODUCTION

The previous chapters laid out a series of frameworks for viewing the information systems activity and each function of IS management. In sum, the book specifies the concrete details as to how one should conduct an information system management audit for the organization. Our final chapter integrates these materials by highlighting the impact of our six major themes. We have chosen to view an organization's information systems activity as a stand-alone *business within a business* and, in particular, to apply the notions of the marketing mix analysis. This view, as will be described below, permits the development of a synthesis of the concepts of organization, planning, control, and strategy formulation for IS.

In this formulation, we will deal in depth with the issues of the marketing mix, strategy formulation, role of the steering committee as a board of directors, and the function of the IS director as the chief executive officer, because these items are particularly relevant in understanding the interface between the two businesses. We will not deal with the operational details of operating strategy, since many of the general elements of IS operations management have already been covered in Chapter 8. Similarly, issues of internal accounting and control within the IS organization will not be covered as they do not impact directly on the interface between the two businesses (IS business and host business). For similar reasons, only the portions of IS organization issues which deal with the IS business's external relations will be covered here.

The IS business is a high-technology and fast-changing business. Depending on the specific IS business one is dealing with, it may be a rapidly growing, more or less steady enterprise, or in a few cases, a declining business. The total territory of the IS business may be conceived as covering the development, maintenance, and operation of all IS technologies in a firm,[1] irrespective of where the various pieces are physically located or where they administratively report.

It is a business whose scope of technologies to be coordinated has expanded tremendously as computers, telecommunications, and office automation have all merged together, and whose product offerings are exploding into new consumer areas, such as electronic mail, editing, and computer-assisted design/computer-assisted manufacturing. The complexity of implementing projects, the magnitude of work to be done, and limited human resources have forced the IS business away from being a primarily production-oriented department to one where a significant percentage of its work is concerned with coordinating the acquisition of outside services for use by its customers (i.e., acting as a *distributor*). This shift has forced major changes in its approach to planning and controls in order to deal effectively with these new products and new sources of supply. Implicit in this formulation, as will be described below, is that, at least *at a policy level,* the overwhelming majority of firms require·an integrated perspective and approach to IS activities. The IS activities include not just the corporate IS center and its directly linked networks but also the distributed islands of mini-micro-computers, distributed systems development activities, outside software company contracts, computer service bureaus, and so forth. *The various users of IS services may be considered to be its consumers,* who possess options in many cases to buy services other than directly from the central IS organization, as noted below.

We believe this formulation of the IS task permits the transfer of disciplines and ways of thinking in other aspects of managerial action to the IS function in a way which can generate new and useful insights. Similarly, as will be discussed below, for general management, we believe the analogy to

---

[1] Throughout this chapter, the term *firm* will refer to the parent holding company of the IS business.

the board of directors is a useful one in thinking through a realistic role for an executive steering committee and other aspects of how they should interface with the IS function. Like all analogies, this one can also be pushed too far and some caution must be taken. For example, the financing of the IS business has no analogy to the corporate capital markets, since its capital support comes directly from the parent firm (with no debt analogy), and its revenues, exclusively in many cases, also come directly from the parent. Similarly, the customer base in many respects is deeply interdependent on common files, etc., and so customers cannot be treated as being entirely independent. On the other hand the IS business is free from many of the legal and governmental constraints that the parent company has. Other legal and governmental constraints, such as the Equal Employment Opportunity Commission (EEOC), may be placed on it primarily in the context of the firm's total corporate posture, with little room or need for the IS business to strike an independent posture.

The rest of this chapter deals with three main topics relating to management of the IS business:

1. The IS marketing mix and its implications for managing the IS business.
2. The role of the IS board of directors and how it can best be managed.
3. The role of the IS chief executive officer.

THE IS MARKETING MIX

Product. The IS product line is a very rapidly changing and continuously evolving one. Exhibit 10-1 notes some of the key aspects of change.

EXHIBIT 10-1 □ IS Product-Line Changes

Past focus	Future
Developing new products	Heavy maintenance of old products meeting obsolescence challenges
Majority of manufacturing inside	Significant percent sourced from outside
Capital intensive (hardware economy of scale dominant need)	People intensive (economy of skill dominant need)
Product mix—mainly large, few medium, many small	Product mix—some large, many medium, thousands small
Strong return on investment	Many projects have intangible benefit justification
New technologies permit new products	New technologies and regroupings of old ones permit new products
Structured services, such as automated accounting and inventory control	Unstructured services, such as executive decision support systems and query systems

Part of the dynamism of the line stems from the enormous proliferation of opportunities afforded by the economics of new technology. The other element of dynamism stems both from changing customer needs as a result of ordinary shifts in business and from new insights (phase 2 learning) as to how this technology can be applied to their specific operations. The products range in size from very small to enormously large (in terms of both development time and complexity to operate on a day-in, day-out basis). The large products (usually a single, one-time customized effort) can have such a long lead time (four years, not dissimilar to rebuilding automobile manufacturing processes) that significant uncertainty exists whether it will really meet customers' needs (often evolving) at time of completion. While for some products, the possibility exists of delaying their introduction with limited damage, for other products, severe damage to consumers will occur if delays of any magnitude take place in development. In terms of day-to-day operations, wide variances exist in terms of the importance of cost, good response time, quality control, etc.

Product obsolescence is a major headache of the IS business. Changing consumer needs (made possible by new technologies) and new manufacturing technologies for existing products offer significant opportunities. The old products become so clumsy over time that it becomes more and more expensive to introduce the necessary enhancements (styling changes) to keep them relevant. In due course, a major factory retooling must be implemented.

The method of delivery of IS products is shifting as the IS customer changes sourcing decisions. As an increasing percentage of IS development expenditures goes to software houses and time-sharing vendors, and production expenditures go to stand-alone minis and micros, IS's role is shifting from one of being primarily a developer and *manufacturer,* to one where it is also a significant *distributor* of products manufactured by others. This distribution role involves identifying and evaluating alternate sources of supply (of both software and production) as well as professionally reviewing those identified by customers.

The products run the gamut from those where the need is clearly (and perhaps correctly) understood by customers and they are knocking down the door for the product (e.g., point-of-sales terminals) to those where there is no perceived need and where considerable and extended sales efforts must take place prior to a sale. They run the gamut from those which are absolutely essential and critical to the customers (inventory control systems) to those which are nice but whose purchase is essentially postponable. Projects at the two extremes require quite different sales approaches.

The situation is complicated by the difference in maturity in the competitive marketplaces for suppliers of different IS technologies. For example, a relatively stable competitive pattern has emerged for suppliers of large mainframe computers. Conversely, the supply side is very turbulent in the microcomputer and office automation markets, with considerable uncertainty as to who the winners will be and what the form of their product offerings will be five years in the future. A competitive pattern, however, is beginning to emerge here. In telecommunications, however, the recent AT&T divestiture has contributed to making the nature of competition very murky for the forseeable future.

Further in the past, monopoly control over product delivery gave IS businesses considerable discretion in timing the introduction of new products to their customers. The changed pattern of competition among suppliers means that in many organizations IS has lost control over the marketing of those products.

In terms of benefits, the products range from those where they can be crisply summarized in an ROI framework for the customer to those whose benefits are more qualitative and intangible in nature. Again, products at each end of the spectrum require a different marketing approach. Some products are absolutely cut-and-dried in focus (certain types of accounting data), while others must be tailored to influence individual tastes and preferences. Further, in many instances, the complexity of the product, and the inherent factors which influence quality, are not easily comprehended by many purchasers. (There are many parallels between the purchase of tires and IS systems.) Finally, some products require tailoring during field installation. These products need quite different field support and distribution staffs than the products without adaption requirements.

The above description of IS product characteristics captures the complexity of the IS marketing task. In terms of developing a marketing strategy, the IS business is one of distributing evolving products which are differentiated by a wide range of characteristics. In other businesses often a strong effort is made to rationalize the product line to permit economy of scale in manufacturing, plus focus and efficiency in distribution. It is the inability to accomplish this in many IS businesses that has contributed to the turbulence associated with their management. Too often they are trying to deliver many different types of products from their traditional monopoly-supplier position with weak promotion, surly sales, and a fixation of being a manufacturer (as opposed to a distributor, when appropriate). What works for one set of products often does not work for another. Recognizing the need for and implementing a differentiated marketing approach is very difficult, particularly for a medium-sized ($5–7 million budget) IS business.

IS Consumer. On many dimensions, the IS consumer is changing in terms of both needs and sophistication. Exhibit 10–2 captures a number of important aspects of these changes. The older consumers, after 20 years of working with the mature technologies, have some sensitivity to the problems of working within their constraints. They are often quite unaware of the newer technologies and the enormous behavioral modifications they must

---

EXHIBIT 10–2 □ IS Consumer Profile Changes

Older consumers	Younger consumers
Experienced with older technologies	Inexperienced in older technologies
Leery of newer technologies	Unsophisticated in newer technologies (but they do not know it)
Identifiable	Often unidentifiable; many more; are at all levels in organizations
Willing to accept IS as experts	Often hostile to IS; wants to develop their own solutions.
Low confidence in their own abilities (often cautious buyers because of cost)	High confidence in their abilities and judgment (often unwarranted)
High turnover rate	High turnover rate

---

make if they are to use them properly. They bring their old purchasing habits to the new environment, without understanding that it is new. The younger consumers, on the other hand, have close familiarity with personal computing and are more intolerant of the inability to get immediate access to it. They also are quite naive about the problems of designing and maintaining information service systems which must run on a regular basis. This generation gap suggests that both classes of consumer have major, but different personal educational needs if they are to be responsible consumers.

The new technologies have made the problem more complicated because many consumers see the opportunity to withdraw from reliance on the IS business and set up their own small business. They are often propelled in this direction by their own entrepreneurs or purchasing agents (i.e., decentralized systems analysts) who are long in hope and short in practical firsthand expertise and realistic risk assessment.

A real challenge to the IS marketing force, in this world of evolving technology, is to assess who the target new consumers are and reach them before they begin to make their own independent decisions. New application clusters and groups of consumers keep rushing to the surface.

Volatility in the consumer composition creates a sustained need for a field sales force. An effective sales job of educating some persons does no good if they move on to other assignments and their successors are both unaware of IS technology and the particular sequence of decisions which got their organization to its current status.

Firsthand personal computing experience and a barrage of advertising in the general press has substantially raised consumer expectations and general level of self-confidence in making IS decisions. Unfortunately, in many cases, this is an entirely misplaced confidence, with a total lack of appreciation for subtle but important nuances, and for the IS hygiene practices which must be installed if there is to be a significant probability of success. This again increases the need for sustained direct sales and follow-up of direct sales efforts.

As will be discussed below, apparently cheap external market prices are another source of confusion to the end consumers. Products essentially similar to those available in-house, appear to be available at much lower prices. It requires great consumer sophistication (often not present) to correctly identify what is a real IS bargain versus that which is really an inferior product. All this takes place in an environment where there is an explosion in the number of potential services from which customers can make a selection.

These facts, in composite, have substantially complicated the IS marketing effort. An unstable group of consumers with diversified, rapidly changing needs requires a far higher level of direct selling effort than do consumers in environments where this cluster of characteristics is not present. The need to spend promotion money on the difficult group has been intensified by the cultural heritage of IS in many settings. Consumers have been left hostile about the quality of IS support and receptive to solutions which will carry them as far as possible away from reliance on the central IS business unit. These consumers, trained to respond in the correct way to many of yesterday's technologies, are inappropriately trained for today's technologies. Underinvestment in marketing to deal with these realities has been a major cause of dissatisfaction.

Cost.   Significant changes from a marketing viewpoint are taking place in both the cost of the product and in delivery systems to get them to the users. Exhibit 10–3 identifies some of the major shifts. On the one hand, the cost of many elements of IS hardware has dropped dramatically and is likely to continue to drop significantly in the foreseeable future. On the other

---

EXHIBIT 10-3 □ Changes in IS Cost Profile—from Consumer Viewpoint

Past cost profile	Future cost profile
Hardware very expensive	Hardware very inexpensive
Major economies of scale in large systems; user stand-alones not feasible in most cases	Limited economy of scale in large systems; user stand-alones very attractive
Systems development expensive	Systems development expense down but not as much as hardware
Limited outside software acquisitions opportunities	Attractive outside software acquisition opportunities
Hard to estimate development and production costs accurately in advance	Still hard to estimate development and production costs accurately
Maintenance expense underestimated	Maintenance a soaring cost of keeping systems alive

hand, progress in reducing the cost of developing software, while positive, has been much slower and is likely to continue to be slow for the near future. On top of this, ability to accurately estimate both development and operating costs in advance for large, high-technology, low-structure systems continues to be both limited and disappointing.

A critical component of cost explosion has been the steady increase in the cost of maintaining already installed products (that is, software). As is true of an auto, these expenses are usually not carefully factored in at the time of purchase, and they tend to grow exponentially with the passage of years as the business grows and changes. The problem can be intensified in that in the short term these costs can be deferred with apparently little damage. In the long term, however, their neglect can cause a virtual collapse of the product.

This change in cost characteristics has accelerated the move of a significant portion of the IS business to the distribution of services. Specialized data bases accessible to many users can be put together in a cost-effective fashion that would be utterly uneconomic if done by single users for their own purposes. A proliferation of packages and software houses has exploded onto the marketplace, and shared software development has become very attractive. For example, a major consortium of 25 regional banks is funding a joint $13 million software development project (in areas such as demand deposit accounting and savings accounts) which will benefit them all. A final recent change has been the large numbers of users who have acquired their own computer capacity. (At a large eastern business school, nearly 40 percent of the faculty now own their own micros.)

As will be discussed in the section on pricing, it is difficult to identify what the total costs are or should be for any particular product or service. In part, this is because a piece of data or software development may be used to support multiple products and consumers, thus generating a concern as to whether they should be treated as joint costs or by-product costs. For any particular product, another complicating issue is the extent to which previously spent R&D costs (to get to today's skill levels) should be treated as part of product cost.

While management and control of costs is a critical component of the IS business strategy, the details of its execution will vary significantly between IS settings. High growth, very product-competitive environments appropriately take a softer line on IS inefficiency and cost control than environments where the IS products are more stable and where the customer mix is more concerned with cost than product quality.

In aggregate, the changing cost structure of IS *products* has forced the IS *business* to reconsider its sourcing decisions and has provided a distinct emphasis for the IS business to take on a much stronger distribution role. Internally, the relative emphasis placed on IS cost control at the expense of product-line growth, quality, and responsiveness of service to consumers depends on the IS business strategy; thus wide variances exist from one setting to another.

Channels of Distribution. As described in Chapters 2, 3, and 4, the number of channels for delivering to users and their relative importance have been shifting rapidly. Exhibit 10–4 shows some of the important changes in this domain. Historically, the major channel for both manufacturing and delivering the IS product has been the IS business itself. In most firms, it had a complete monopoly; changing cost factors and shifts in user preferences have put this channel under great pressure and have caused great pain inside the IS business as it has tried to adapt to the new challenges of a competitive market—which it cannot totally serve in a cost-effective fashion from its manufacturing facility. The IS business has had to adapt to a new mission and is now *not* the sole channel, but rather one of many sources of manufacturing, with a major new role being that of identification and assessment of cost, quality, etc. of products in other channels. Although for many IS businesses, adaptation to this new role has been very uncomfortable psychologically (involving incorrect notions of loss of power, etc.), successful and rapid adaptation by the IS business is critical for the health of its present and future consumers. This is because the new channels, while offering very attractive products and cost structures, in many cases also carry with them sizable risks. The most important of these risks include the following:

1. Misassessment of the real development and operations costs of the

---

EXHIBIT 10–4 □ Changes in the IS Channels of Distribution

Past profile	Future profile
Heavy development and production role; central IS	Significant development but lower percent of total
Limited direct purchase of hardware/software by user	Major direct purchases hardware/software by user
Individual user limited to service from large shared system	Individual user can obtain powerful independent system for use
Time-sharing service bureaus sell time	Time-sharing service bureaus sell products and time bundled together
Limited use of external data bases via time-sharing	Major use of external data bases via time-sharing
Only crude external software and processing services available	Large amount of external software and processing services available
Limited development of software by users	Major development of software by users (packages and user-friendly languages)
Retention of contract analysis/programmers	Less retention of contract analysts/programmers; more applications specialists

products in the channel. Important elements of short-term and (more important) long-term costs may be completely overlooked.

2. Consumer vulnerability to abuse of data by not controlling access, documenting procedures, and implementing data disciplines.
3. Financial vulnerability of the supplier. Is there a possibility of failure and, if so, what are the operational implications to the consumer? Is there an easy way to protect the consumer's fundamental interests if the worst occurs?
4. Obsolescence of products. Is the supplier likely to keep the products modernized (at a suitable cost, of course) for the consumer over the years? If not, what are the safety valves for the consumer and is it important that there be safety valves (obviously, a financial transaction processing system may be more vulnerable in the long-term in this regard than a decision support model)?

Considerable marketing and internal adjustment of perspectives are needed by the IS business unit if its consumers are to feel that they can rely on the IS staff to objectively evaluate alternate channels (instead of pushing their own manufacturing facility at every opportunity). It is probable that the long-run solution will develop knowledgeable consumers. Failure to execute this mission will ultimately cripple its effectiveness to service consumer needs. This will occur through fragmentation of data needed by many consumers, proliferation of redundant development efforts, and an increase of poorly conceived and managed local factories.

Competition. Of the elements in the marketing mix, the one where this analogy is weakest in describing administrative practice and *problems* is competition. In a generic sense, the IS business appears to have *two principal competitors*. These are:

1. The consumers going their own independent way to find solutions without engaging IS in either its manufacturing or its distribution capacity.
2. The potential consumers failing to recognize that they have problems or opportunities which can be addressed by IS technologies.

In the first case, competition has arisen by poor performance of the IS unit. Their inability to formulate and implement sensible, useful guidelines to assist the consumers in their purchasing decisions is a failure of IS to adapt its product line to meet the needs of the changing times. (It is worth noting that, for the broad purposes of the firm, it may be useful to run this aspect of the IS business as a loss leader.) It should be emphasized that loss of manufacturing business in a *planned* or managed way to other channels should not be seen as a competitive loss to the IS business, but simply as a restructuring of its product line to meet changing consumer needs. One of the most successful IS businesses the authors have seen in the past four years has halved its central IS manufacturing capacity. Under a rubric of general policies and controls, it has created a series of smaller manufacturing centers near major clusters of users (i.e., at divisional headquarters), including an explosion of stand-alone office automation systems under user control of all phases of the systems life cycle except the construction phase.

The second competitor, which is really cost-of-delayed-market opportunity, arises as a result of ineffective management of price, product, or distribution policies. These actions permit consumers in an imperfect market to allocate funds to projects which may have less payoff than IS products. However, the notion of aggressive external competition through pricing, product innovation, and creative distribution hurting the IS business is not appropriate in this setting. Defined the way we have done it, the IS business has a monopoly responsibility—sometimes producing a product, in other cases choosing the role of stimulating consumer awareness of appropriate external sources of supply.

Promotion. The rapid changes in IS technology, plus turnover in consumers, make promotion one of the most important elements to manage of the marketing mix because, unlike the previous items, it is largely within the control of IS management. Phase 2 learning by its consumers is at the core of a successful IS business. Even as today's mature technologies are being delivered to consumers, a strong need exists to cultivate tomorrow's consumers with tomorrow's products. Price discounts (introductory offers), branch offices (decentralized analysts), and a central IS sales force are key to making this happen. For example, one large multinational electronics company has a 400-person central IS manufacturing facility near corporate headquarters. Included in this staff are five international marketing representatives. Their job consists of preparation of brochure material to distribute to potential consumers, organization of educational seminars, and frequent trips to countries where they have a major presence to constantly promote new IS products and services. Their job is to develop a close professional relationship with the consumers. These relationships have permitted both effective dissemination of services and acquisition of insights as to performance of existing products and need for new products. This level of expenditure was regarded as being absolutely essential to the IS business in achieving its goals. In another firm, 7 APPLE 2s with VISICALC were distributed in the controller's department at no expense to the users by IS management, to help stimulate awareness of new financial analysis technology. Six months later, retroactively, the controller purchased the machines and ordered four more. This type of high profile *pilot project,* (or test market) to spark consumer interest, is another critical promotion tool.

In large part, this need to adapt is due to the recent shift in the industry. Most vendors who initially executed an overwhelming industrial marketing approach now have added a retail marketing one. From the beginning of the industry to the late 1970s, the large information systems suppliers sold primarily to the IS managers. Recently, in office automation and computers, the suppliers have not only opened a series of retail stores but also are attempting to sell directly to the end users. This has forced the IS business to promote the validity of its guidelines within the firm to protect the users from unintentional fiascoes.

A number of IS businesses have found it attractive to organize both their development and production control activities around market structure as opposed to manufacturing technology (that is, have designated development staffs dedicated to specific clusters of consumers rather than a traditional development group, a programming group, and a maintenance group). This structure permits the development of deep long-term relationships and better understanding and action on operating problems as they arise. Within these market units, it is appropriate to fund specific integrating and liaison positions as opposed to pure technical positions. This approach is critical since, as a result of past performance and poor marketing, the IS business is often in a worse position relatively than an outside software company with its large marketing staff. Money spent this way, although large, is often among the IS unit's most important expenditure, and should be the last to be cut back.

IS newsletters on new services and product announcements (that is, advertising or promotional material) should be sent to key present and potential consumers on a regular basis. Similarly, a program of IS-conducted consumer educational programs, as well as identification of appropriate external educational programs, can significantly assist the marketing effort. When complemented by an appropriate set of sales calls, this can accelerate phase 2 learning.

Consequently, the mix of these promotional tools will vary widely by organizational setting. Just as industrial and consumer companies have very different promotion programs, so also should different IS units. The strategic relevance of its products to its consumers, stability and mix of sophistication of consumers, consumer geographic location, are examples of items which all legitimately impact the structure of an appropriate promotion process.

Price. As noted in Chapter 6, the selection of IS prices is a very emotional and rapidly changing process. It is, however, a very important element in establishing a businesslike, professional relationship between the IS business and its consumers. Indeed, addressing pricing policies aggressively with a marketing view gives significant legitimacy to the notion of the stand-alone IS business. Issues which make pricing a very complicated topic include the following:

1. *Inefficient Market.* The establishment of rational and competitive criteria is very complicated for the following reasons:

a. Product quality is largely hidden and is very elusive to all but the most sophisticated and meticulous consumer. Prices that on the surface appear to be widely apart, if meticulously analyzed, often turn out to be quite comparable.

b. Different vendors have quite different goals, product mixes, and stability. A small vendor who is trying to buy into a market can come up with a very attractive price with which to defuse discussions concerning his financial viability.

c. Vendors may produce very attractive prices because they are pricing a service as a by-product of some other necessary business and thus produce very favorable numbers in relation to a system which attempts to make each user bear a proportionate share of the full cost of the manufacturing operation. This is particularly true for in-house operations which are trying to dispose of excess capacity for some "financial contribution." The long-term stability of this should be a matter of concern to the informed consumer. (What are the implications of his output becoming the main product and the other consumer's output the by-product?)

d. Excess capacity considerations may produce attractive *short-term* marginal prices which are not sustainable on a *long-term* basis as direct costing issues evolve into full costing ones. A variant of this is a bargain entry-level price to attract the consumer. Once captured, it is then easy to elevate prices significantly. This is particularly true for large, internally developed telecommunications systems.

2. *Introductory Offers.* To stimulate phase 2 learning, and stimulate long-term demand, it is often appropriate to offer deep discounts on early business to generate access to a stream of long-term profits at either quite different price structures or cost structures, once the initial learning is completed.

3. *Monopoly Issues.* Review and regulation of pricing decisions by senior management in many areas is needed because of IS's de facto monopoly position. Highly confidential data and data bases needed by multiple users in geographically remote locations are examples of IS products which cannot be supplied by manufacturers other than the IS business. It is important that the prices of these services be appropriately regulated to prevent possible abuses.

4. *Unbundling.* An effective pricing strategy involves two important elements not in widespread practice. The first is the unbundling of development, maintenance, operations, and special turnaround requirements into special packages, each having its own price. The establishment of these prices at an arm's-length basis in advance is a critical element in ensuring a professional relationship with the consumers. The prices need to be negotiated in as much depth and with as much care by the IS business as contracts between outside software companies and consumers. Often this negotiation can be a useful education program to alert users to the "true nature" of service cost. The second element is a need to produce understandable prices for the consumers. Prices established for reports, number of customer records, price per invoice, etc., are much easier for the consumer to relate to than prices in terms of utilization of IS resource units such as CPU cycles, MIPS, etc. The added risk undertaken (if any) by the IS business

in terms of a horror-struck consumer, who has just been educated in the facts of life, tends to be more than offset by much better communication with the ultimate consumer.

5. *Profit.* A final pricing issue, which again strains the independent business analogy, is how far notions of a profitable business should be pressed. It is not clear that, in the short term (in some cases, even in the long term), an IS business should make a profit, or even break even in some settings. Environments where consumers need a lot of education, and where a lot of phase 1 and 2 experimentation is needed, may appropriately run at a deficit for a long period of time. This issue must be resolved prior to the establishment of an appropriate pricing policy. (The answer to this may evolve over time.)

The establishment of an appropriate IS pricing policy is one of the most complex pricing decisions to be made in industry. An appropriate resolution is critical to establishing a healthy relationship with the consumer. This resolution, however, involves weaving a course between monopolistic and genuine competitive issues, dealing with imperfect markets, and resolving ambiguities concerning the role of profits.

ROLE OF THE BOARD OF DIRECTORS

A question of general interest, which first surfaced in Chapter 1, is: What should be the relationship of the firm's general management to the IS business? We find it useful to think of its participation as being similar to the role of a board of directors for any business. (In many situations, this is given de facto recognition through the creation of an executive steering committee.) Viewing its role in this way, we believe the key tasks of general management can be summarized as follows:

1. The appointment and continued assessment of the performance of the IS chief executive officer (a normal function of the nominating committee).
2. Assuring that appropriate standards are in place and are being adhered to. This includes the receipt of appropriate reports on the subject from the IS auditor and a more cursory review from the firm's external auditors (a normal function of the audit committee).
3. Ensuring that the board is constructed to provide overall guidance to the IS business from its various interested constituencies. Unlike a publicly held firm, the IS board does not need a representation of lawyers, bankers, investment bankers, etc. It does need senior user managers who can and are willing to provide user perspective. (As the strategic impact of the IS business on the business as a whole drops, the level of these managers will also appropriately drop.) At the same time, R&D (IS technology planning) and production (IS development and operations

backgrounds) need to be present to ensure that the art of the possible is represented in these sessions.

4. Providing broad guidance for the strategic direction of the IS business, ensuring detailed planning processes are present within the IS business, and satisfying themselves that the outputs of the planning processes fit the strategic direction. Practically, this surveillance will be executed through a combination of the following:

    a. General presentations to the board by IS management on market development and product planning, as well as financial plans.

    b. Review by the board of summary documentation of overall direction.

    c. Formal and informal briefings of board members by other members concerning current issues as to how the IS business is supporting (or not supporting) their legitimate business needs.

    d. Request for and receipt of internal and external reviews of these issues as they seem appropriate.

This definition of the role of the board is designed to deal with the realities of members' background and availability for this kind of work in relation to the other demands on their time. Wallowing in operational or technical detail is unlikely to be suitable or effective. In many settings, periodic (on a one- or two-year basis) education sessions for the board members have turned out to be useful both in making them more comfortable in executing their responsibilities and in bringing them up to date on broad trends within the IS business as well as in the IS industry in general.

ROLE OF IS CHIEF EXECUTIVE OFFICER

A historically high turnover job, the IS chief executive position has been a very difficult and demanding one, with a steadily shifting mix of skills required to be effective over time. Critical special responsibilities which must be managed by the CEO include the following:

1. Maintaining board relationships personally. This includes keeping the board appropriately informed about major policy issues and problems and being fully responsive to their needs and concerns. There is a strong link between the board and the customers that is not present in many settings.

2. Ensuring that the strategy-formulating processes are adequately evolved and that appropriate detailed action programs are developed. As in any high-technology business, high-quality technical scanning is absolutely essential. Its interpretation is crucial and may well lead to major changes in organization, product mix, and marketing strategy. Without

aggressive leadership from the top, the forces of cultural inertia may cause the IS business to delay far too long.

3. Paying close attention to salary, personnel practices, and thus to employee quality-of-life issues. The work force in the IS business is far more mobile and less easily replaceable in these businesses than an average employee.

4. Giving high priority to factory security. (It is more important for the IS business than for most manufacturing technologies; a single, disgruntled employee can do vast—and often undetected for long periods of time—amounts of damage.)

5. Making certain that there is an appropriate management balance between the marketing, manufacturing, and control parts of the business. Of the three, marketing in its broadest sense is the one most often neglected. The CEO, who often comes out of the factory and has been seared by operations fiascoes, has potentially more sensitivity to these issues. However, since this experience was at a particular time with a particular mix of technology assimilation problems, and a particular set of control responses, the CEO's perspectives in these areas may be too narrow, and inappropriate for the current challenges.

6. Developing an IS esprit. A key factor in the success of the IS business is its belief in the value and potential of information for the profit of the firm. Senior IS managers must develop team spirit and lead their organizations with enthusiasm into new ventures. At the same time, they must develop the confidence of the board by good judgment—not only taking risks but also making wise decisions on where to limit the market or when to knowingly forgo a useful technology. If they assess that the customer is not ready, they must balance keeping abreast versus the receptiveness of the market.

SUMMARY

The above discussion captures, we believe, several important complicating aspects of the IS business. Complex and shifting products, changing consumers, new major channels of distribution, and evolving cost structure have forced a major reanalysis and redirection of both its product offerings and its marketing efforts. This changed marketing environment is not only very complex to manage but has forced significant changes in the IS factory, organization and appropriate control systems, and most fundamentally, its perception of its strategic mission. Ted Levitt's great classic *Marketing Myopia*[2] best captured this as he noted the great growth business of the 19th century—the railroads—collapsed because the managers saw themselves in

---

[2] *Harvard Business Review*, (September–October), 1975.

the *railroad,* not the *transportation* business. The analogy to the information systems business is that it is not in the electronic-based *computer,* telecommunications, or office automation business. Rather, it is in the business of bringing a sustained stream of innovation in information services to change the company's internal operations and in many cases (banks, American Express, etc.) also its external products. Far too many directors of data processing centers myopically believe they are running a computer center. Failure to perceive and act on their broader role will lead to a collapse of their operations, probable loss of jobs, and great disservice to the customer base.

When IS is defined in this way, the dynamism in the elements of the successful marketing mix in the early 1980s suddenly snaps into focus. Reliance on existing product structure, more efficient ways of delivering the old technology, and old organization is a recipe for an uncontrolled dissolution of the IS business. This IS organization has been a group of change agents to their customers for 30 years. The change agent itself, however, must change to be relevant.

General Management Library
for the IS Manager

Ackoff, Russell L. *Creating the Corporate Future: Plan or Be Planned For*. New York: John Wiley & Sons, 1981.

Anthony, Robert N. *Planning and Control Systems—A Framework for Analysis*. Boston: Division of Research, Harvard Graduate School of Business Administration, 1965.

[This book introduces the framework of operational control, management control, and strategic planning which has been a major contributor to thinking about the different areas of IS application and their different management problems.]

Anthony, Robert N., and James S. Reece. *Accounting Principles*. Homewood, Ill.: Richard D. Irwin, 1979.

[This is a comprehensive treatment of current accounting and management control thinking. It is very relevant to a broad consideration of IS management control problems.]

Beer, Michael. *Organizational Change and Development: A Systems View*. Santa Monica, Calif.: Goodyear Publishing, 1980.

[A thoughtful, useful discussion on managing organizational change by a leading practitioner/academician.]

Bower, Joseph L. *Managing the Resource Allocation Process—A Study of Corporate Planning and Investment*. Boston: Division of Research, Harvard Graduate School of Business Administration, 1970.

[This in-depth analysis of corporate planning and capital budgeting provides critical insights relevant to both the role of steering committees and how IS planning can be effectively done.]

Chandler, Alfred. *Strategy and Structure: Chapters in the History of the Industrial Enterprise*. Cambridge, Mass.: MIT Press, 1967.

[This classic by the preeminent business historian examines the inexorable relationship between corporate strategy and its organization structure. Its insights are relevant to many facets of IS organization and planning.]

Christensen, C. Roland; Kenneth R. Andrews; and Joseph L. Bower. *Business Policy: Text and Cases.* Homewood, Ill.: Richard D. Irwin, 1978.

Ennis, Ben M., and Keith Cox, eds. *Marketing Classics: A Selection of Influential Articles.* 4th ed. Boston: Allyn & Bacon, 1981.

[A collection of the best of current marketing literature, it provides a series of insights on how best to market the IS business.]

Lawrence, Paul R., and Jay W. Lorsch. *Organization and Environment: Managing Integration and Differentiation.* Boston: Division of Research, Harvard Graduate School of Business Administration, 1967.

[This classic presents the underlying thinking of the need for specialized departments and how they should interface to the rest of the organization. It is relevant for all IS organizational decisions.]

Kimberly Miles and Associates. *The Organizational Life Cycle.* San Francisco: Jossey-Bass, 1981.

[Reports, findings, and analyses of key issues concerning the creation, transformation, and decline of organizations.]

Porter, Michael E. *Competitive Strategy—Techniques for Analyzing Industries and Competition.* New York: Free Press, 1980.

[This book provides a new way of looking at corporate strategy and is invaluable in thinking about how to start IS planning.]

Schein, Edgar H. *Organizational Psychology.* 3d ed. Englewood Cliffs, N.J.: Prentice-Hall, 1980.

[The classic book on the field focusing on how to manage the tension between the individual and the organization.]

Simon, Herbert A. *Administrative Behavior: A Study of Decision-Making Processes in Administrative Organization.* New York: Free Press, 1976.

[This classic destroys many of the classic notions of administrative behavior and introduces more powerful and useful ones. Its generalizations are applicable to all aspects of the IS business.]

Skinner, Wickham. *Manufacturing in the Corporate Strategy.* New York: John Wiley & Sons, 1978.

[This very broad and powerful book on manufacturing strategy provides critical insights for how the IS operations function should be viewed and managed.]

Stonich, Paul. *Zero-Based Budgeting.* Homewood, Ill.: Dow Jones-Irwin, 1977.

[A workmanlike book on zero-based budgeting, it is must reading for the IS director · who plans to do ZBB.]

Vancil, Richard F. *Decentralization: Managerial Ambiguity by Design.* Homewood, Ill.: Dow Jones-Irwin, 1979.

[A study of the managerial issues posed by decentralizing a firm's operations. It provides valuable context for IS organizational and management control decisions.]

Warren, E. Kirby. *Long-Range Planning: The Executive Viewpoint.* Englewood Cliffs, N.J.: Prentice-Hall, 1966.

[The classic in corporate planning, it provides valuable insights to how IS planning can be conducted.]

IS Library for the General Manager

Ackoff, R. L. "Management Misinformation System." *Management Science,* vol. 14, no. 4 (December 1967), pp. B140–B156.

[A classic, this article provides an early categorization of the real management issues in IS administration.]

Blumenthal S. *MIS—A Framework for Planning and Development.* Englewood Cliffs, N.J.: Prentice-Hall, 1969.

[This is the first book on IS planning which gave the subject a comprehensive and realistic treatment.]

Davis, Gordon B. *Management Information Systems: Conceptual Foundations,* Structure and Development. New York: McGraw-Hill, 1978.

[A good treatment of contemporary IS technology.]

Davis, William S., and McCormack, A. *The Information Age.* Reading, Mass.: Addison-Wesley Publishing, 1979.

[A well-written introduction to the jargon of computer-based systems and their important issues.]

Gorry, G. A., and M. S. Scott-Morton. "A Framework for Management Information Systems." *Sloan Management Review,* vol. 13, no. 1 (1971), pp. 55–70.

[A classic article which lays out the domain for IS technology application. It clearly identifies why the IS applications of the 1980s provide such different problems from the 1970s.]

Lucas, Henry C., Jr. *Information Systems Concepts for Management.* New York: McGraw-Hill, 1978.

[A useful guide on how to think about IS management issues.]

Hussain, Donna, and K. M. Hussain. *Information Processing Systems for Management.* Homewood, Ill.: Richard D. Irwin, 1981.

[A good conventional treatment of what the elements of IS technology are and how to approach their management.]

Maciariello, Joseph. *Program Management Control Systems.* New York: John Wiley & Sons, 1978.

[A contemporary analysis of how to manage the project life cycle to ensure good results in IS projects.]

"Managing and Using Computers" Harvard Business Review, no. 21340, reprint series, 1981.

[A compendium of recent *HBR* articles on IS management, it covers from a broad perspective many of the key IS management issues.]

Martin, James. *Introduction to Teleprocessing.* Englewood Cliffs, N.J.: Prentice-Hall, 1972.

[A primer on the basics of communication technology.]

McLean, Ephraim R., and John V. Soden, *Strategic Planning for MIS.* New York: John Wiley & Sons, 1977.

[A comprehensive and relevant treatment of IS planning issues and how it can be done more effectively.]

Nolan, Richard L. *Managing the Data Resource Function.* 2d ed. St. Paul, Minn.: West Publishing, 1982.

[A collection of classics which influenced current IS management thinking.]

Rodgers, William. *Think: A Biography of the Watsons and IBM.* New York: Mentor Books, 1974.

Sayles, Leonard, and Margaret Chandler. *Managing Large Systems—Organization for the Future.* New York: Harper & Row, 1971.

[A comprehensive treatment of the project management insights gained in the Apollo Moon Program. It is invaluable for the manager concerned with large complex IS projects.]

Scott-Morton, Michael, and Peter Keen. *Decision Support Systems.* Reading, Mass.: Addison-Wesley Publishing, 1978.

[This book identifies the type of systems which have followed the large transaction-oriented ones and their special managerial issues. This has been followed by a number of working papers by the authors and others under the auspices of MIT's Center for Information Systems Research (CISR).]

Synnott, William R., and William H. Gruber. *Information Resource Management— Opportunities and Strategies for the 1980s.* New York: John Wiley & Sons, 1981.

[A contemporary analysis of the tactical approaches to ensuring a successful MIS operation.]

Index

This book has been set VIP, in 10 and 9 point Optima, leaded 2 points. Chapter numbers and titles are 16 point Optima. The size of the type page is 30 by 47 picas.